SUPERMAN BATMAN

ABSOLUTE POWER

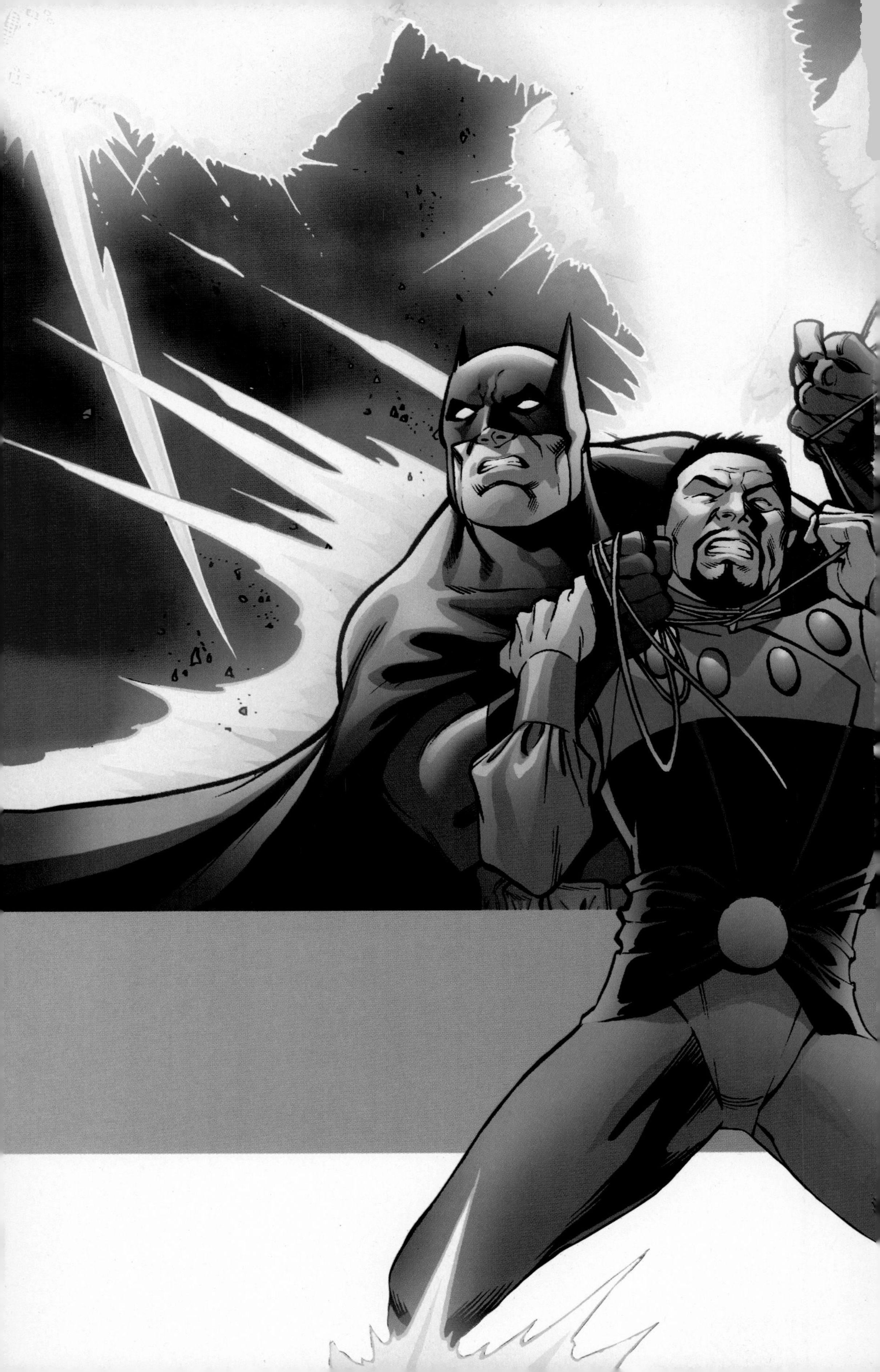

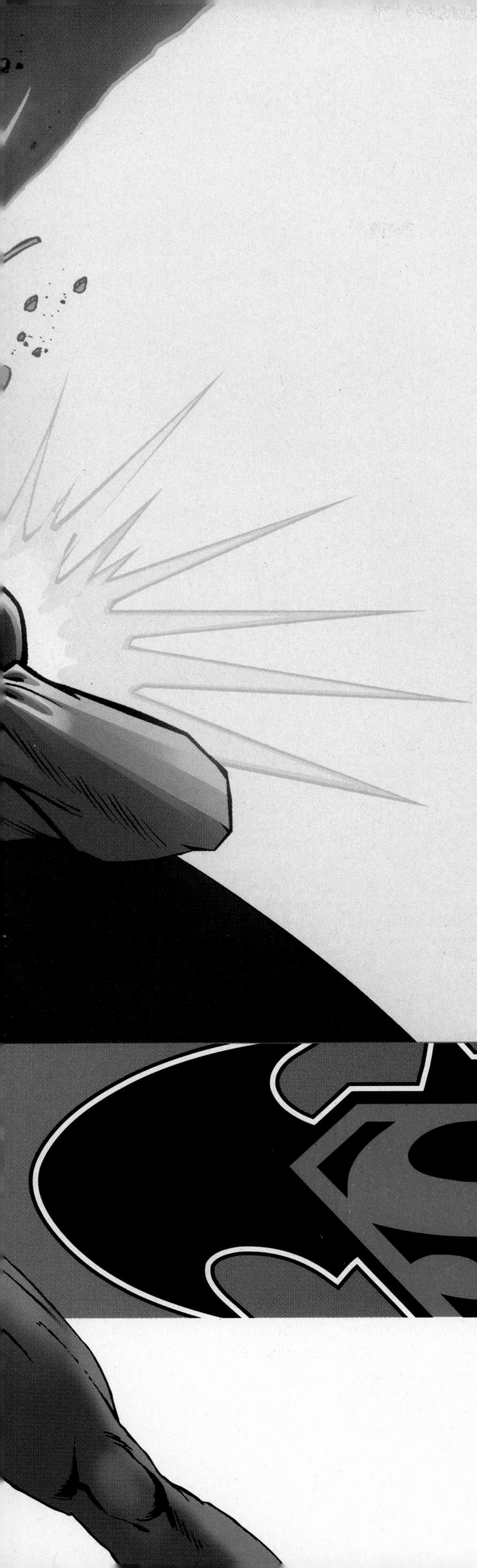

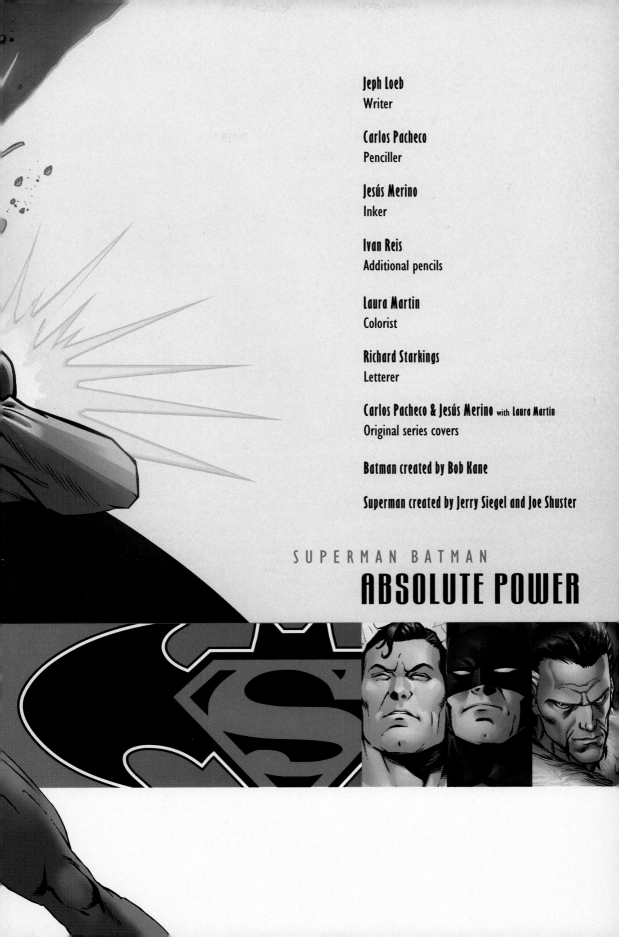

Jeph Loeb
Writer

Carlos Pacheco
Penciller

Jesús Merino
Inker

Ivan Reis
Additional pencils

Laura Martin
Colorist

Richard Starkings
Letterer

Carlos Pacheco & Jesús Merino with Laura Martin
Original series covers

Batman created by Bob Kane

Superman created by Jerry Siegel and Joe Shuster

SUPERMAN BATMAN

ABSOLUTE POWER

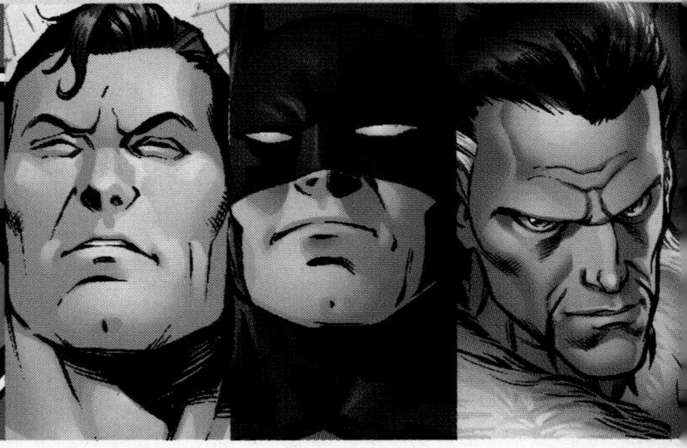

DAN DIDIO VP-Executive Editor   EDDIE BERGANZA Editor-original series   TOM PALMER, JR. Associate Editor-original series   ANTON KAWASAKI Editor-collected edition

ROBBIN BROSTERMAN Senior Art Director   PAUL LEVITZ President & Publisher   GEORG BREWER VP-Design & Retail Product Development   RICHARD BRUNING Senior VP-Creative Director

PATRICK CALDON Senior VP-Finance & Operations   CHRIS CARAMALIS VP-Finance   TERRI CUNNINGHAM VP-Managing Editor   STEPHANIE FIERMAN Senior VP-Sales & Marketing

ALISON GILL VP-Manufacturing   RICH JOHNSON VP-Book Trade Sales   HANK KANALZ VP-General Manager, WildStorm   LILLIAN LASERSON Senior VP & General Counsel

JIM LEE Editorial Director-WildStorm   PAULA LOWITT Senior VP-Business & Legal Affairs   DAVID MCKILLIPS VP-Advertising & Custom Publishing

JOHN NEE VP-Business Development   GREGORY NOVECK Senior VP-Creative Affairs   CHERYL RUBIN Senior VP-Brand Management   BOB WAYNE VP-Sales

SUPERMAN/BATMAN: ABSOLUTE POWER
Published by DC Comics. Cover and compilation copyright © 2005 DC Comics. All Rights Reserved.
Originally published in single magazine form in SUPERMAN/BATMAN: SUPERGIRL #14-18. Copyright © 2005 DC Comics. All Rights Reserved. All characters, their distinctive likenesses and related
elements featured in this publication are trademarks of DC Comics. The stories, characters and incidents featured in this publication are entirely fictional. DC Comics does not read or accept
unsolicited submissions of ideas, stories or artwork.
DC Comics, 1700 Broadway, New York, NY 10019. A Warner Bros. Entertainment Company. Printed in Canada. First Printing.
Hardcover ISBN: 1-4012-0447-3. Softcover ISBN: 1-4012-0714-6.
Cover art by Carlos Pacheco & Jesús Merino with Laura Martin.
Special thanks to Larry Molinar.

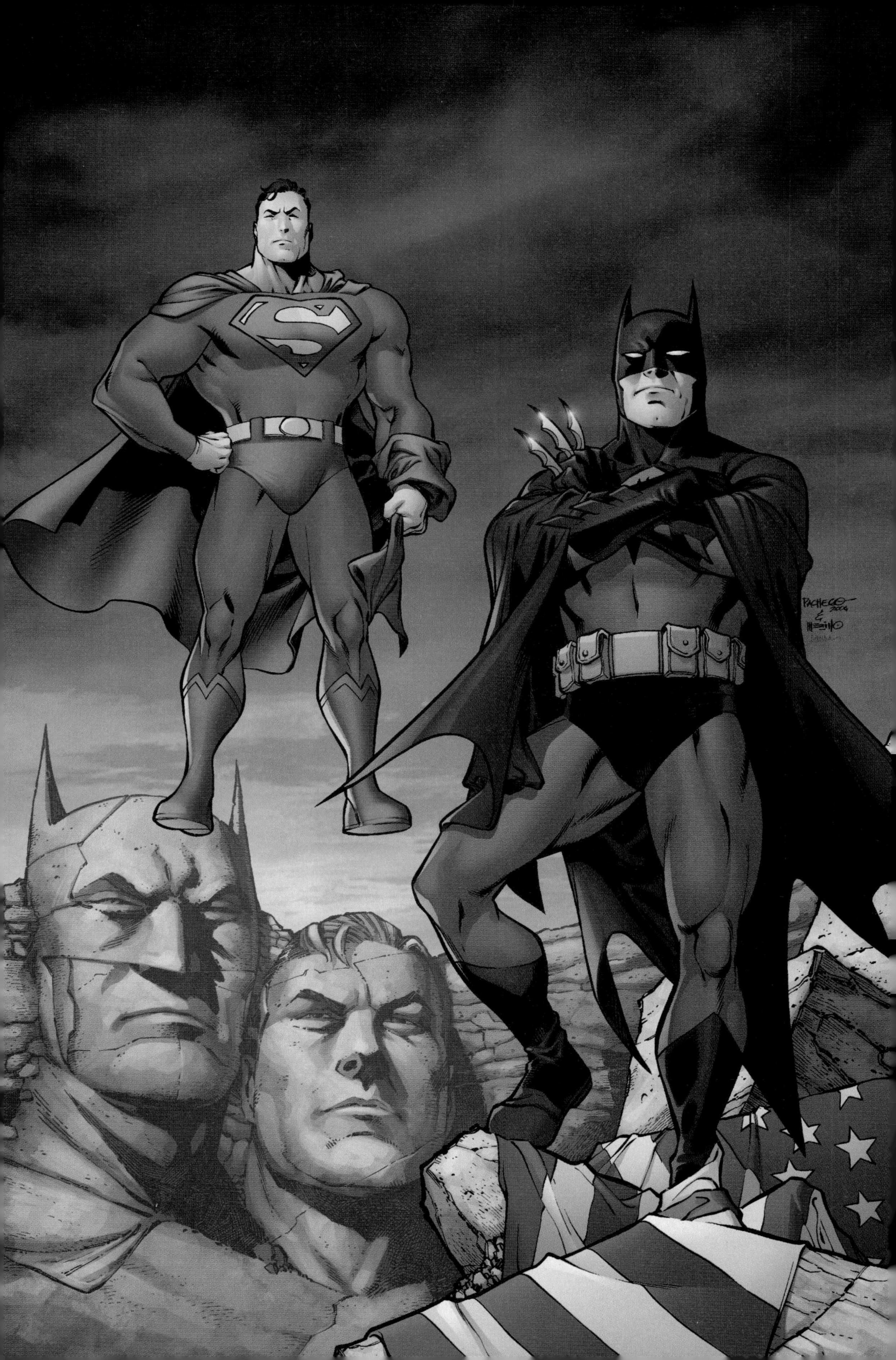
PACHECO 2004

"I PLEDGE ALLEGIANCE..."

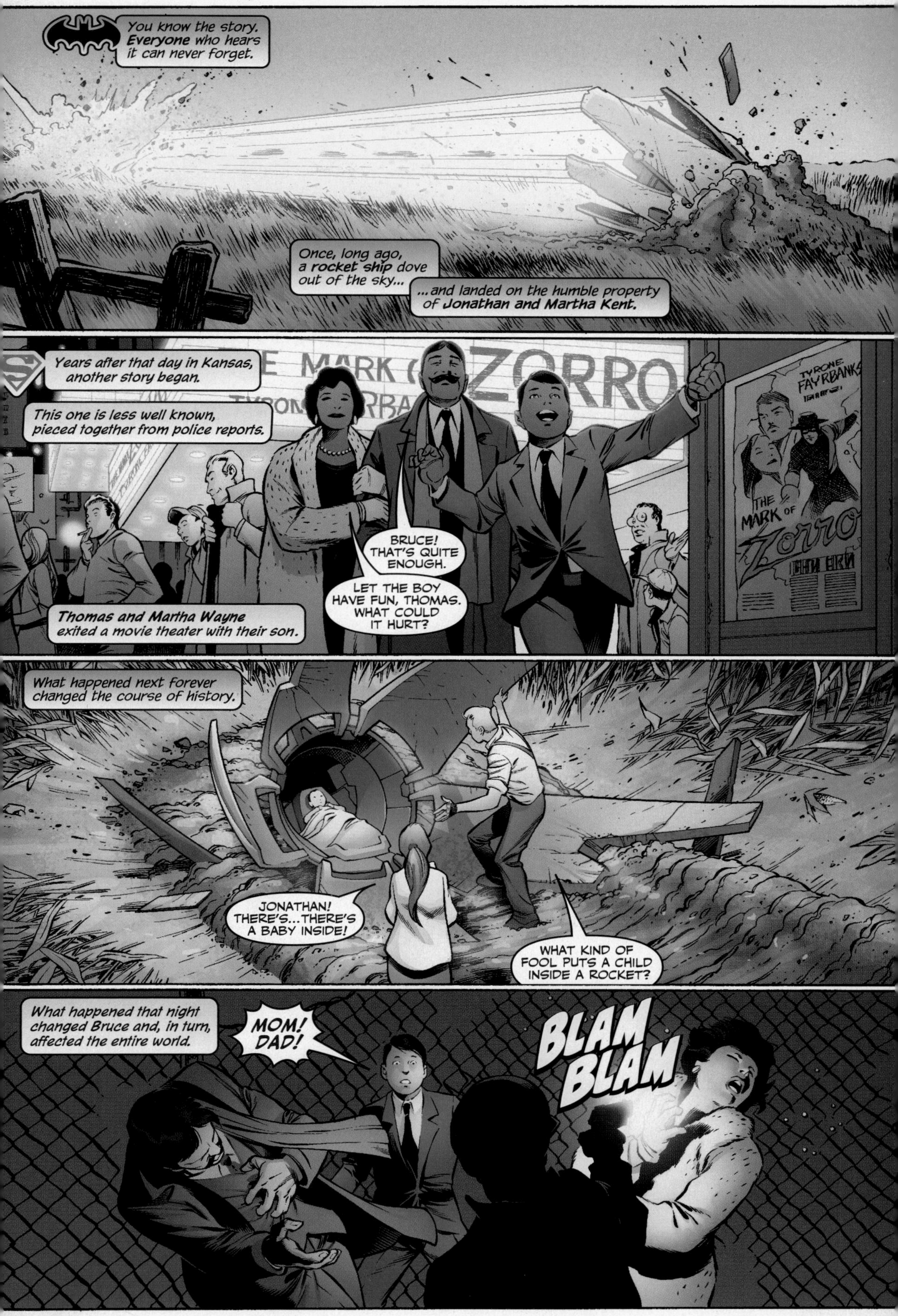

You know the story. Everyone who hears it can never forget.
Once, long ago, a rocket ship dove out of the sky...
...and landed on the humble property of Jonathan and Martha Kent.
Years after that day in Kansas, another story began.
This one is less well known, pieced together from police reports.
THE MARK OF ZORRO
TYRONE FAYRBANKS
THE MARK OF ZORRO
BRUCE! THAT'S QUITE ENOUGH.
LET THE BOY HAVE FUN, THOMAS. WHAT COULD IT HURT?
Thomas and Martha Wayne exited a movie theater with their son.
What happened next forever changed the course of history.
JONATHAN! THERE'S...THERE'S A BABY INSIDE!
WHAT KIND OF FOOL PUTS A CHILD INSIDE A ROCKET?
What happened that night changed Bruce and, in turn, affected the entire world.
MOM! DAD!
BLAM BLAM

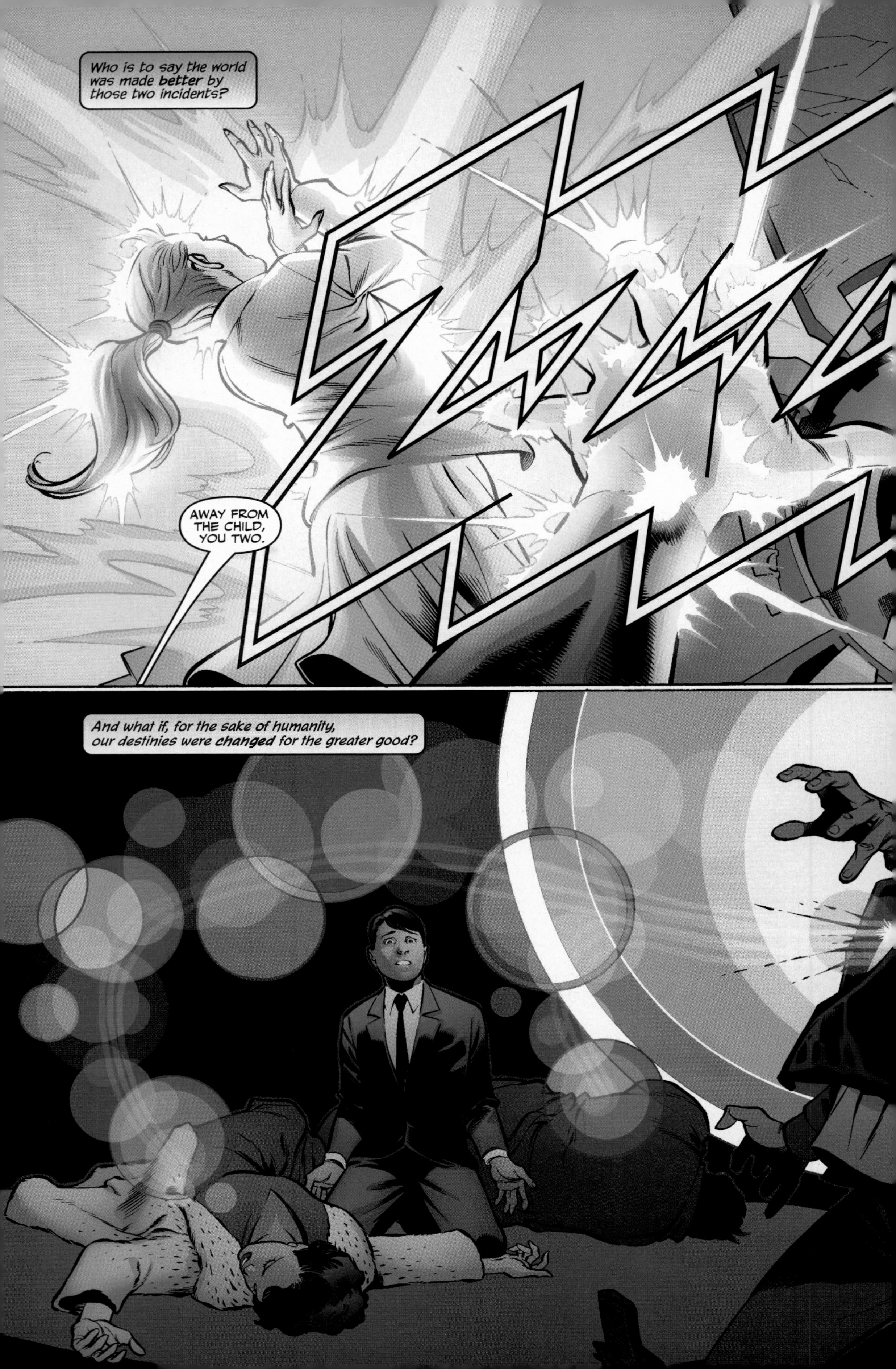
Who is to say the world was made **better** by those two incidents?
AWAY FROM THE CHILD, YOU TWO.
And what if, for the sake of humanity, our destinies were **changed** for the greater good?

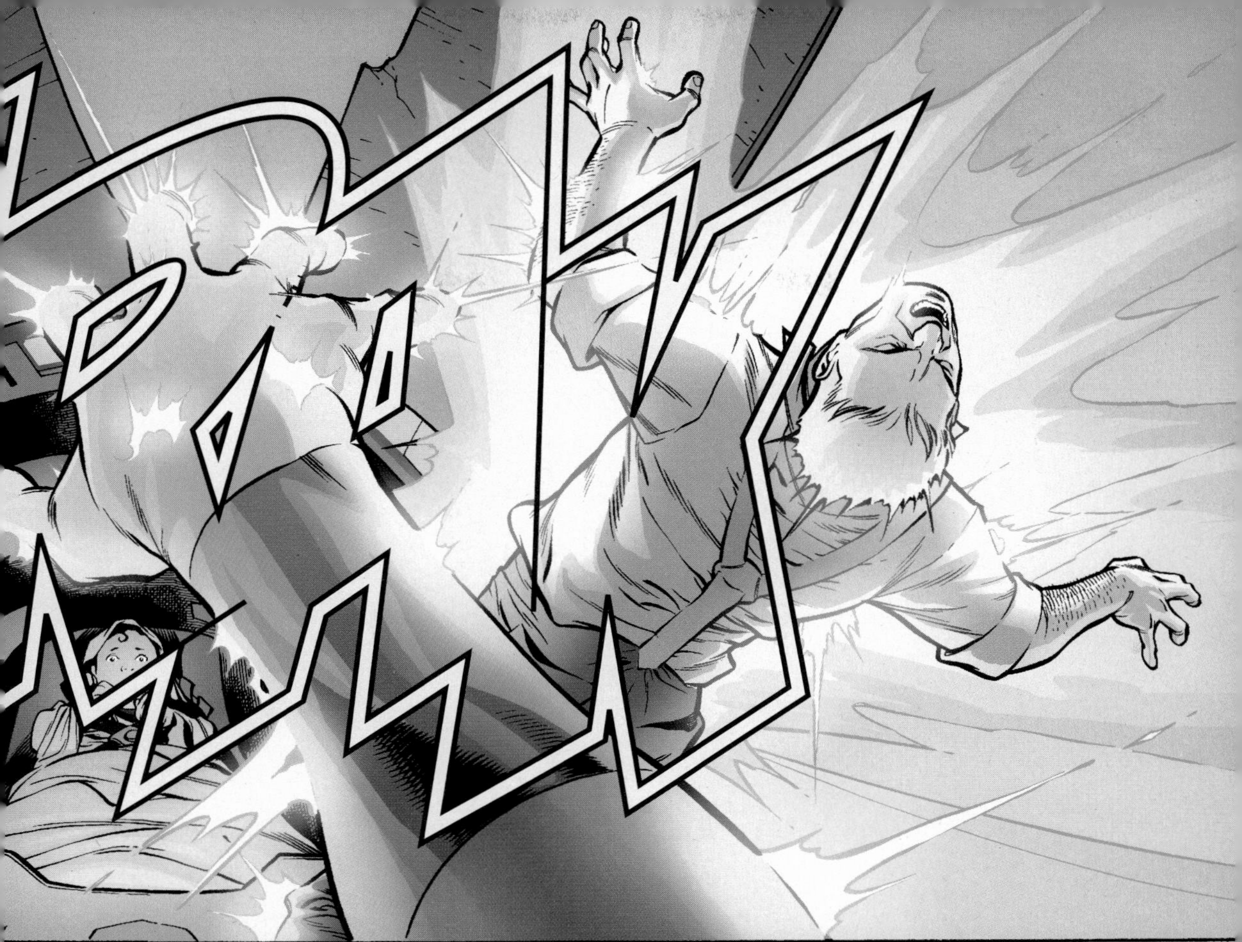

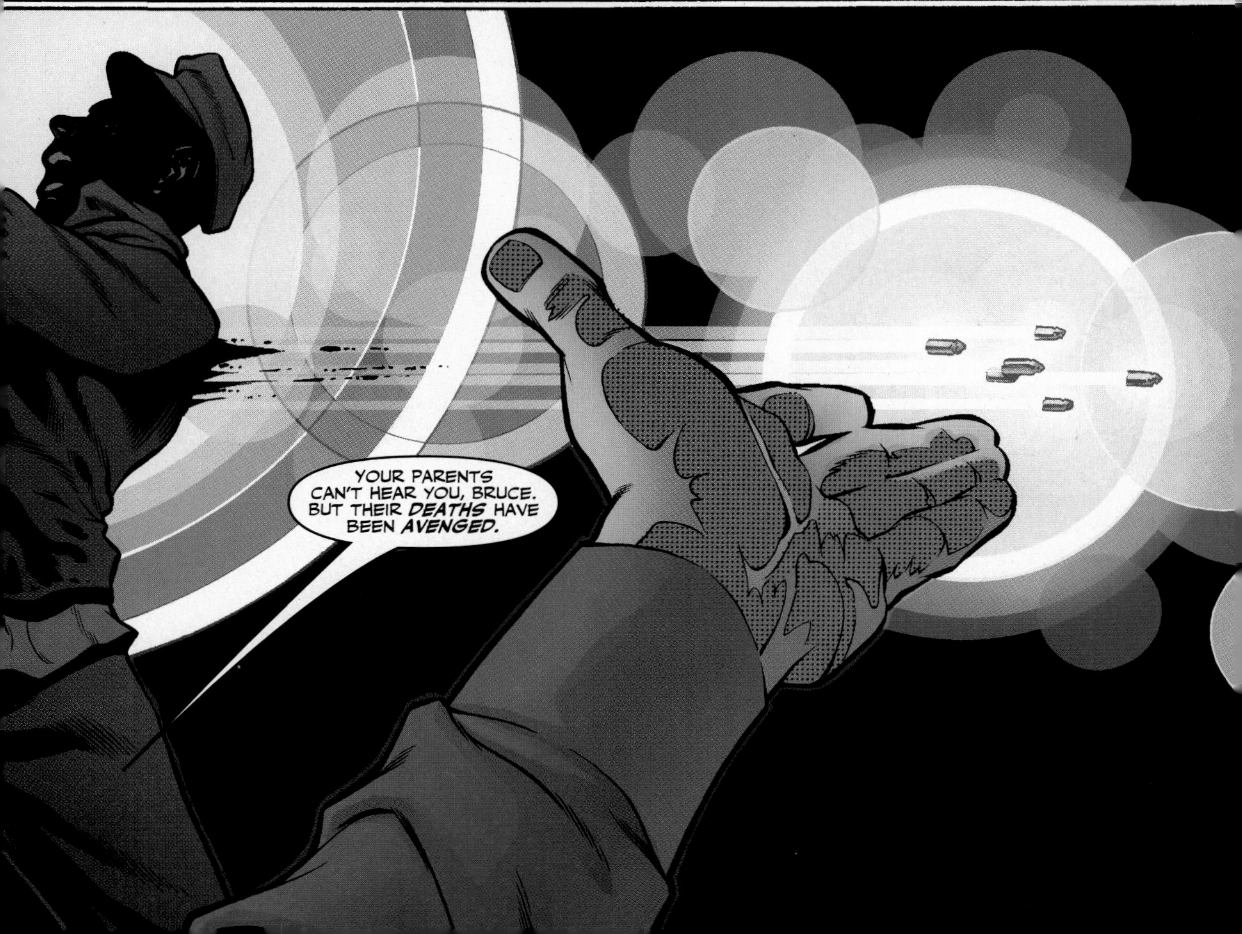
YOUR PARENTS CAN'T HEAR YOU, BRUCE. BUT THEIR DEATHS HAVE BEEN AVENGED.

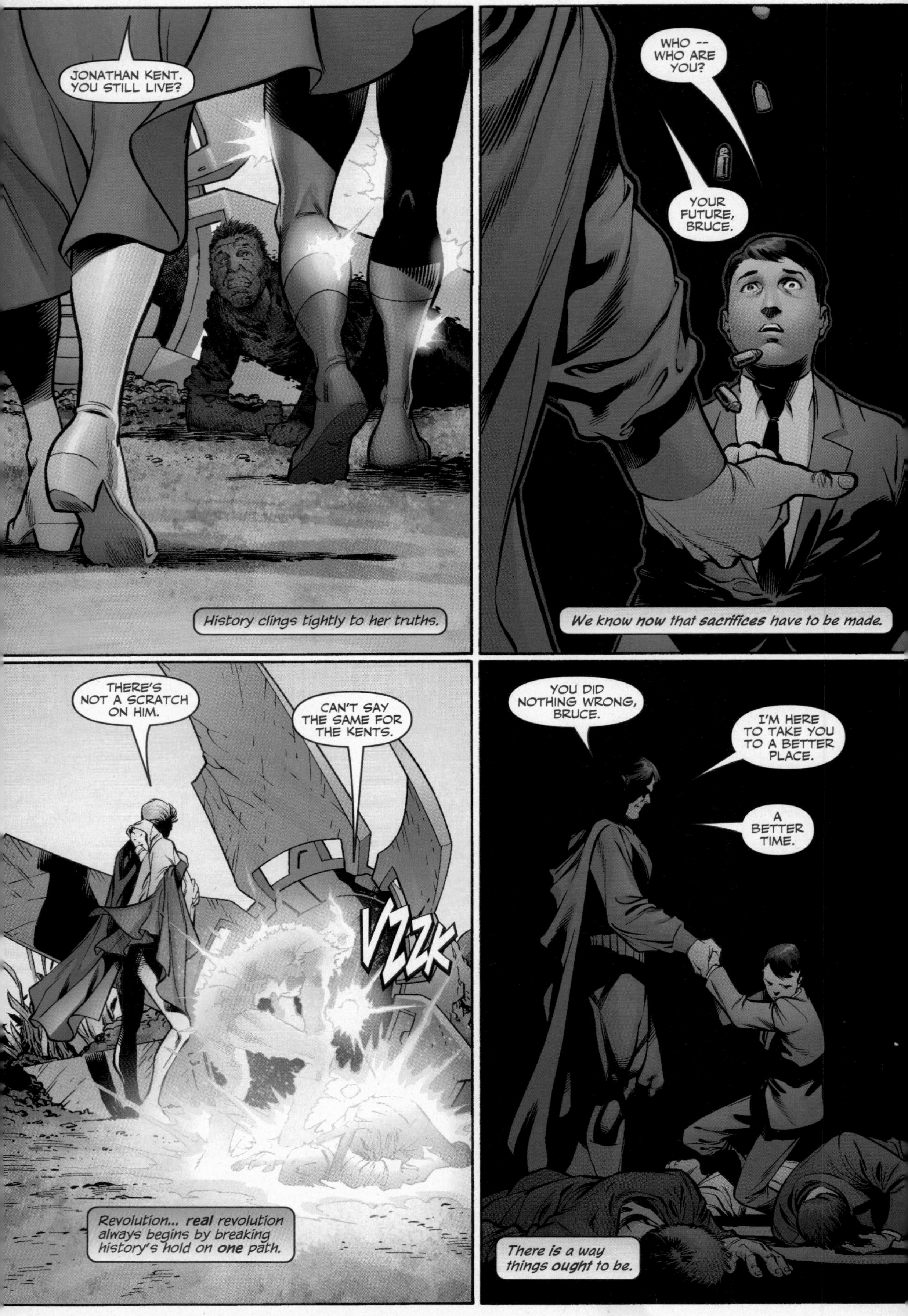
JONATHAN KENT. YOU STILL LIVE?
History clings tightly to her truths.
WHO -- WHO ARE YOU?
YOUR FUTURE, BRUCE.
We know now that sacrifices have to be made.
THERE'S NOT A SCRATCH ON HIM.
CAN'T SAY THE SAME FOR THE KENTS.
VZZK
Revolution... real revolution always begins by breaking history's hold on one path.
YOU DID NOTHING WRONG, BRUCE.
I'M HERE TO TAKE YOU TO A BETTER PLACE.
A BETTER TIME.
There is a way things ought to be.

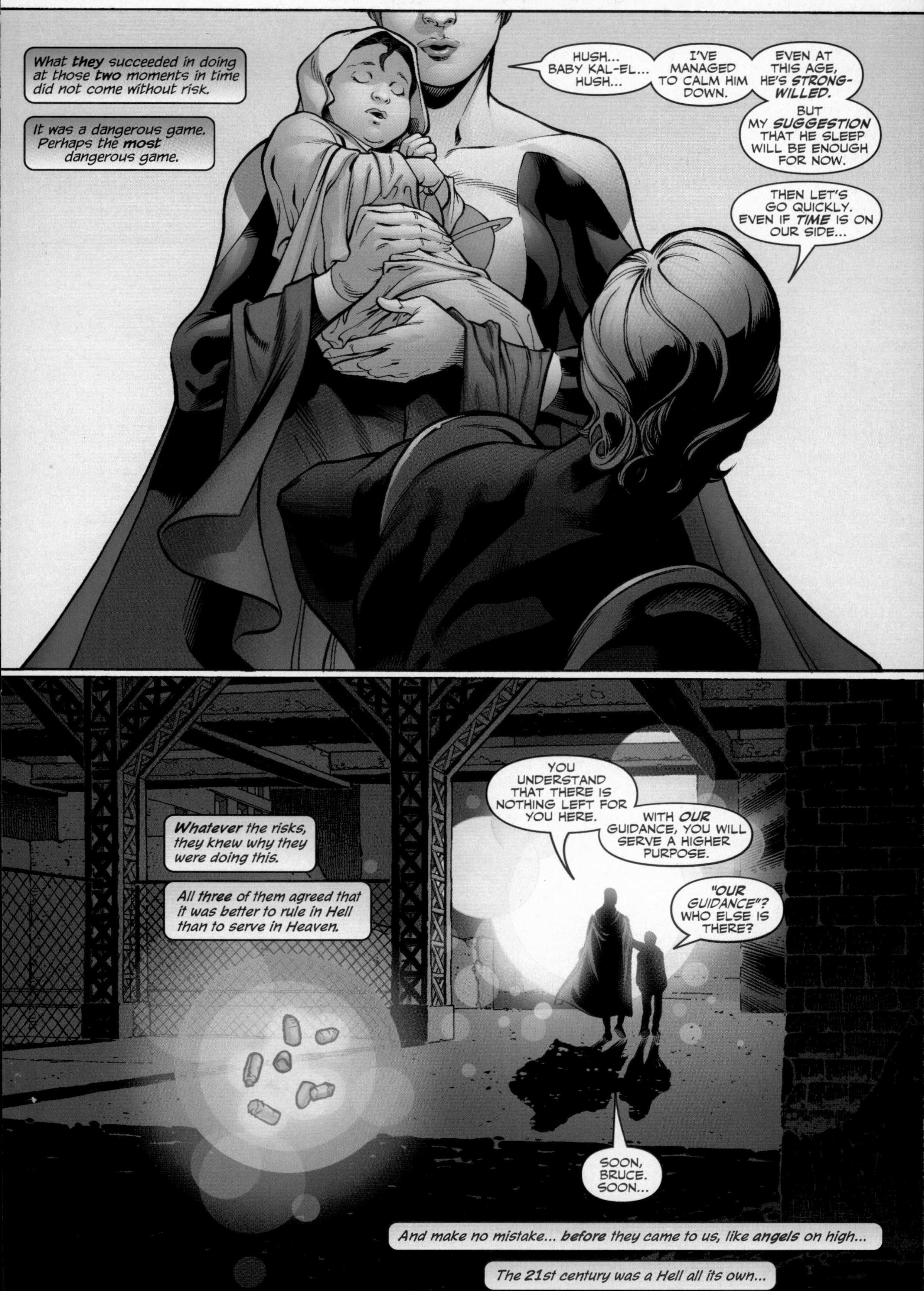

What they succeeded in doing at those two moments in time did not come without risk.
It was a dangerous game. Perhaps the most dangerous game.
HUSH... BABY KAL-EL... HUSH...
I'VE MANAGED TO CALM HIM DOWN.
EVEN AT THIS AGE, HE'S STRONG-WILLED.
BUT MY SUGGESTION THAT HE SLEEP WILL BE ENOUGH FOR NOW.
THEN LET'S GO QUICKLY. EVEN IF TIME IS ON OUR SIDE...
Whatever the risks, they knew why they were doing this.
All three of them agreed that it was better to rule in Hell than to serve in Heaven.
YOU UNDERSTAND THAT THERE IS NOTHING LEFT FOR YOU HERE.
WITH OUR GUIDANCE, YOU WILL SERVE A HIGHER PURPOSE.
"OUR GUIDANCE"? WHO ELSE IS THERE?
SOON, BRUCE. SOON...
And make no mistake... before they came to us, like angels on high...
The 21st century was a Hell all its own...

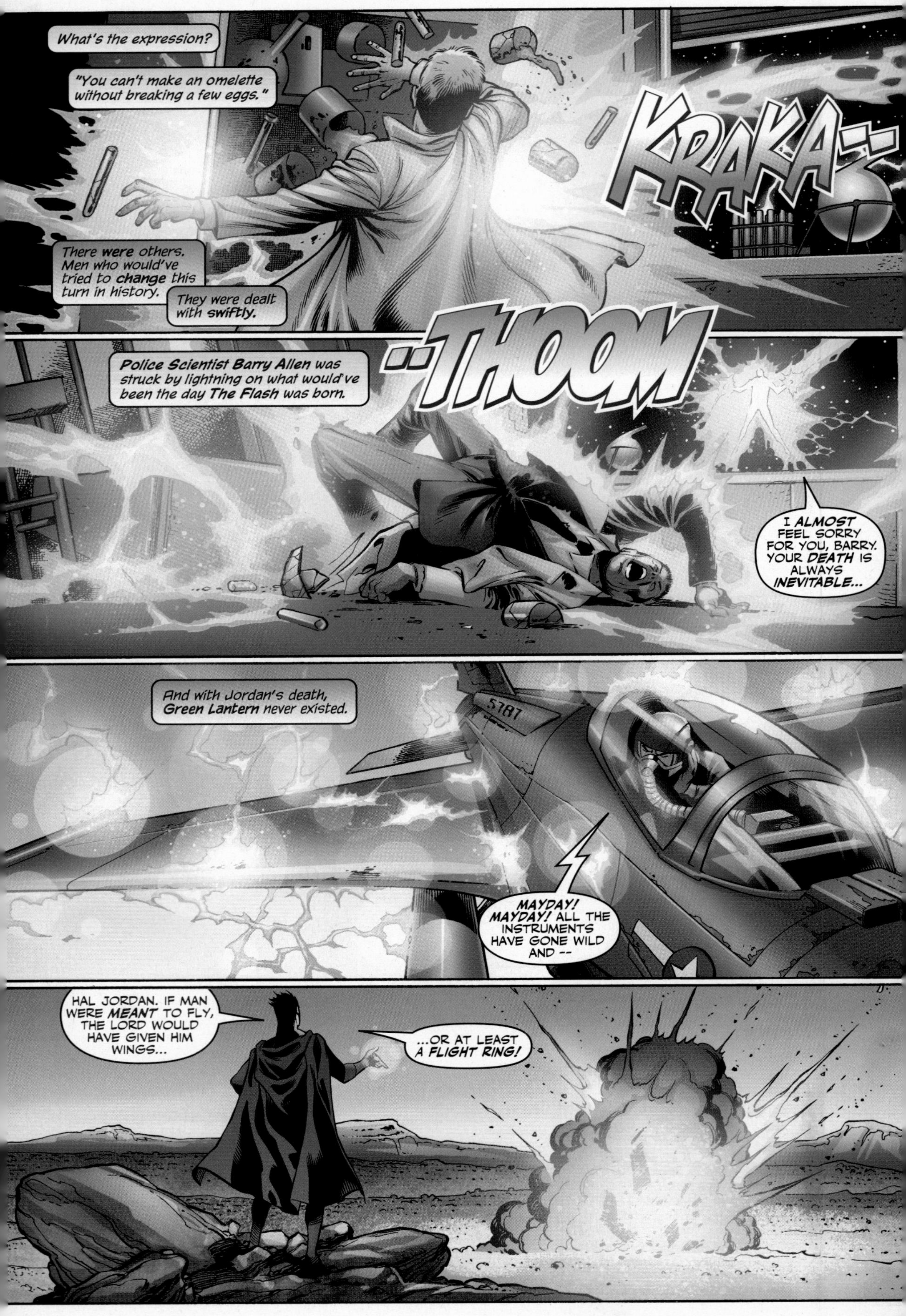
What's the expression?
"You can't make an omelette without breaking a few eggs."
KRAKA--
There were others. Men who would've tried to change this turn in history.
They were dealt with swiftly.
--THOOM
Police Scientist Barry Allen was struck by lightning on what would've been the day The Flash was born.
I ALMOST FEEL SORRY FOR YOU, BARRY. YOUR DEATH IS ALWAYS INEVITABLE...
And with Jordan's death, Green Lantern never existed.
5787
MAYDAY! MAYDAY! ALL THE INSTRUMENTS HAVE GONE WILD AND --
HAL JORDAN. IF MAN WERE MEANT TO FLY, THE LORD WOULD HAVE GIVEN HIM WINGS...
...OR AT LEAST A FLIGHT RING!

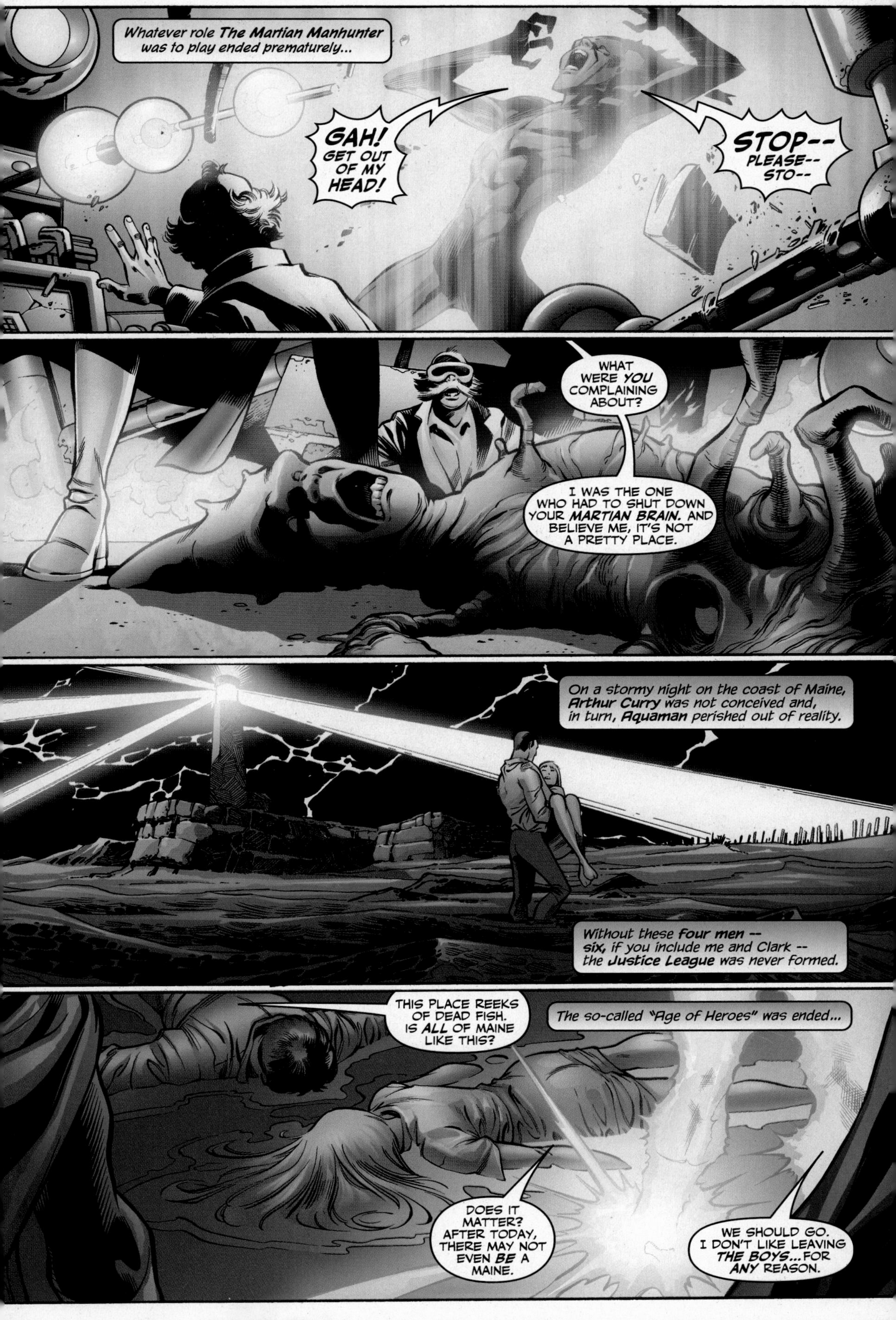
Whatever role The Martian Manhunter was to play ended prematurely...
GAH! GET OUT OF MY HEAD!
STOP-- PLEASE-- STO--
WHAT WERE YOU COMPLAINING ABOUT?
I WAS THE ONE WHO HAD TO SHUT DOWN YOUR MARTIAN BRAIN. AND BELIEVE ME, IT'S NOT A PRETTY PLACE.
On a stormy night on the coast of Maine, Arthur Curry was not conceived and, in turn, Aquaman perished out of reality.
Without these four men -- six, if you include me and Clark -- the Justice League was never formed.
THIS PLACE REEKS OF DEAD FISH. IS ALL OF MAINE LIKE THIS?
The so-called "Age of Heroes" was ended...
DOES IT MATTER? AFTER TODAY, THERE MAY NOT EVEN BE A MAINE.
WE SHOULD GO. I DON'T LIKE LEAVING THE BOYS...FOR ANY REASON.

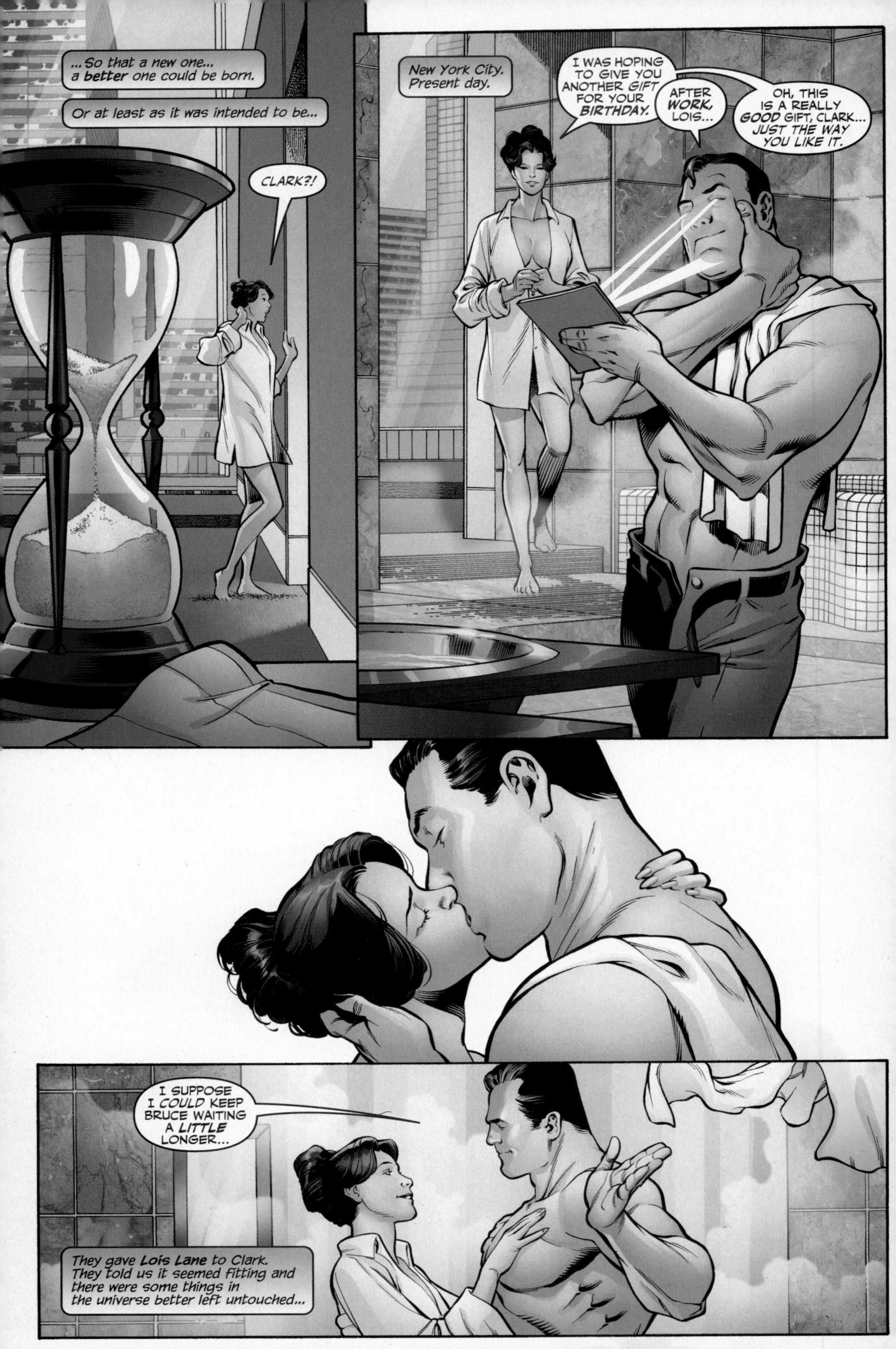
...So that a new one... a **better** one could be born.
Or at least as it was intended to be...
CLARK?!
New York City. Present day.
I WAS HOPING TO GIVE YOU ANOTHER *GIFT* FOR YOUR *BIRTHDAY.*
AFTER *WORK,* LOIS...
OH, THIS IS A REALLY *GOOD* GIFT, CLARK... *JUST THE WAY YOU LIKE IT.*
I SUPPOSE I *COULD* KEEP BRUCE WAITING A *LITTLE* LONGER...
They gave **Lois Lane** to Clark. They told us it seemed fitting and there were some things in the universe better left untouched...

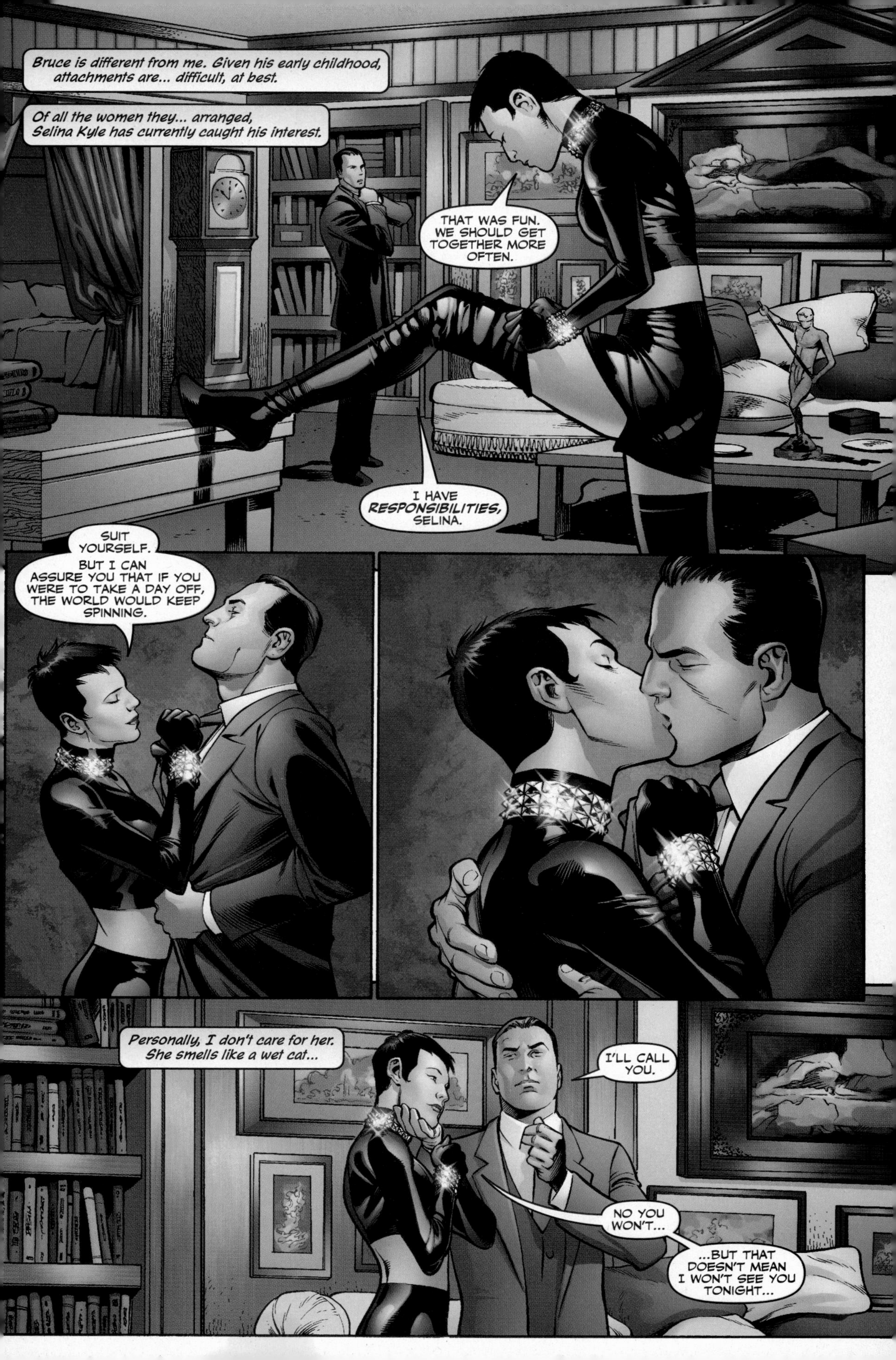
Bruce is different from me. Given his early childhood, attachments are... difficult, at best.
Of all the women they... arranged, Selina Kyle has currently caught his interest.
THAT WAS FUN. WE SHOULD GET TOGETHER MORE OFTEN.
I HAVE RESPONSIBILITIES, SELINA.
SUIT YOURSELF.
BUT I CAN ASSURE YOU THAT IF YOU WERE TO TAKE A DAY OFF, THE WORLD WOULD KEEP SPINNING.
Personally, I don't care for her. She smells like a wet cat...
I'LL CALL YOU.
NO YOU WON'T...
...BUT THAT DOESN'T MEAN I WON'T SEE YOU TONIGHT...

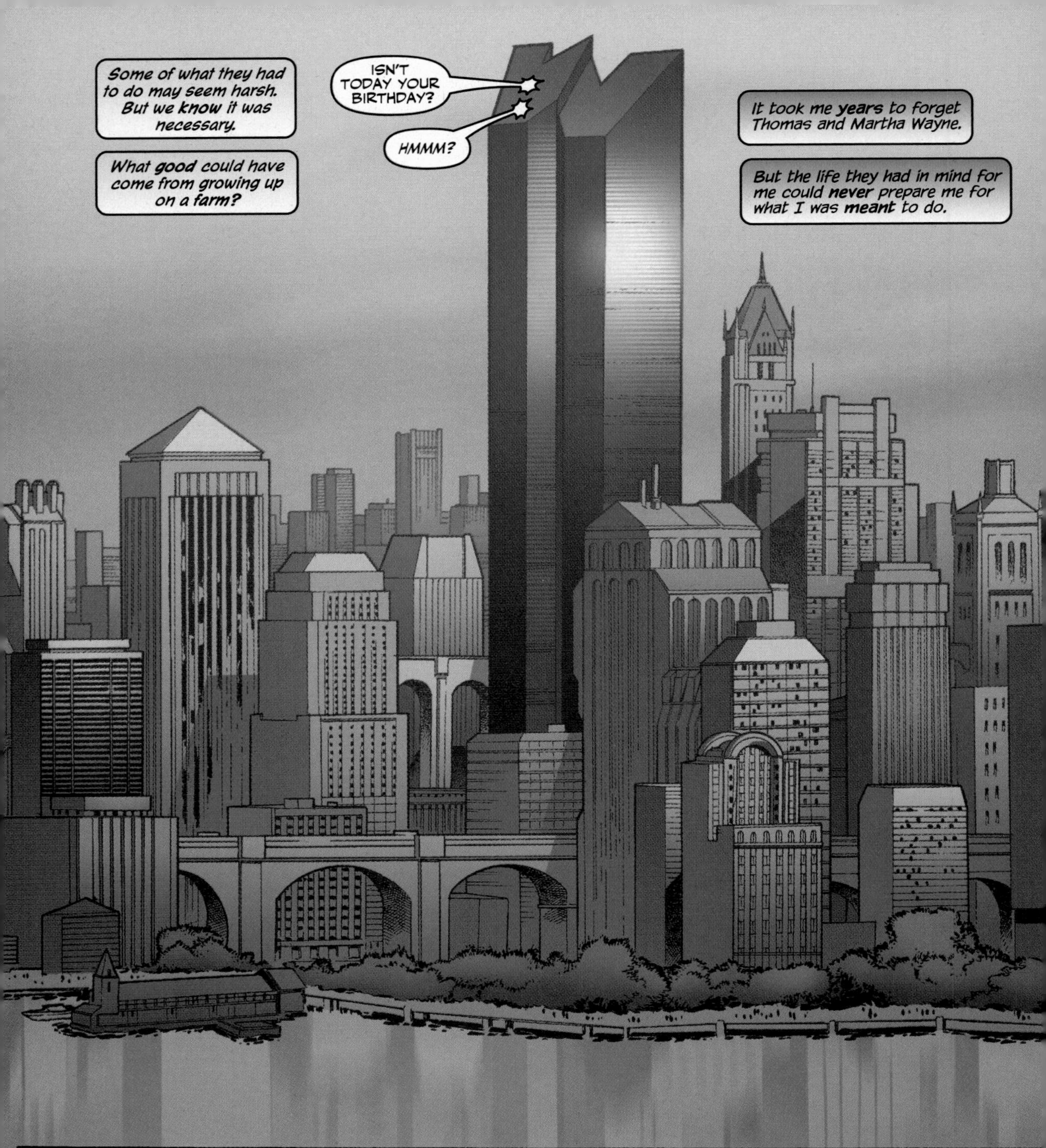
Some of what they had to do may seem harsh. But we *know* it was necessary.
What *good* could have come from growing up on a farm?
ISN'T TODAY YOUR BIRTHDAY?
HMMM?
It took me *years* to forget Thomas and Martha Wayne.
But the life they had in mind for me could *never* prepare me for what I was *meant* to do.

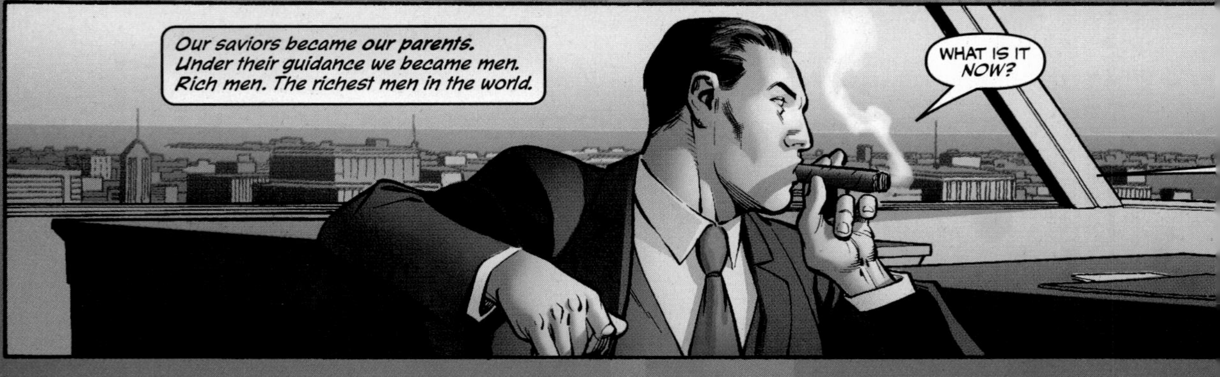
Our saviors became our *parents.* Under their guidance we became men. Rich men. The richest men in the world.
WHAT IS IT *NOW?*

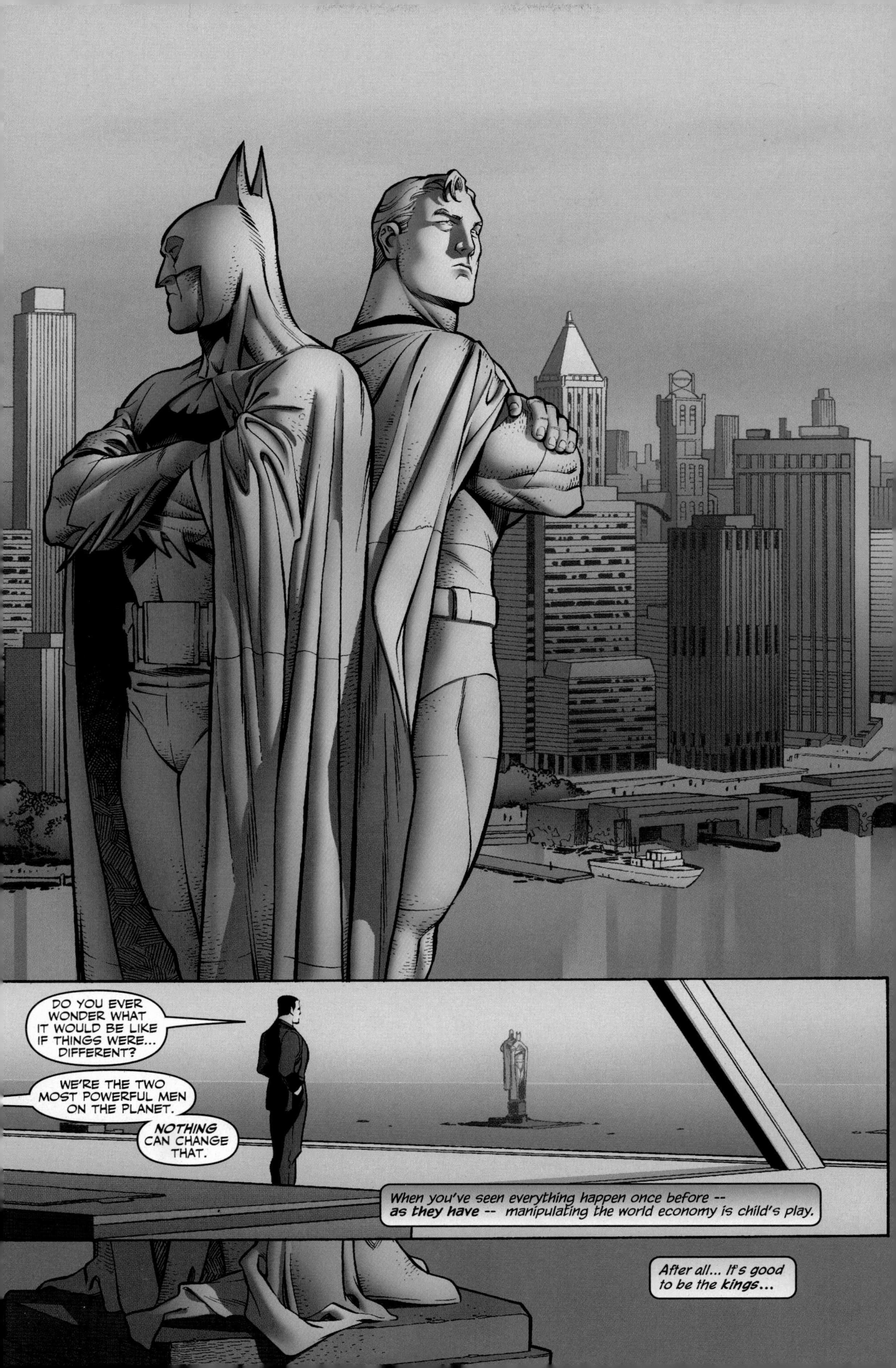
DO YOU EVER WONDER WHAT IT WOULD BE LIKE IF THINGS WERE... DIFFERENT?
WE'RE THE TWO MOST POWERFUL MEN ON THE PLANET.
NOTHING CAN CHANGE THAT.
When you've seen everything happen once before -- as they have -- manipulating the world economy is child's play.
After all... It's good to be the kings...

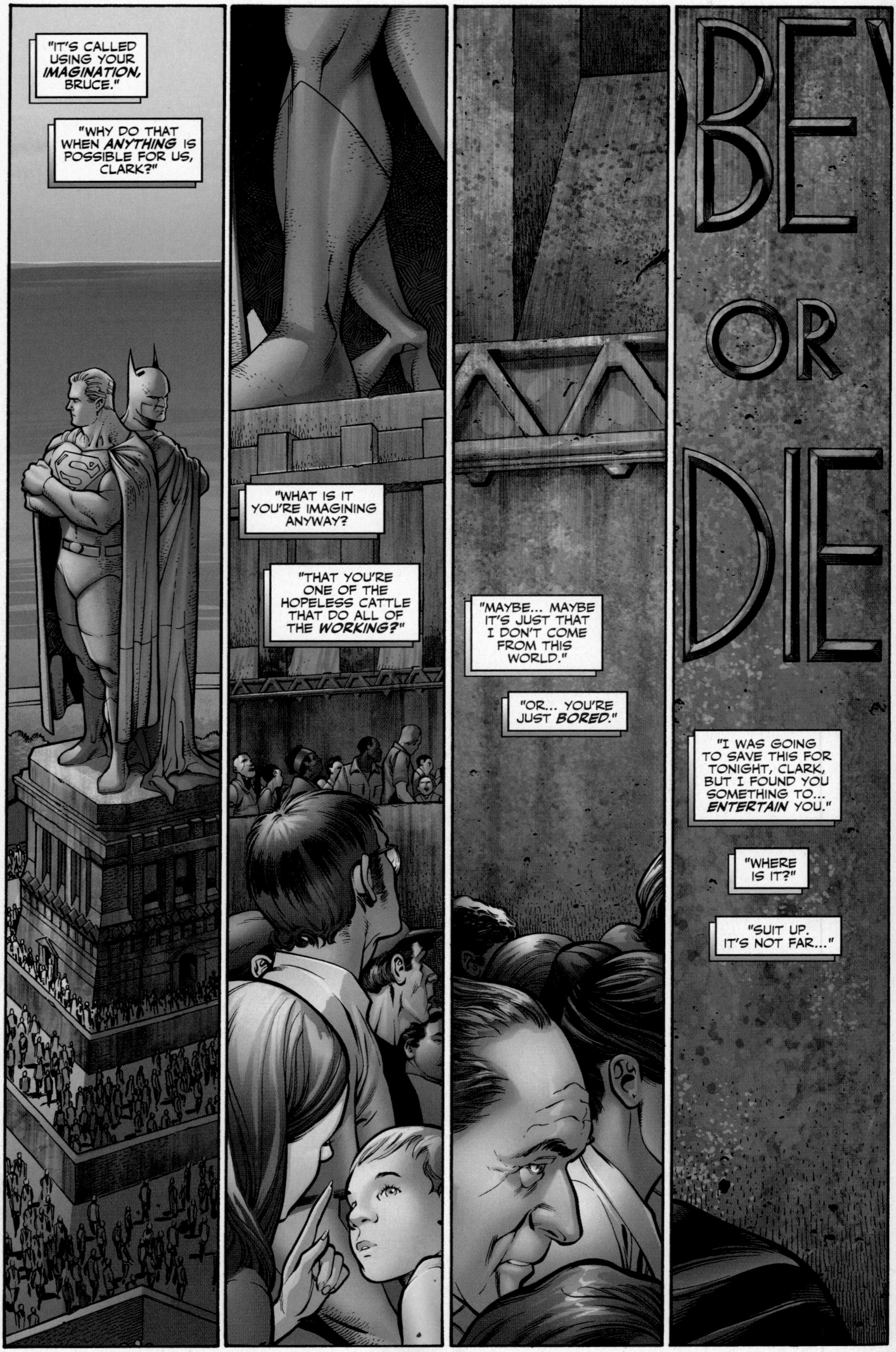
"IT'S CALLED USING YOUR *IMAGINATION,* BRUCE."
"WHY DO THAT WHEN *ANYTHING* IS POSSIBLE FOR US, CLARK?"
"WHAT IS IT YOU'RE IMAGINING ANYWAY?
"THAT YOU'RE ONE OF THE HOPELESS CATTLE THAT DO ALL OF THE *WORKING?*"
"MAYBE... MAYBE IT'S JUST THAT I DON'T COME FROM THIS WORLD."
"OR... YOU'RE JUST *BORED.*"
BE
OR
DIE
"I WAS GOING TO SAVE THIS FOR TONIGHT, CLARK, BUT I FOUND YOU SOMETHING TO... *ENTERTAIN* YOU."
"WHERE IS IT?"
"SUIT UP. IT'S NOT FAR..."

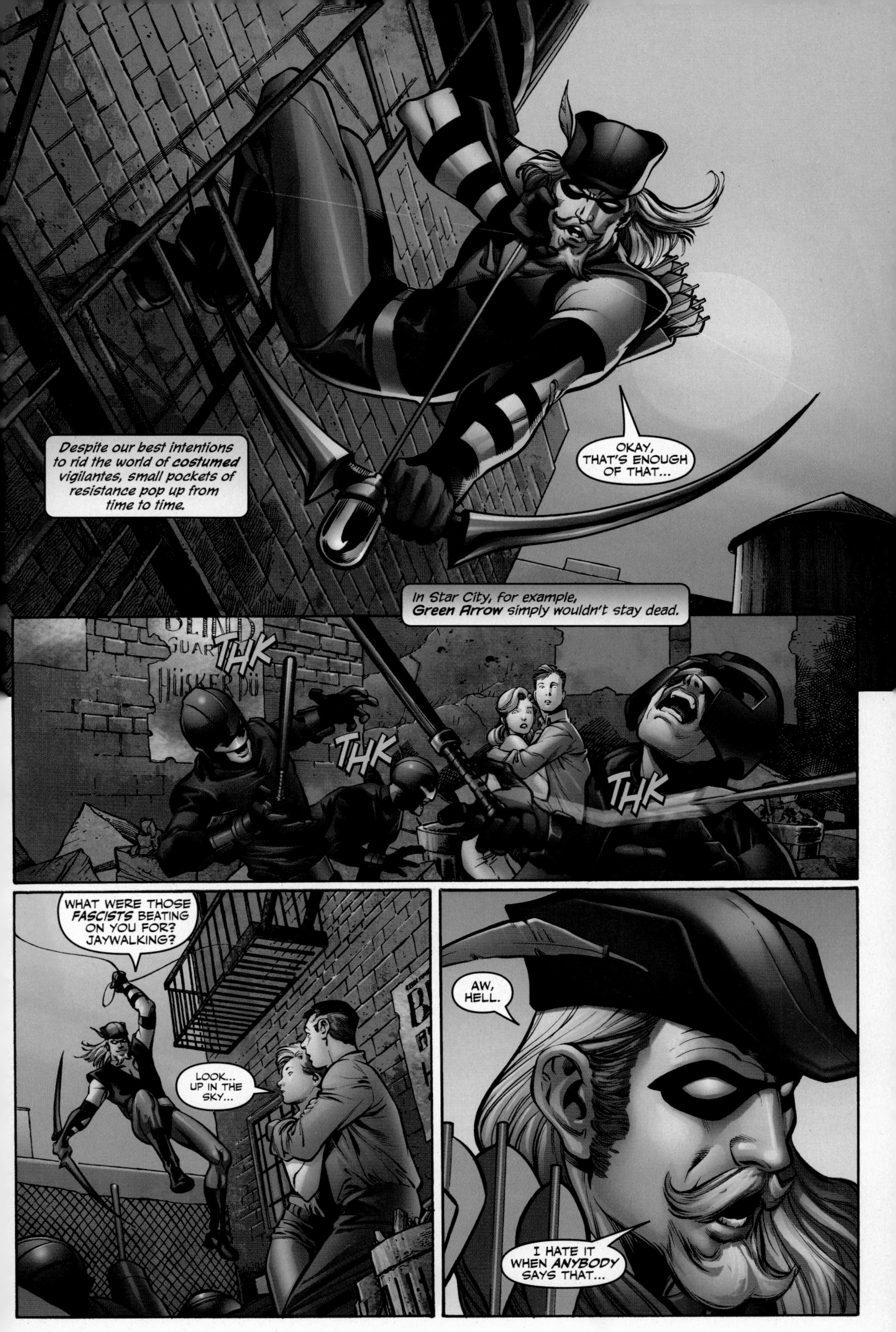

Despite our best intentions to rid the world of costumed vigilantes, small pockets of resistance pop up from time to time.
OKAY, THAT'S ENOUGH OF THAT...
In Star City, for example, Green Arrow simply wouldn't stay dead.
HÜSKER DÜ
THK
THK
THK
WHAT WERE THOSE FASCISTS BEATING ON YOU FOR? JAYWALKING?
LOOK... UP IN THE SKY...
AW, HELL.
I HATE IT WHEN ANYBODY SAYS THAT...

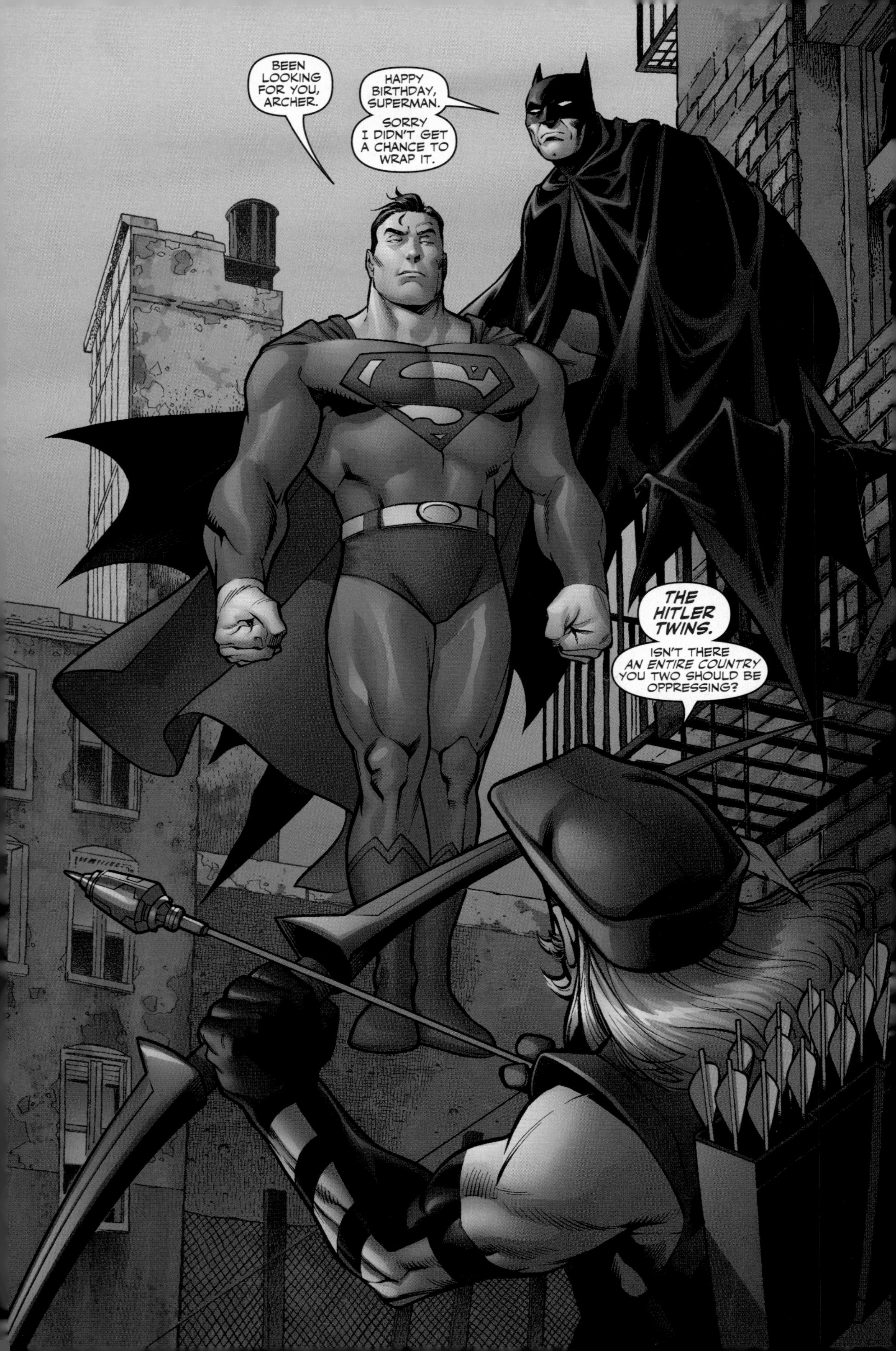
BEEN LOOKING FOR YOU, ARCHER.
HAPPY BIRTHDAY, SUPERMAN.
SORRY I DIDN'T GET A CHANCE TO WRAP IT.
THE HITLER TWINS.
ISN'T THERE AN ENTIRE COUNTRY YOU TWO SHOULD BE OPPRESSING?

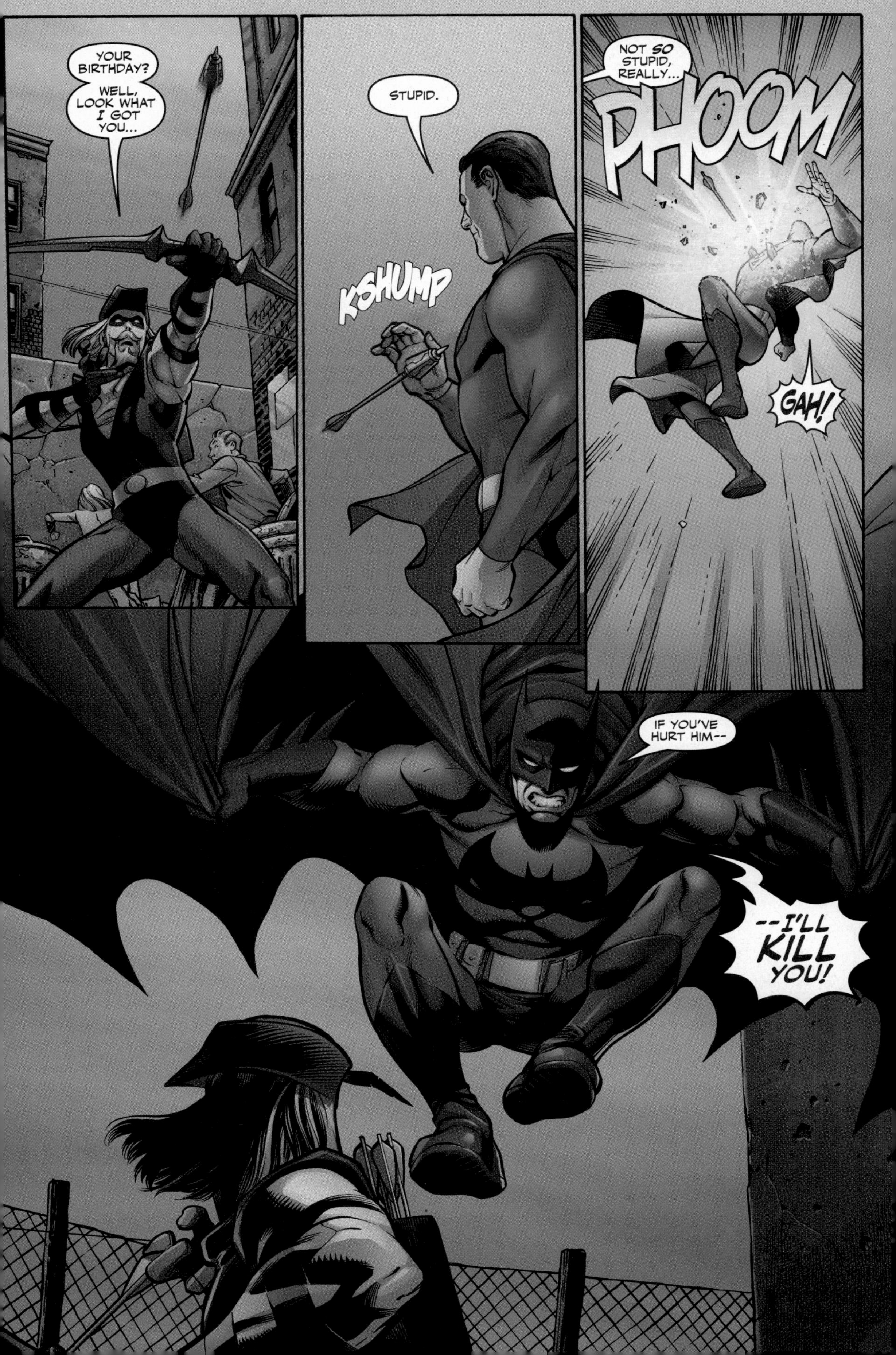
YOUR BIRTHDAY?
WELL, LOOK WHAT I GOT YOU...
STUPID.
KSHUMP
NOT SO STUPID, REALLY...
PHOOM
GAH!
IF YOU'VE HURT HIM--
--I'LL KILL YOU!

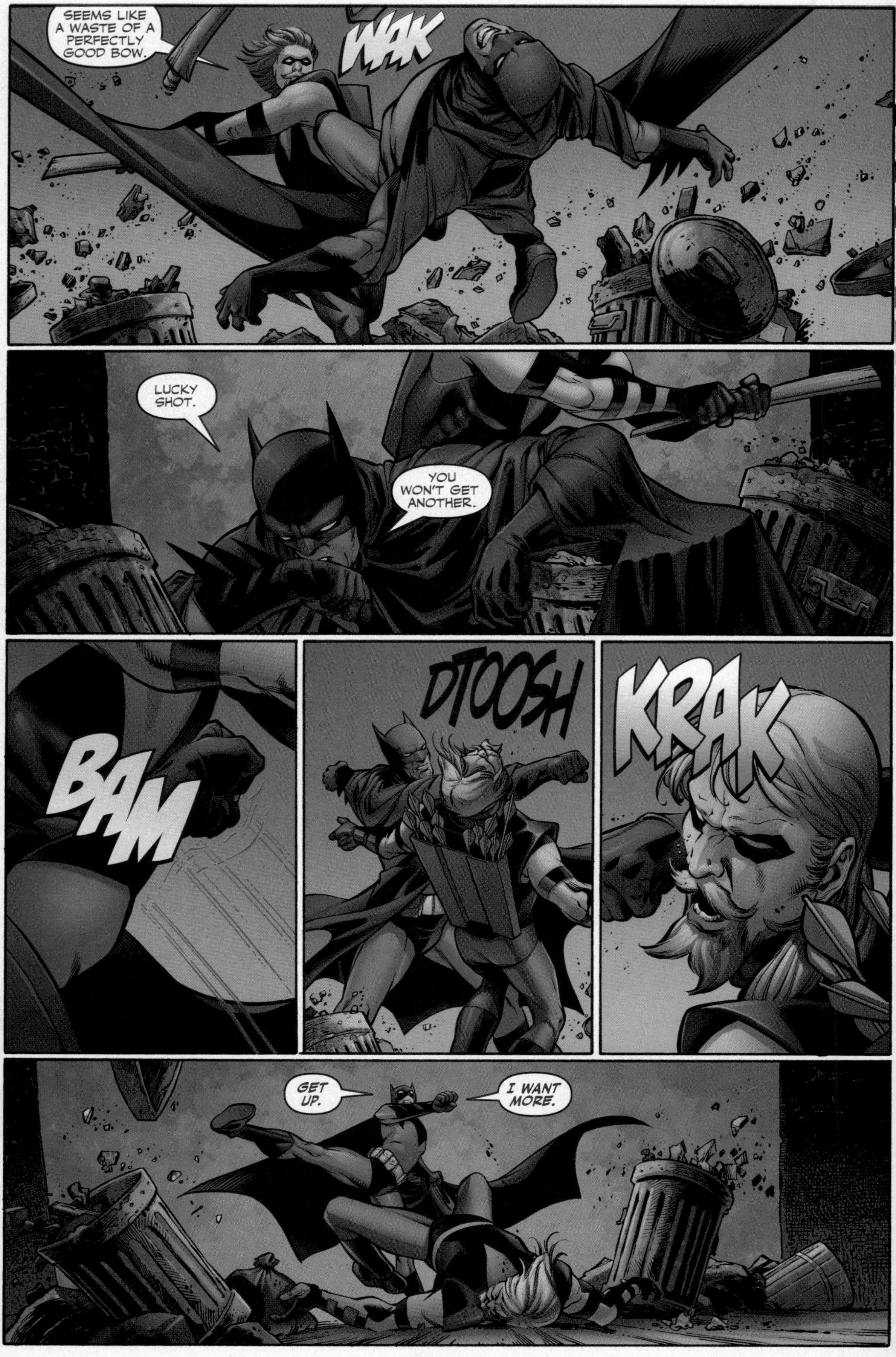
SEEMS LIKE A WASTE OF A PERFECTLY GOOD BOW.
WAK
LUCKY SHOT.
YOU WON'T GET ANOTHER.
BAM
DTOOSH
KRAK
GET UP.
I WANT MORE.

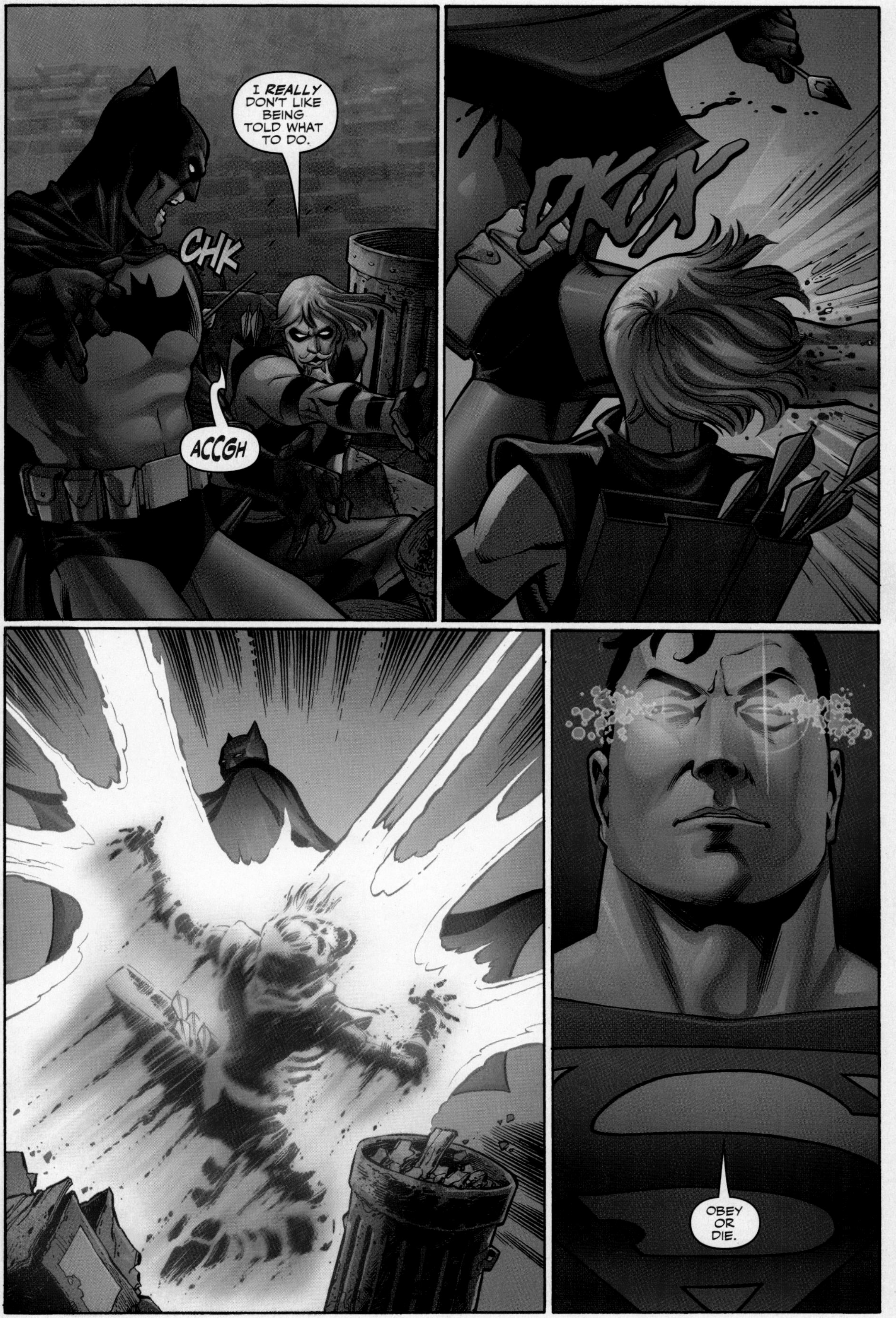
I *REALLY* DON'T LIKE BEING TOLD WHAT TO DO.
CHK
ACCGH
OBEY OR DIE.

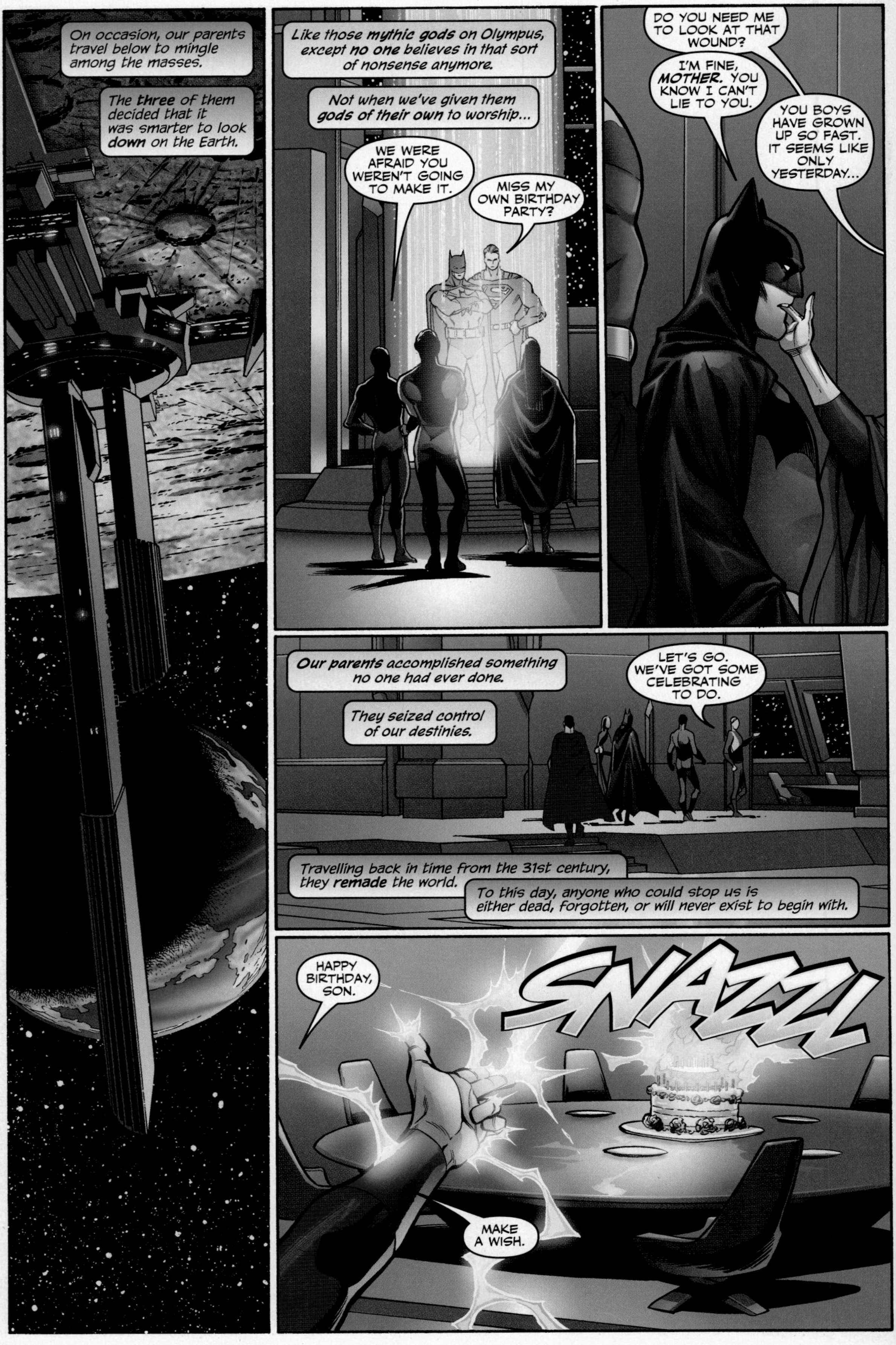
On occasion, our parents travel below to mingle among the masses.
The three of them decided that it was smarter to look down on the Earth.
Like those mythic gods on Olympus, except no one believes in that sort of nonsense anymore.
Not when we've given them gods of their own to worship...
WE WERE AFRAID YOU WEREN'T GOING TO MAKE IT.
MISS MY OWN BIRTHDAY PARTY?
DO YOU NEED ME TO LOOK AT THAT WOUND?
I'M FINE, MOTHER. YOU KNOW I CAN'T LIE TO YOU.
YOU BOYS HAVE GROWN UP SO FAST. IT SEEMS LIKE ONLY YESTERDAY...
Our parents accomplished something no one had ever done.
They seized control of our destinies.
LET'S GO. WE'VE GOT SOME CELEBRATING TO DO.
Travelling back in time from the 31st century, they remade the world.
To this day, anyone who could stop us is either dead, forgotten, or will never exist to begin with.
HAPPY BIRTHDAY, SON.
SNAZZL
MAKE A WISH.

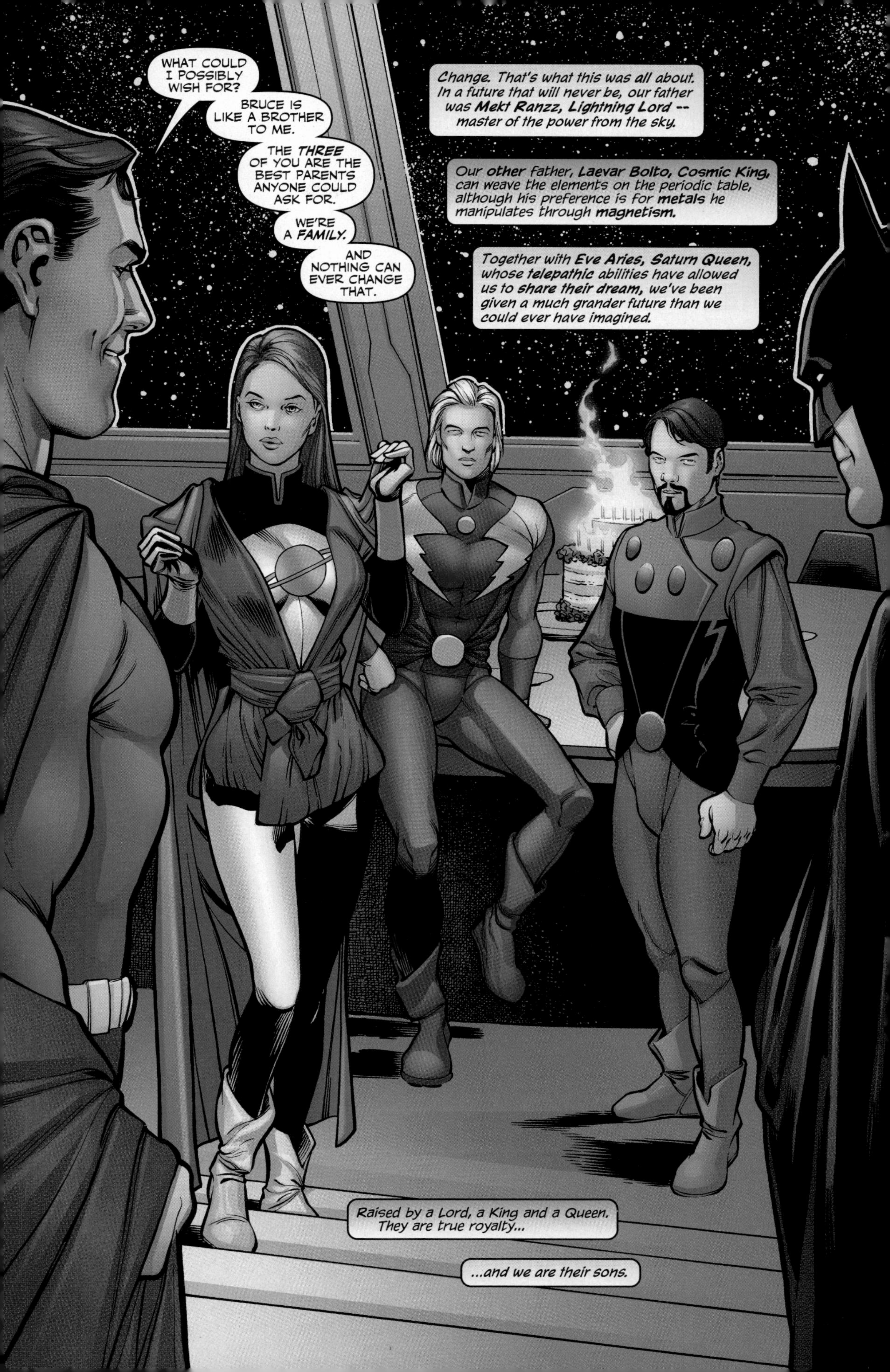

WHAT COULD I POSSIBLY WISH FOR?
BRUCE IS LIKE A BROTHER TO ME.
THE THREE OF YOU ARE THE BEST PARENTS ANYONE COULD ASK FOR.
WE'RE A FAMILY.
AND NOTHING CAN EVER CHANGE THAT.
Change. That's what this was all about. In a future that will never be, our father was Mekt Ranzz, Lightning Lord -- master of the power from the sky.
Our other father, Laevar Bolto, Cosmic King, can weave the elements on the periodic table, although his preference is for metals he manipulates through magnetism.
Together with Eve Aries, Saturn Queen, whose telepathic abilities have allowed us to share their dream, we've been given a much grander future than we could ever have imagined.
Raised by a Lord, a King and a Queen. They are true royalty...
...and we are their sons.

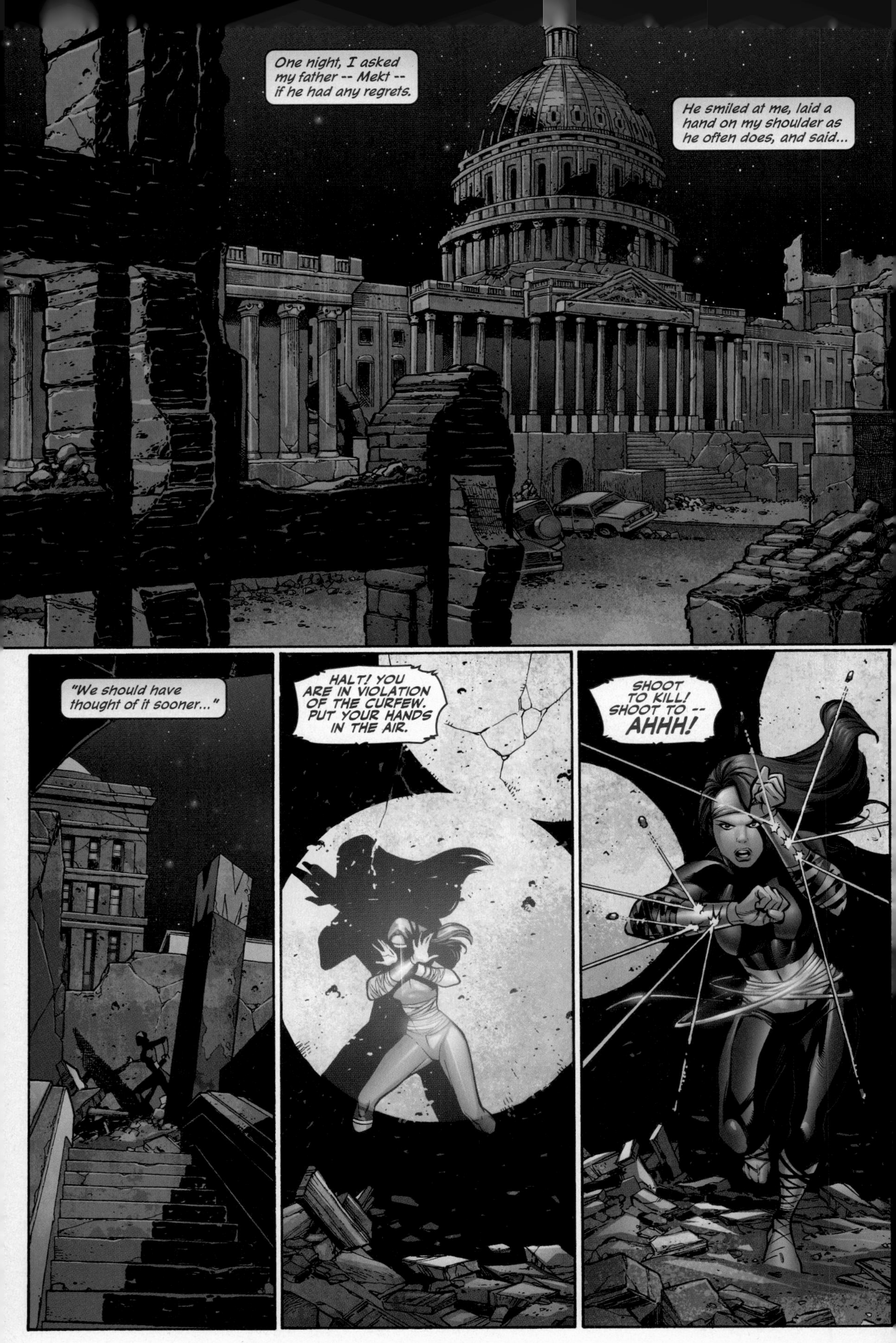
One night, I asked my father -- Mekt -- if he had any regrets.
He smiled at me, laid a hand on my shoulder as he often does, and said...
"We should have thought of it sooner..."
HALT! YOU ARE IN VIOLATION OF THE CURFEW. PUT YOUR HANDS IN THE AIR.
SHOOT TO KILL! SHOOT TO -- AHHH!

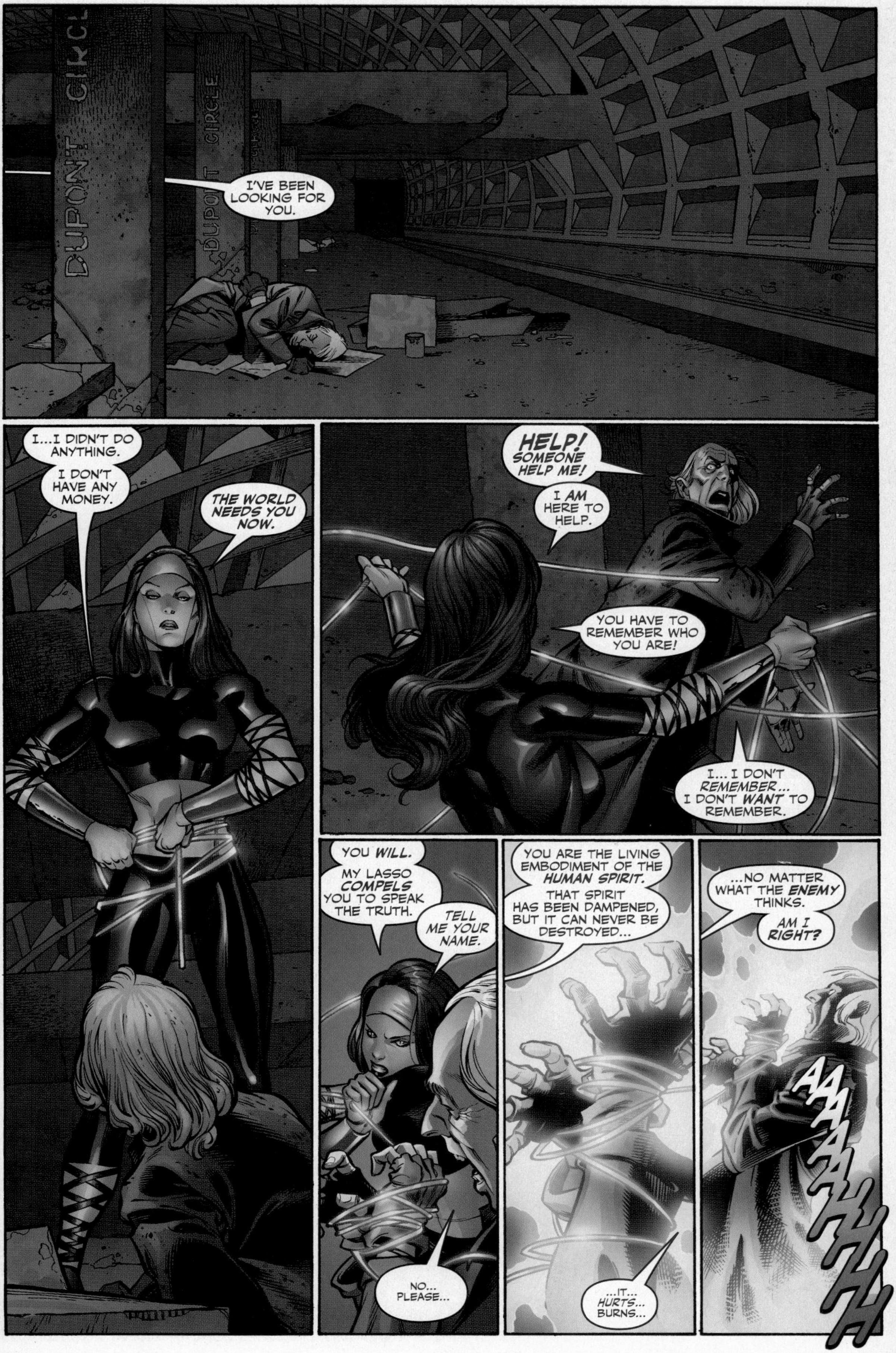
DUPONT CIRCLE
DUPONT CIRCLE
I'VE BEEN LOOKING FOR YOU.
I...I DIDN'T DO ANYTHING.
I DON'T HAVE ANY MONEY.
THE WORLD NEEDS YOU NOW.
HELP! SOMEONE HELP ME!
I AM HERE TO HELP.
YOU HAVE TO REMEMBER WHO YOU ARE!
I... I DON'T REMEMBER... I DON'T WANT TO REMEMBER.
YOU WILL.
MY LASSO COMPELS YOU TO SPEAK THE TRUTH.
TELL ME YOUR NAME.
NO... PLEASE...
YOU ARE THE LIVING EMBODIMENT OF THE HUMAN SPIRIT.
THAT SPIRIT HAS BEEN DAMPENED, BUT IT CAN NEVER BE DESTROYED...
...IT... HURTS... BURNS...
...NO MATTER WHAT THE ENEMY THINKS.
AM I RIGHT?
AAAAAHHHHH

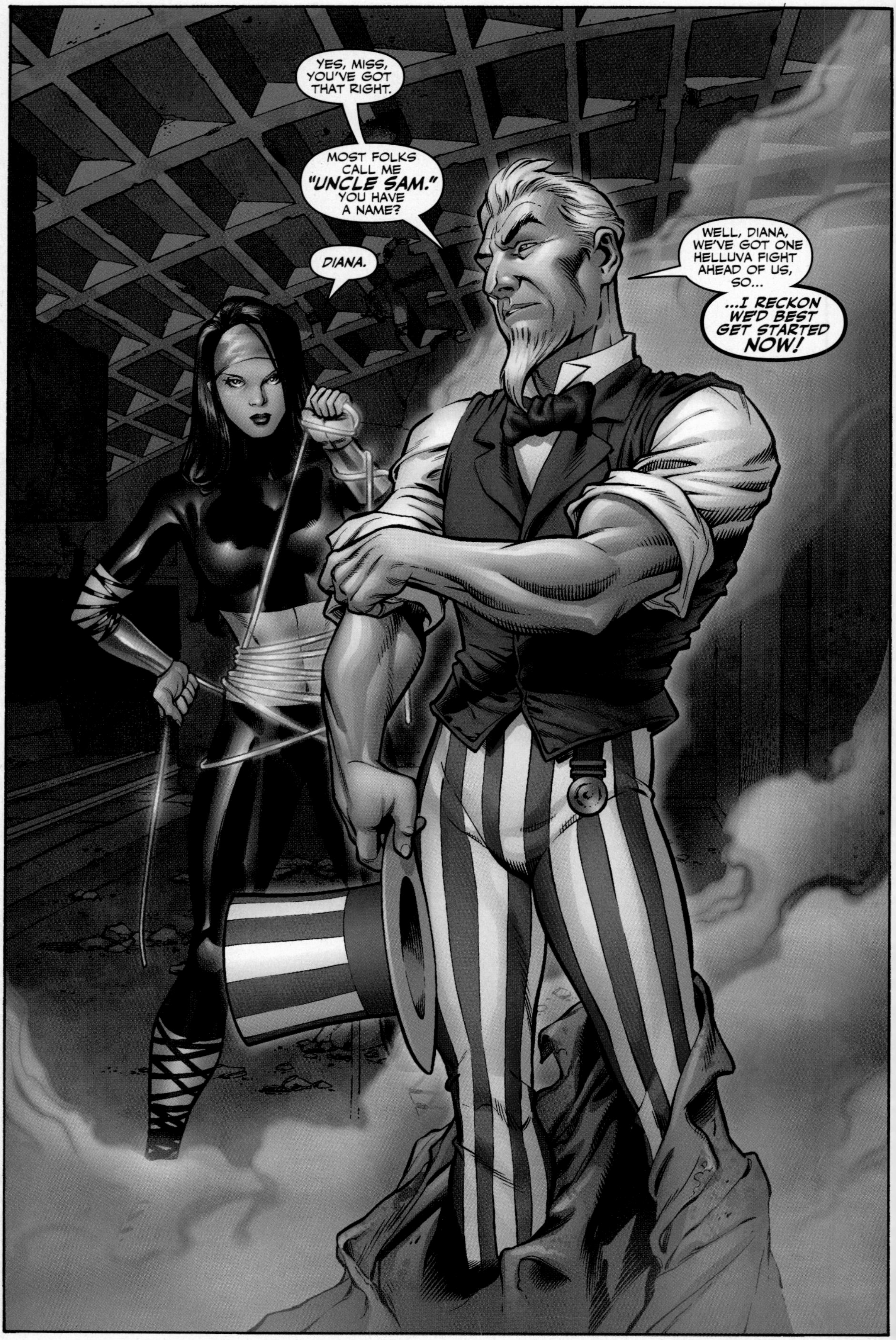
YES, MISS, YOU'VE GOT THAT RIGHT.
MOST FOLKS CALL ME "UNCLE SAM." YOU HAVE A NAME?
DIANA.
WELL, DIANA, WE'VE GOT ONE HELLUVA FIGHT AHEAD OF US, SO...
...I RECKON WE'D BEST GET STARTED NOW!

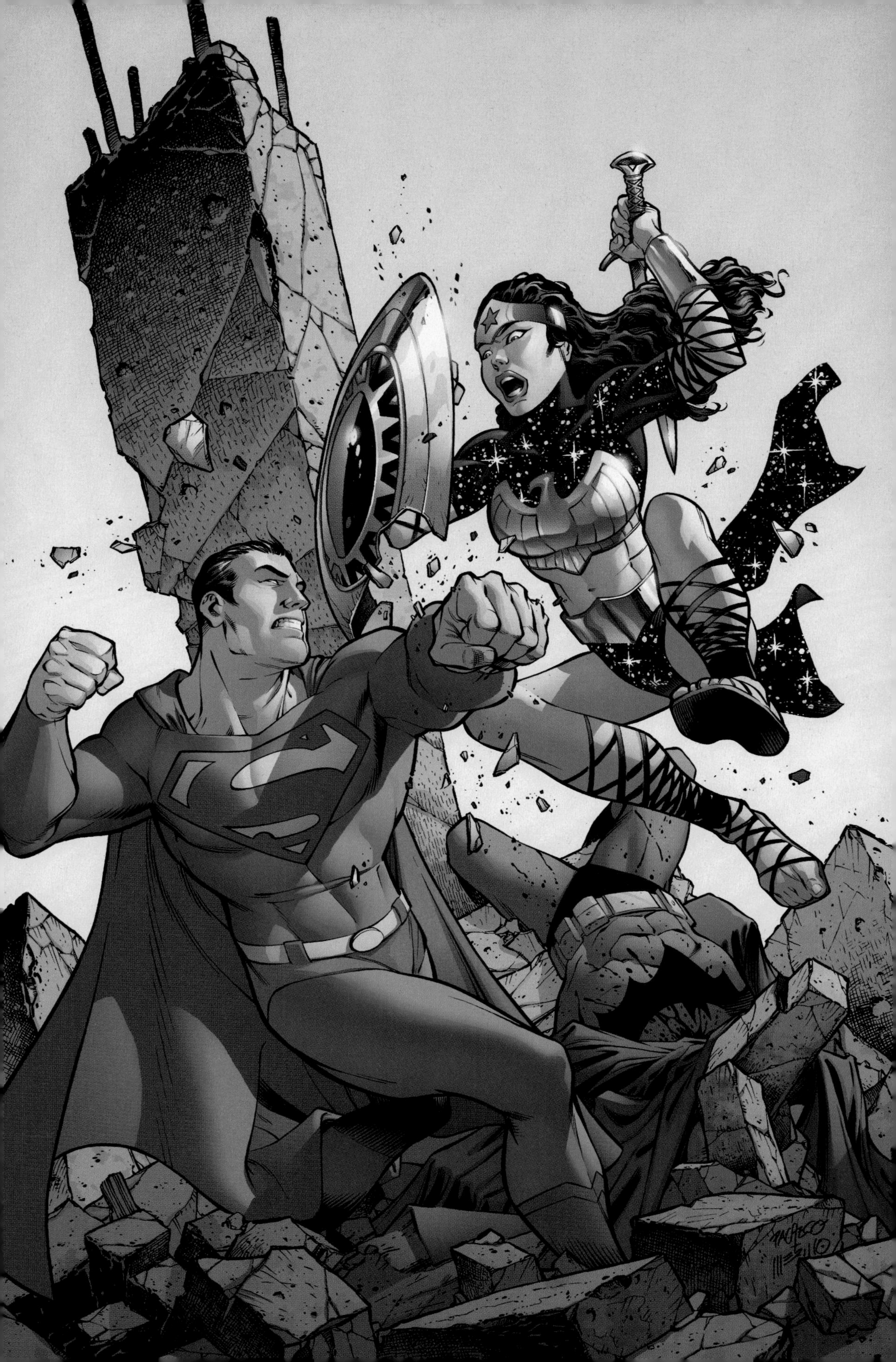

"WHAT PRICE FREEDOM...?"

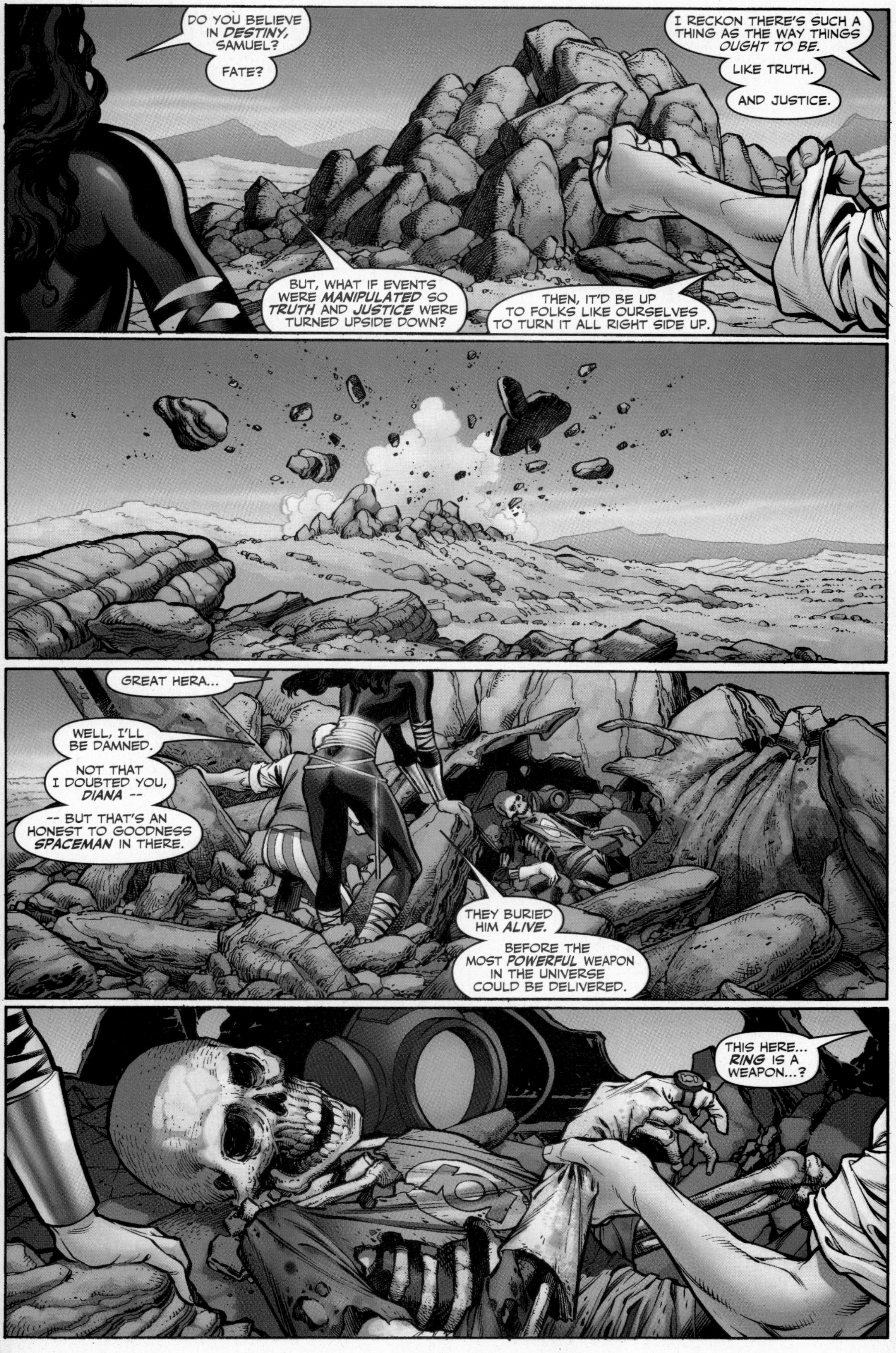
DO YOU BELIEVE IN DESTINY, SAMUEL?
FATE?
I RECKON THERE'S SUCH A THING AS THE WAY THINGS OUGHT TO BE.
LIKE TRUTH.
AND JUSTICE.
BUT, WHAT IF EVENTS WERE MANIPULATED SO TRUTH AND JUSTICE WERE TURNED UPSIDE DOWN?
THEN, IT'D BE UP TO FOLKS LIKE OURSELVES TO TURN IT ALL RIGHT SIDE UP.
GREAT HERA...
WELL, I'LL BE DAMNED.
NOT THAT I DOUBTED YOU, DIANA --
-- BUT THAT'S AN HONEST TO GOODNESS SPACEMAN IN THERE.
THEY BURIED HIM ALIVE.
BEFORE THE MOST POWERFUL WEAPON IN THE UNIVERSE COULD BE DELIVERED.
THIS HERE... RING IS A WEAPON...?

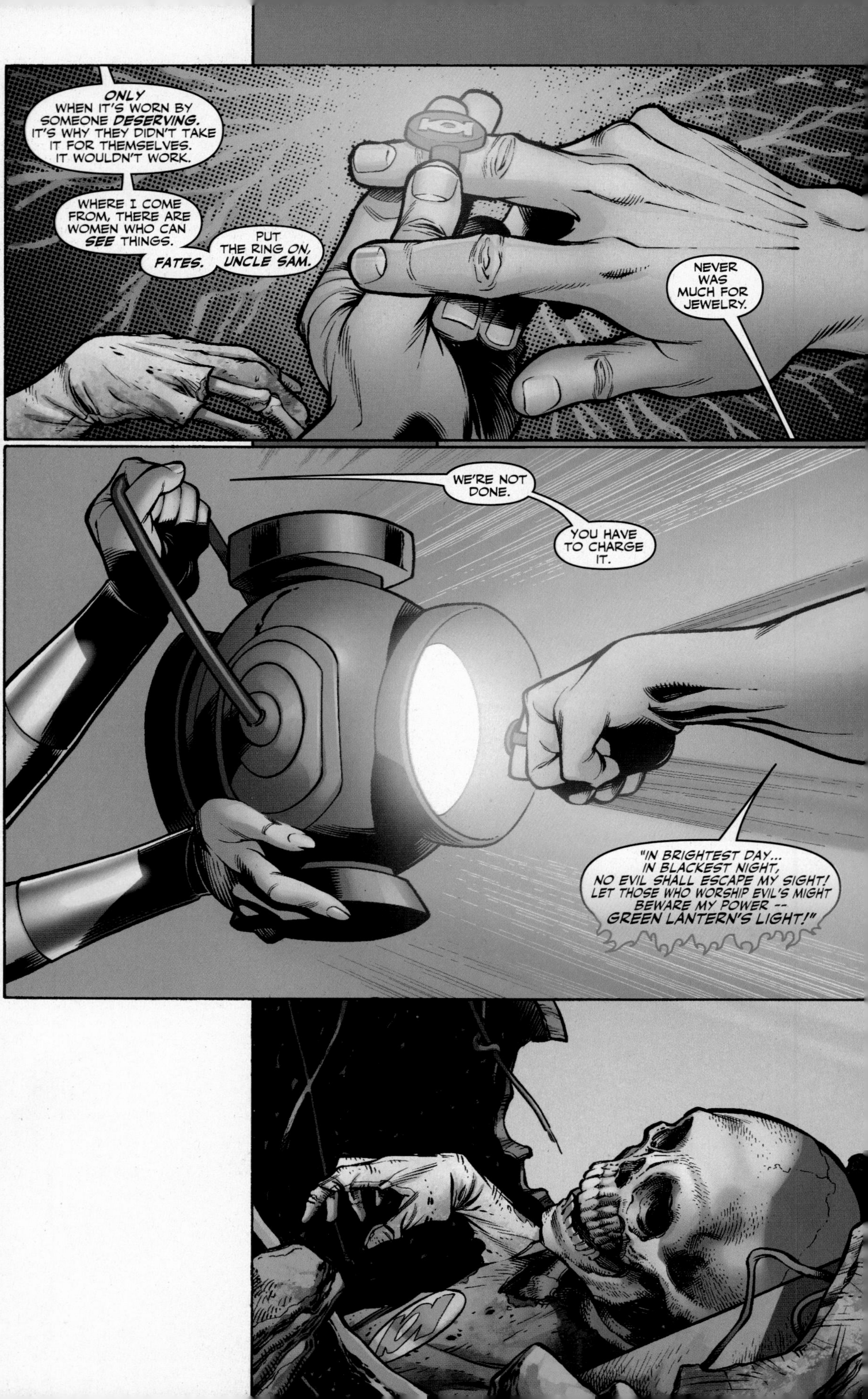
ONLY WHEN IT'S WORN BY SOMEONE DESERVING. IT'S WHY THEY DIDN'T TAKE IT FOR THEMSELVES. IT WOULDN'T WORK.
WHERE I COME FROM, THERE ARE WOMEN WHO CAN SEE THINGS.
FATES.
PUT THE RING ON, UNCLE SAM.
NEVER WAS MUCH FOR JEWELRY.
WE'RE NOT DONE.
YOU HAVE TO CHARGE IT.
"IN BRIGHTEST DAY... IN BLACKEST NIGHT, NO EVIL SHALL ESCAPE MY SIGHT! LET THOSE WHO WORSHIP EVIL'S MIGHT BEWARE MY POWER -- GREEN LANTERN'S LIGHT!"

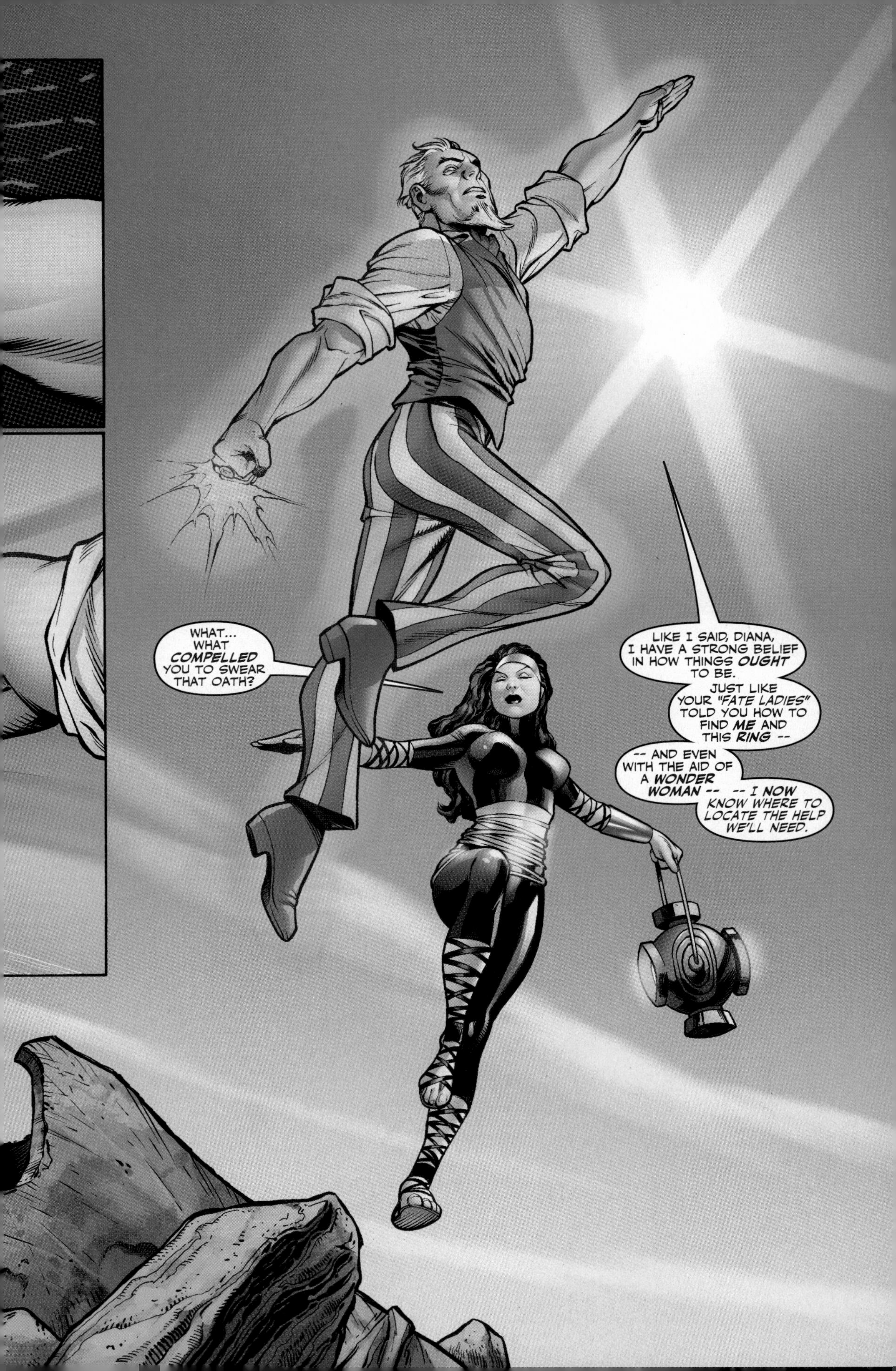
WHAT... WHAT COMPELLED YOU TO SWEAR THAT OATH?
LIKE I SAID, DIANA, I HAVE A STRONG BELIEF IN HOW THINGS OUGHT TO BE.
JUST LIKE YOUR "FATE LADIES" TOLD YOU HOW TO FIND ME AND THIS RING --
-- AND EVEN WITH THE AID OF A WONDER WOMAN --
-- I NOW KNOW WHERE TO LOCATE THE HELP WE'LL NEED.

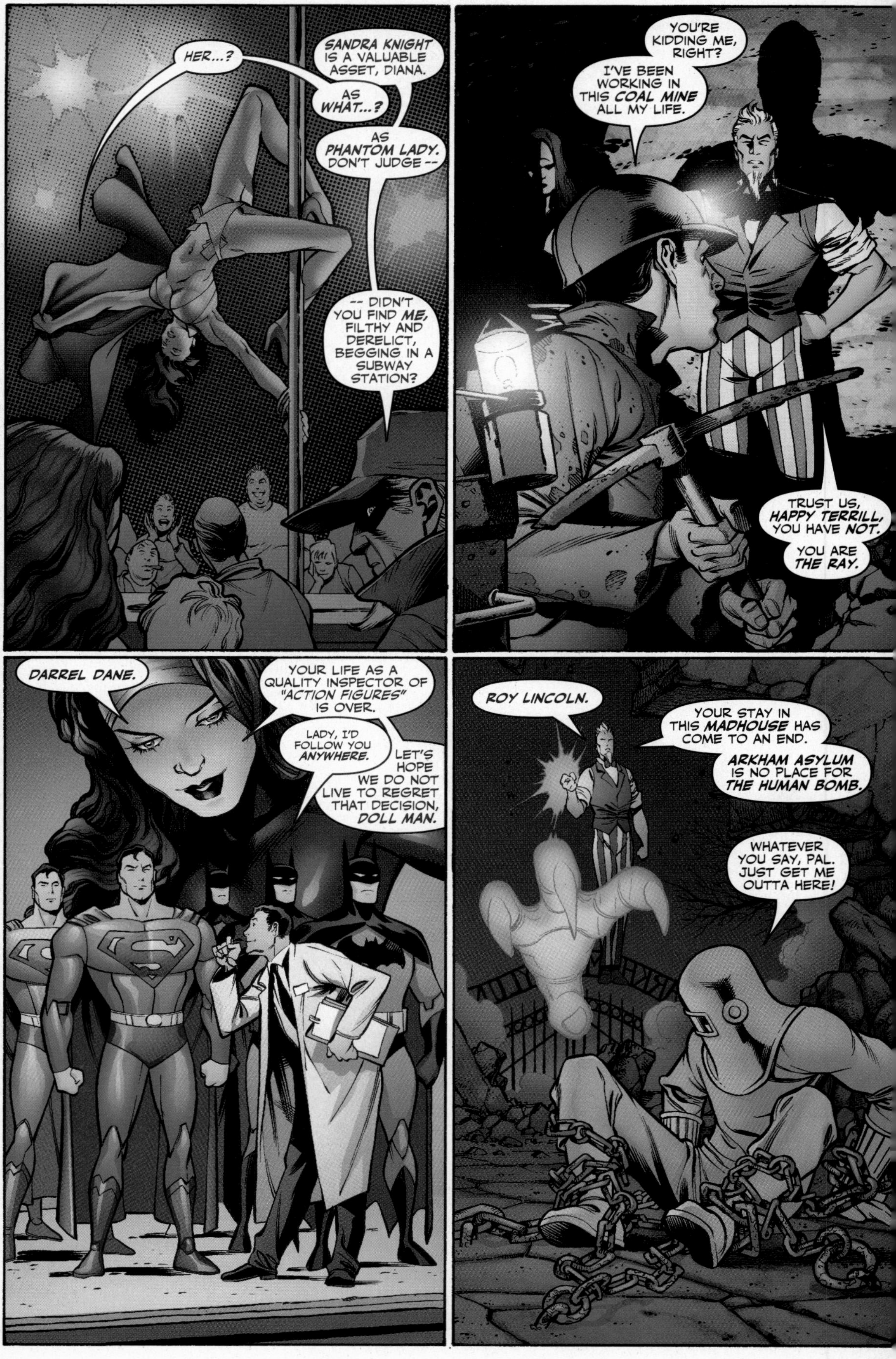
HER...?
SANDRA KNIGHT IS A VALUABLE ASSET, DIANA.
AS WHAT...?
AS PHANTOM LADY. DON'T JUDGE --
-- DIDN'T YOU FIND ME, FILTHY AND DERELICT, BEGGING IN A SUBWAY STATION?
YOU'RE KIDDING ME, RIGHT?
I'VE BEEN WORKING IN THIS COAL MINE ALL MY LIFE.
TRUST US, HAPPY TERRILL, YOU HAVE NOT.
YOU ARE THE RAY.
DARREL DANE.
YOUR LIFE AS A QUALITY INSPECTOR OF "ACTION FIGURES" IS OVER.
LADY, I'D FOLLOW YOU ANYWHERE.
LET'S HOPE WE DO NOT LIVE TO REGRET THAT DECISION, DOLL MAN.
ROY LINCOLN.
YOUR STAY IN THIS MADHOUSE HAS COME TO AN END.
ARKHAM ASYLUM IS NO PLACE FOR THE HUMAN BOMB.
WHATEVER YOU SAY, PAL. JUST GET ME OUTTA HERE!

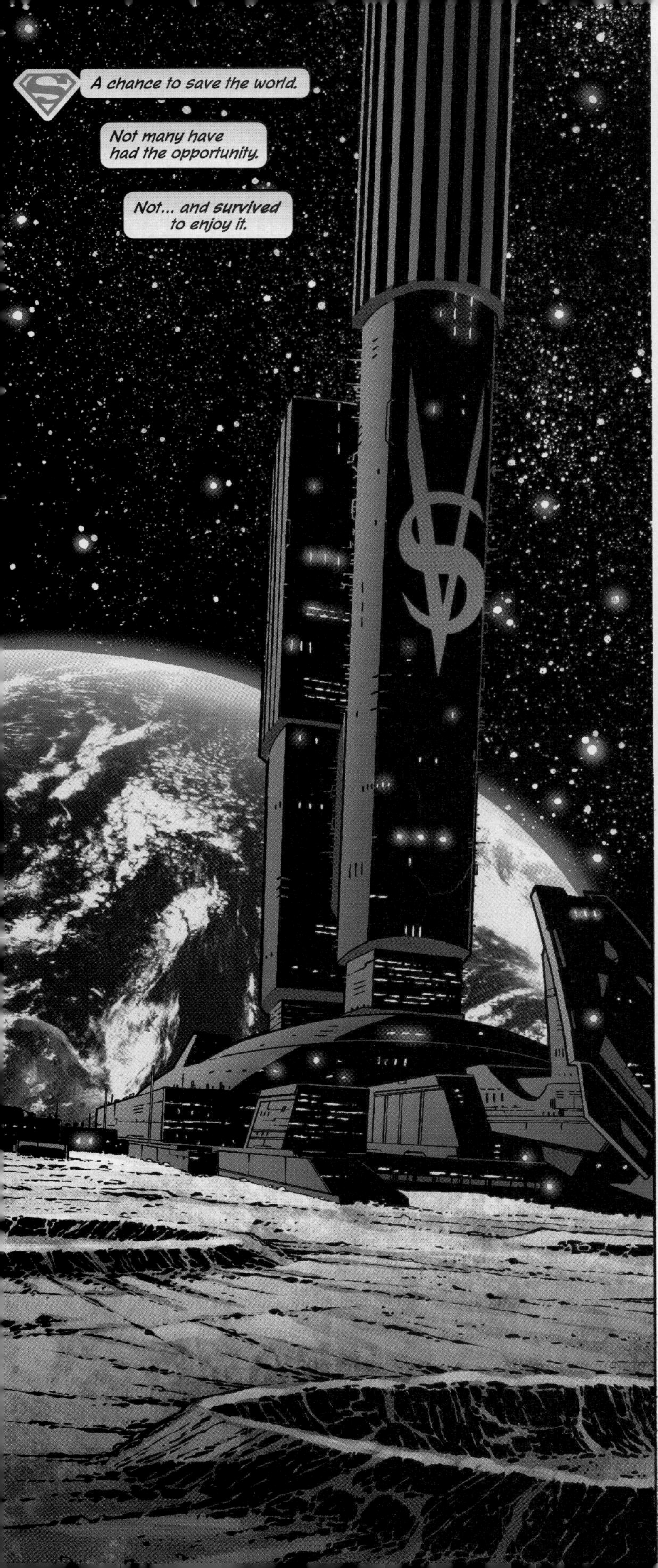
A chance to save the world.
Not many have had the opportunity.
Not... and survived to enjoy it.

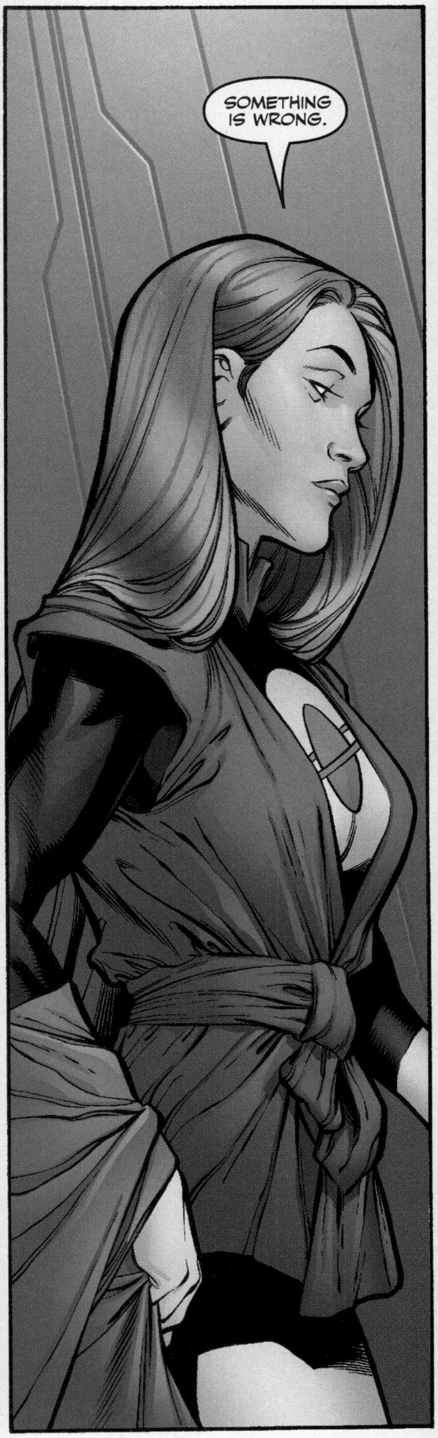
SOMETHING IS WRONG.

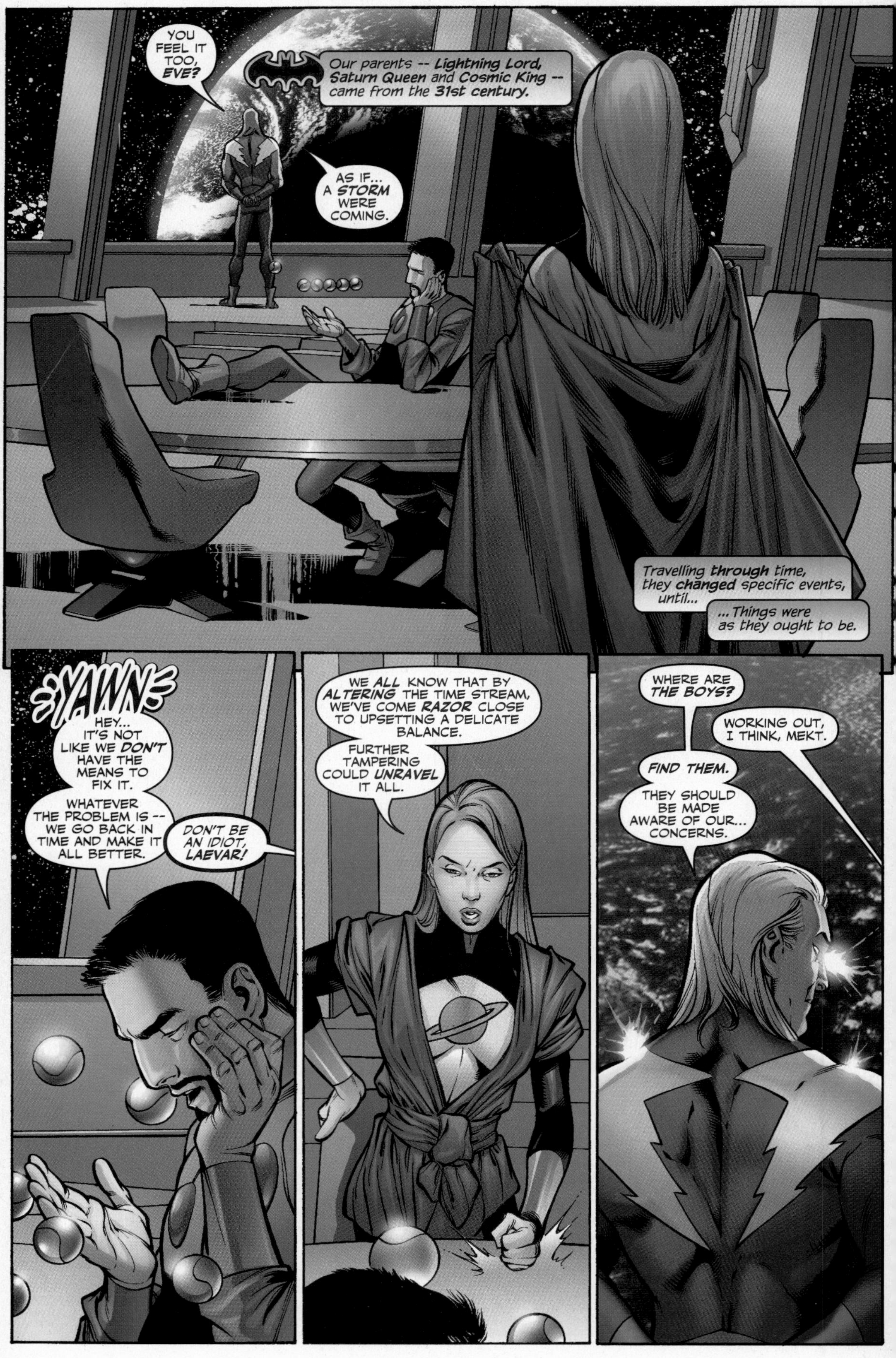
YOU FEEL IT TOO, EVE?
Our parents -- Lightning Lord, Saturn Queen and Cosmic King -- came from the 31st century.
AS IF... A STORM WERE COMING.
Travelling through time, they changed specific events, until...
...Things were as they ought to be.
YAWN
HEY... IT'S NOT LIKE WE DON'T HAVE THE MEANS TO FIX IT.
WHATEVER THE PROBLEM IS -- WE GO BACK IN TIME AND MAKE IT ALL BETTER.
DON'T BE AN IDIOT, LAEVAR!
WE ALL KNOW THAT BY ALTERING THE TIME STREAM, WE'VE COME RAZOR CLOSE TO UPSETTING A DELICATE BALANCE.
FURTHER TAMPERING COULD UNRAVEL IT ALL.
WHERE ARE THE BOYS?
WORKING OUT, I THINK, MEKT.
FIND THEM.
THEY SHOULD BE MADE AWARE OF OUR... CONCERNS.

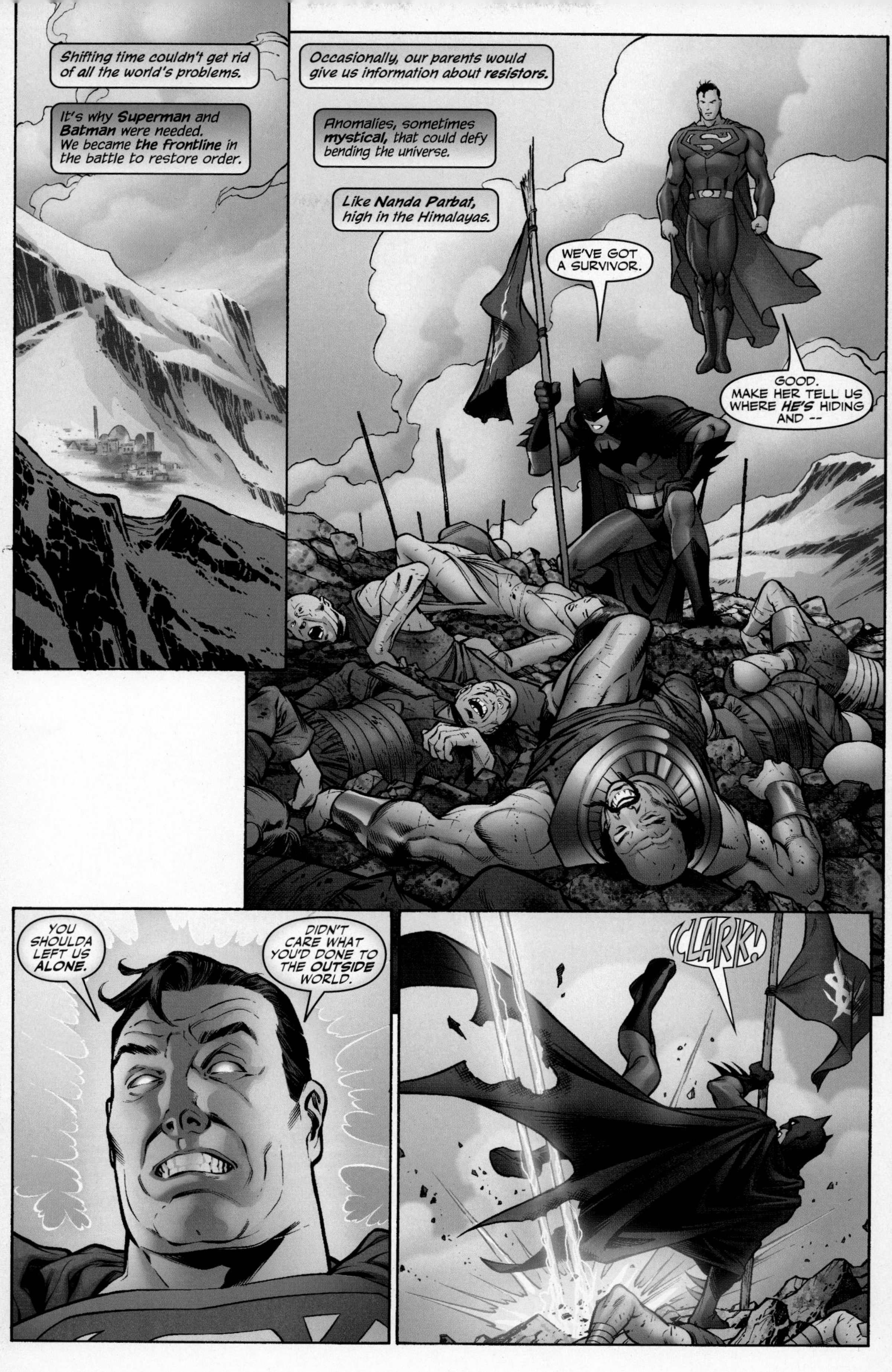
Shifting time couldn't get rid of all the world's problems.
It's why Superman and Batman were needed. We became the frontline in the battle to restore order.
Occasionally, our parents would give us information about resistors.
Anomalies, sometimes mystical, that could defy bending the universe.
Like Nanda Parbat, high in the Himalayas.
WE'VE GOT A SURVIVOR.
GOOD. MAKE HER TELL US WHERE HE'S HIDING AND --
YOU SHOULDA LEFT US ALONE.
DIDN'T CARE WHAT YOU'D DONE TO THE OUTSIDE WORLD.
CLARK!

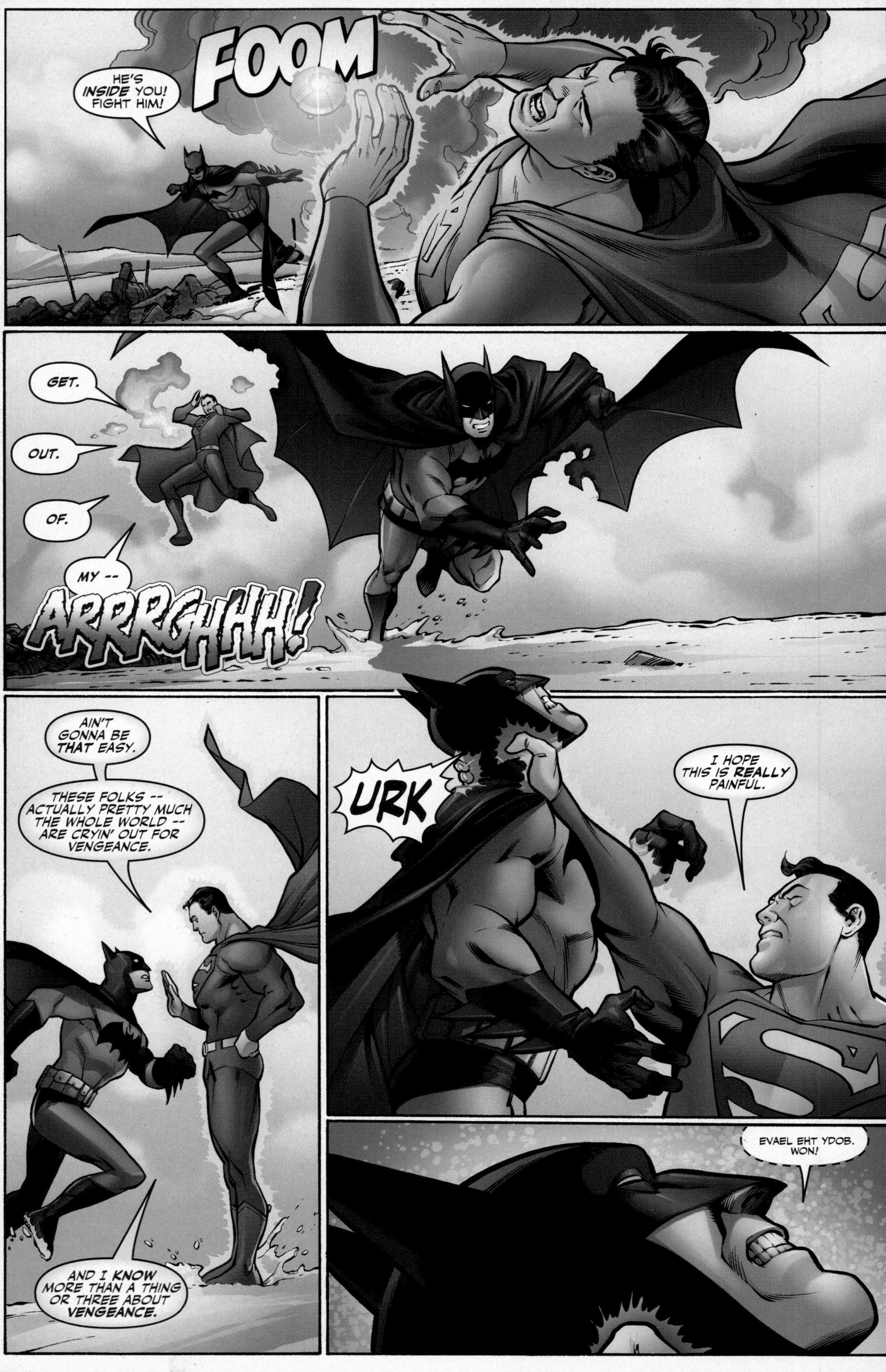
FOOM
HE'S INSIDE YOU! FIGHT HIM!
GET.
OUT.
OF.
MY --
ARRRGHHH!
AIN'T GONNA BE THAT EASY.
THESE FOLKS -- ACTUALLY PRETTY MUCH THE WHOLE WORLD -- ARE CRYIN' OUT FOR VENGEANCE.
AND I KNOW MORE THAN A THING OR THREE ABOUT VENGEANCE.
URK
I HOPE THIS IS REALLY PAINFUL.
EVAEL EHT YDOB. WON!

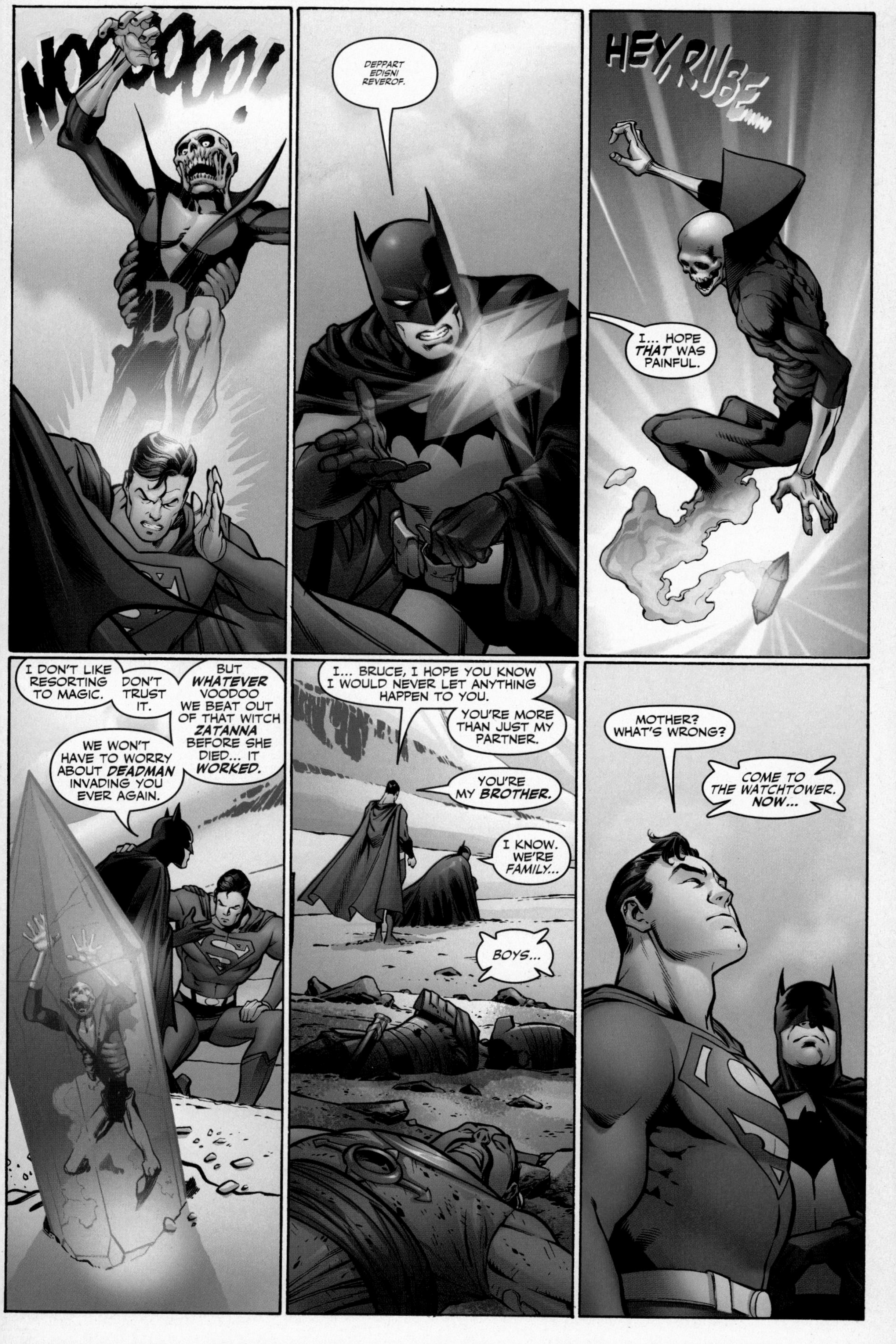
NOOOOO!
DEPPART EDISNI REVEROF.
HEY, RUBE...
I... HOPE THAT WAS PAINFUL.
I DON'T LIKE RESORTING TO MAGIC.
DON'T TRUST IT.
BUT WHATEVER VOODOO WE BEAT OUT OF THAT WITCH ZATANNA BEFORE SHE DIED... IT WORKED.
WE WON'T HAVE TO WORRY ABOUT DEADMAN INVADING YOU EVER AGAIN.
I... BRUCE, I HOPE YOU KNOW I WOULD NEVER LET ANYTHING HAPPEN TO YOU.
YOU'RE MORE THAN JUST MY PARTNER.
YOU'RE MY BROTHER.
I KNOW. WE'RE FAMILY...
BOYS...
MOTHER? WHAT'S WRONG?
COME TO THE WATCHTOWER. NOW...

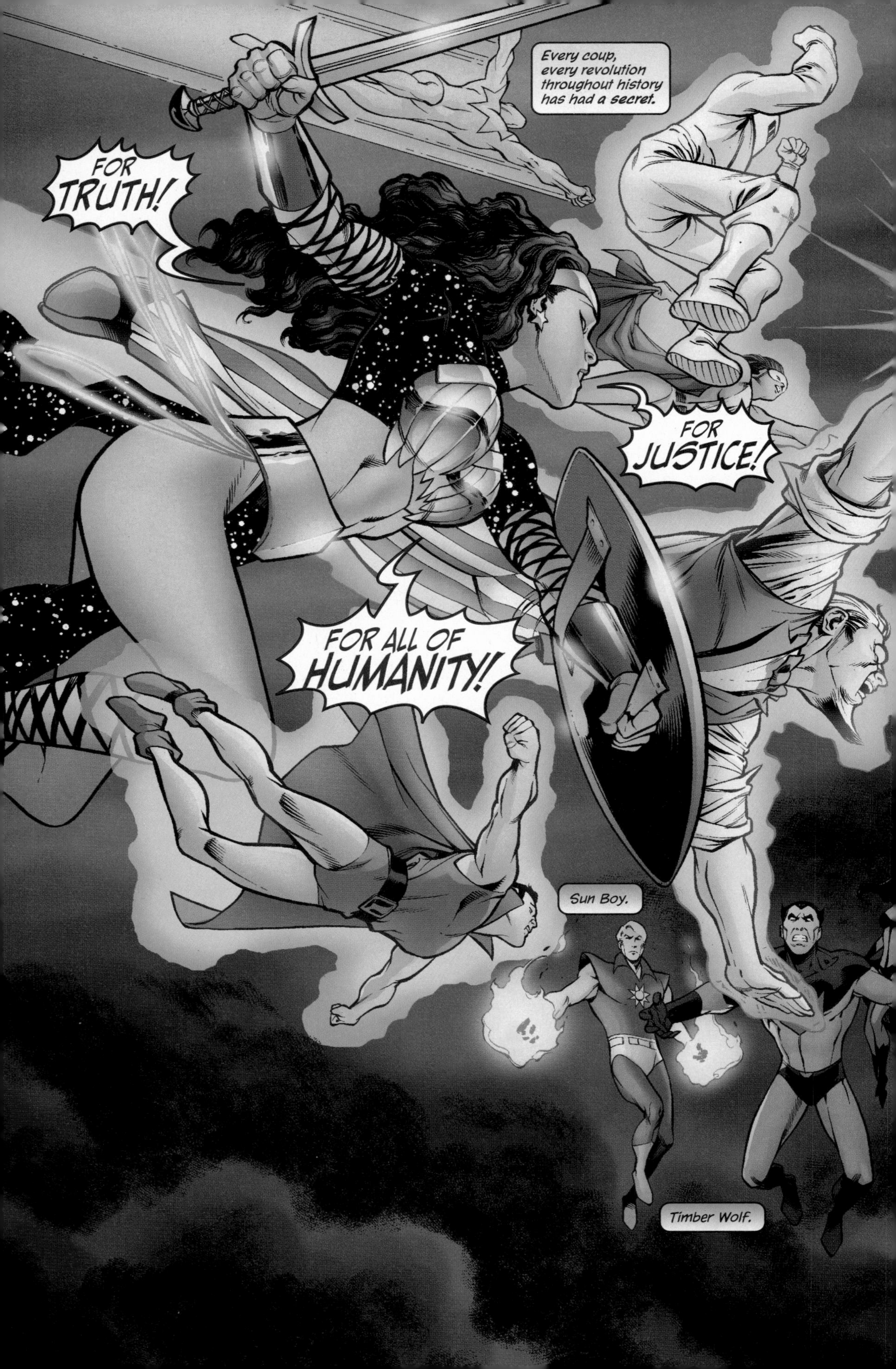
Every coup, every revolution throughout history has had a secret.
FOR TRUTH!
FOR JUSTICE!
FOR ALL OF HUMANITY!
Sun Boy.
Timber Wolf.

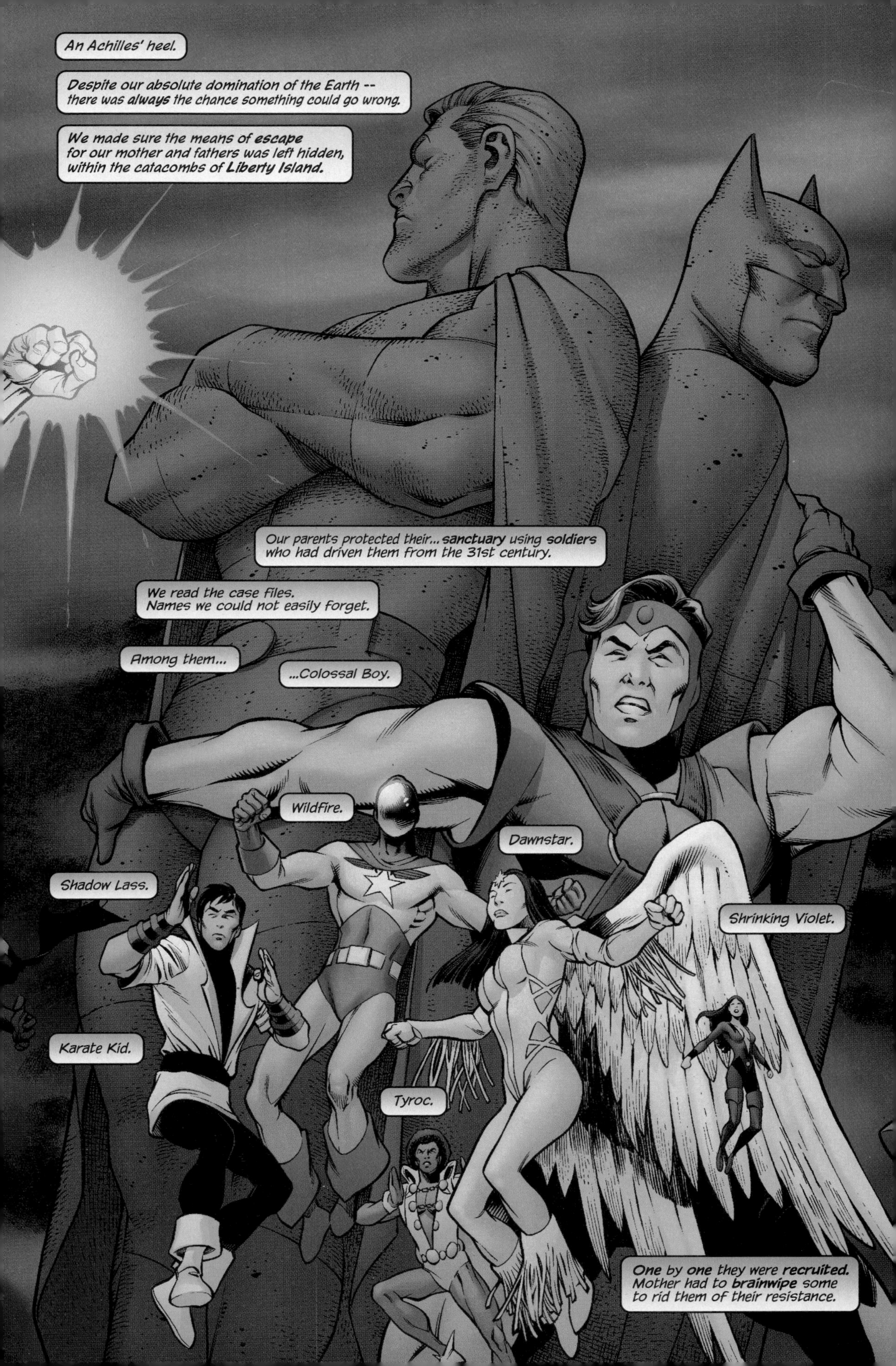
An Achilles' heel.
Despite our absolute domination of the Earth -- there was **always** the chance something could go wrong.
We made sure the means of **escape** for our mother and fathers was left hidden, within the catacombs of **Liberty Island.**
Our parents protected their... **sanctuary** using **soldiers** who had driven them from the 31st century.
We read the case files. Names we could not easily forget.
Among them...
...Colossal Boy.
Wildfire.
Dawnstar.
Shadow Lass.
Shrinking Violet.
Karate Kid.
Tyroc.
One by one they were **recruited.** Mother had to **brainwipe** some to rid them of their resistance.

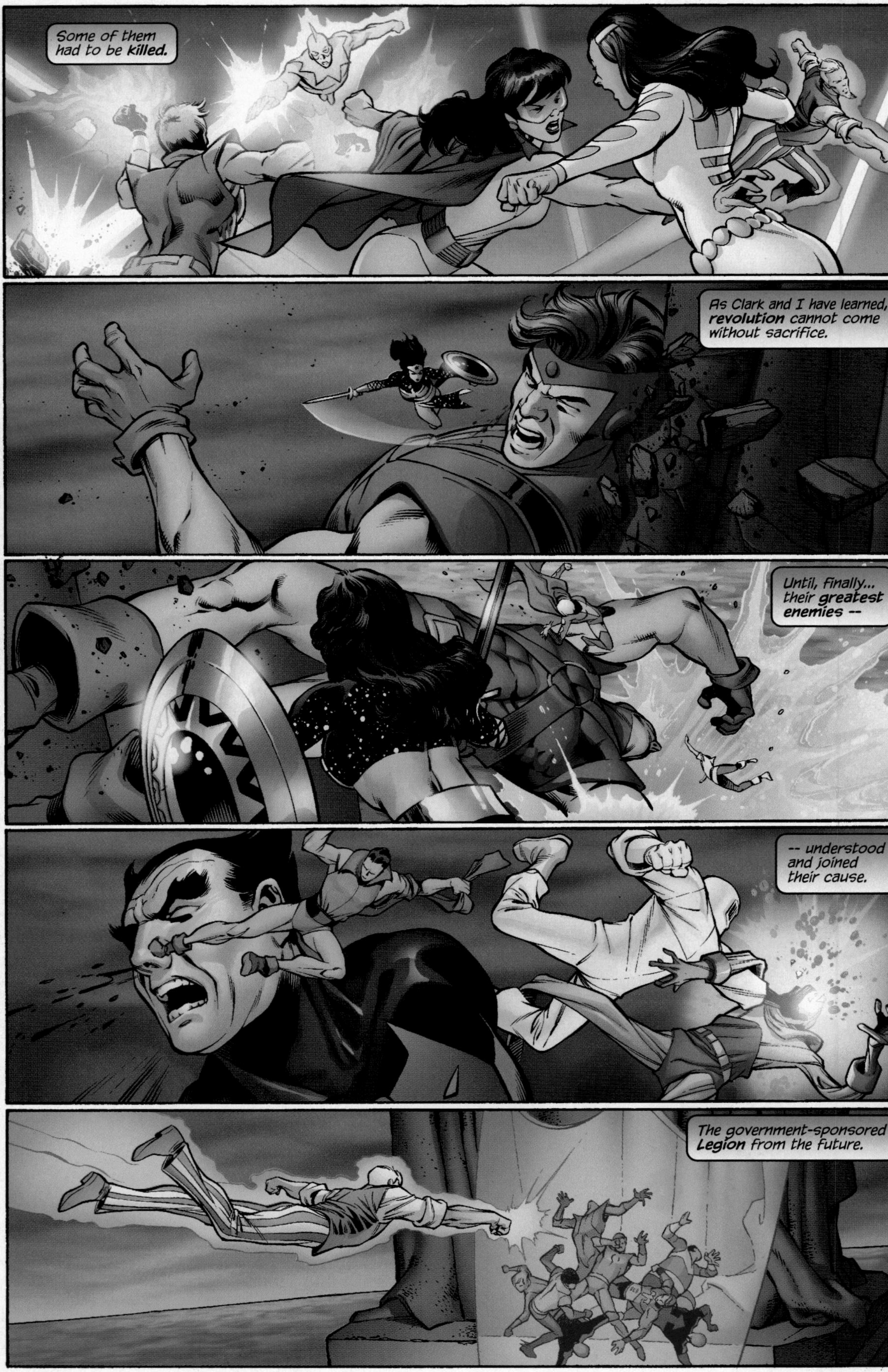
Some of them had to be **killed.**
As Clark and I have learned, **revolution** cannot come without sacrifice.
Until, finally... their **greatest enemies --**
-- understood and joined their cause.
The government-sponsored **Legion** from the future.

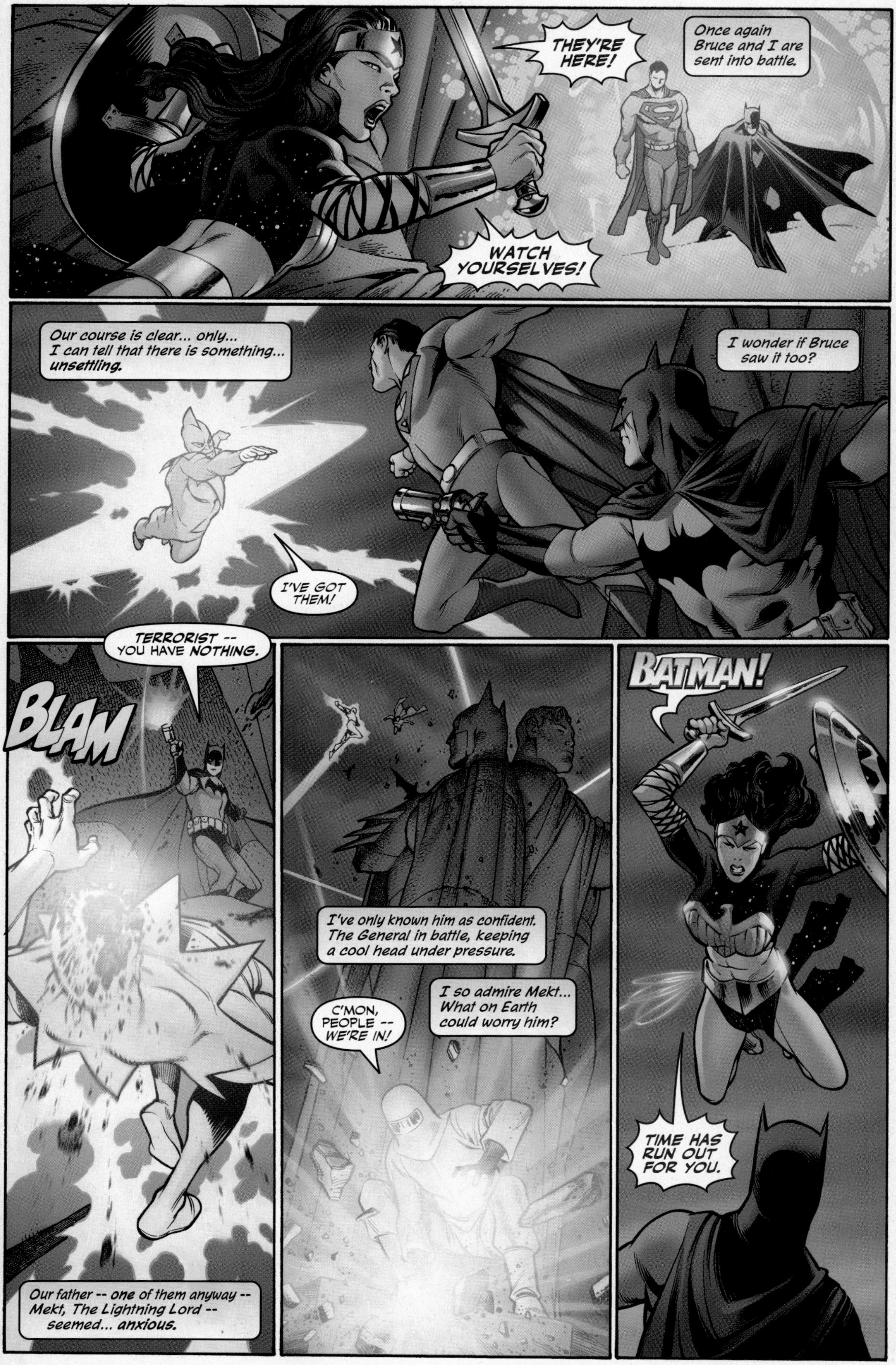
THEY'RE HERE!
Once again Bruce and I are sent into battle.
WATCH YOURSELVES!
Our course is clear... only... I can tell that there is something... unsettling.
I wonder if Bruce saw it too?
I'VE GOT THEM!
TERRORIST -- YOU HAVE NOTHING.
BLAM
Our father -- one of them anyway -- Mekt, The Lightning Lord -- seemed... anxious.
I've only known him as confident. The General in battle, keeping a cool head under pressure.
I so admire Mekt... What on Earth could worry him?
C'MON, PEOPLE -- WE'RE IN!
BATMAN!
TIME HAS RUN OUT FOR YOU.

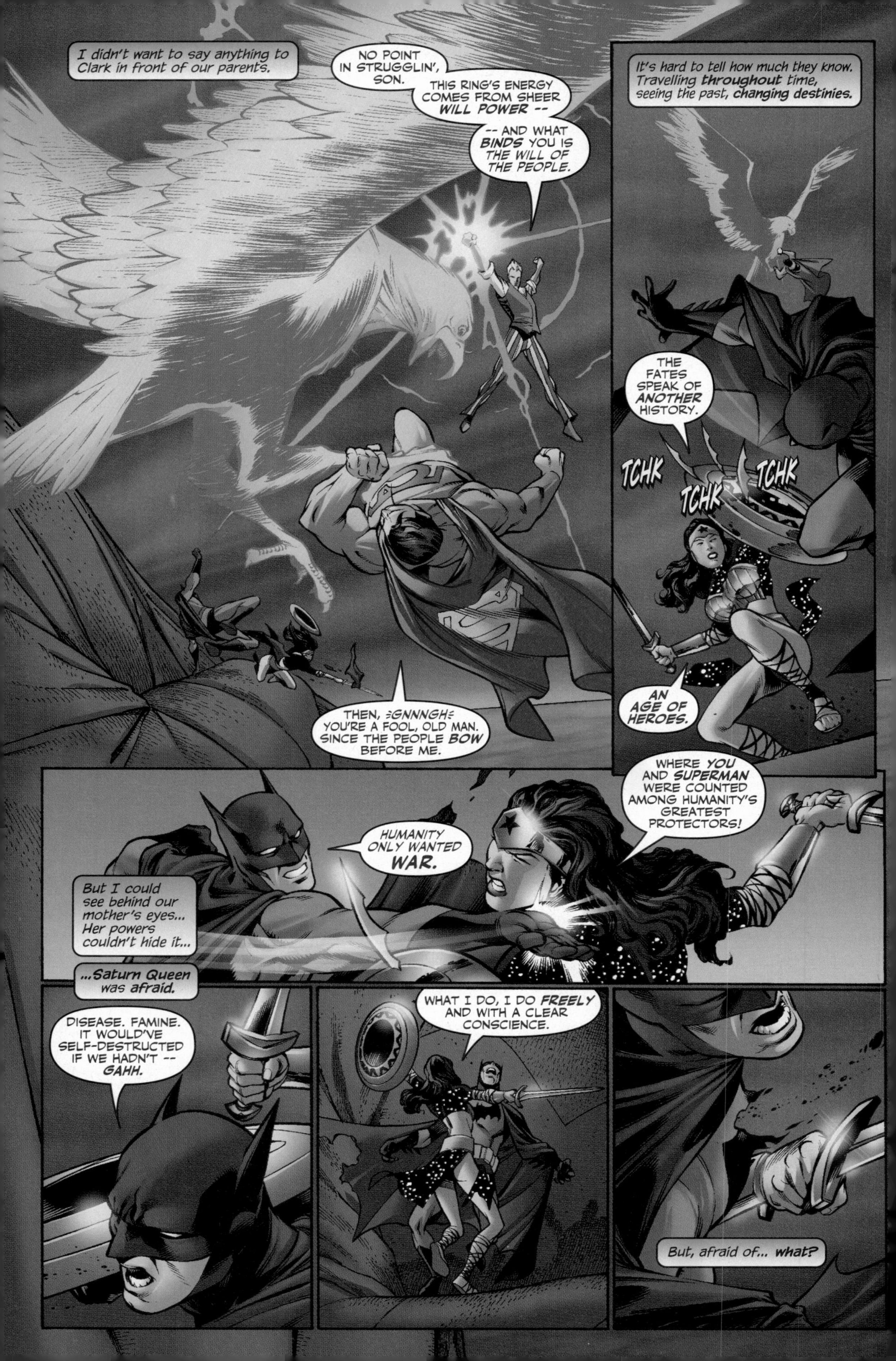
I didn't want to say anything to Clark in front of our parents.
NO POINT IN STRUGGLIN', SON.
THIS RING'S ENERGY COMES FROM SHEER WILL POWER --
-- AND WHAT BINDS YOU IS THE WILL OF THE PEOPLE.
THEN, GNNNGH YOU'RE A FOOL, OLD MAN. SINCE THE PEOPLE BOW BEFORE ME.
It's hard to tell how much they know. Travelling throughout time, seeing the past, changing destinies.
THE FATES SPEAK OF ANOTHER HISTORY.
TCHK
TCHK
TCHK
AN AGE OF HEROES.
WHERE YOU AND SUPERMAN WERE COUNTED AMONG HUMANITY'S GREATEST PROTECTORS!
HUMANITY ONLY WANTED WAR.
But I could see behind our mother's eyes... Her powers couldn't hide it...
...Saturn Queen was afraid.
DISEASE. FAMINE. IT WOULD'VE SELF-DESTRUCTED IF WE HADN'T -- GAHH.
WHAT I DO, I DO FREELY AND WITH A CLEAR CONSCIENCE.
But, afraid of... what?

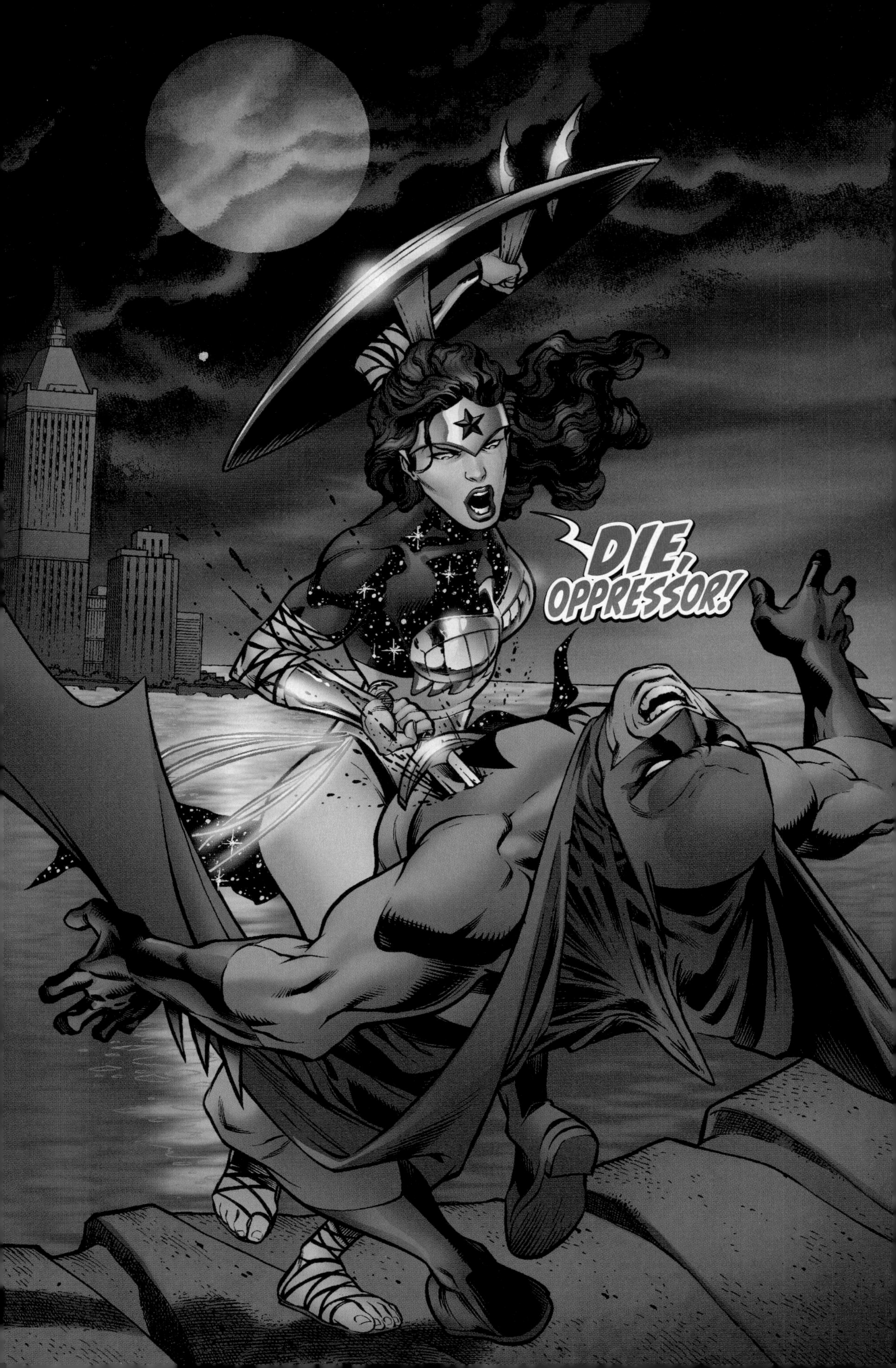
DIE, OPPRESSOR!

BRUCE! NO!

WHAT KIND OF EVIL ARE YOU?!

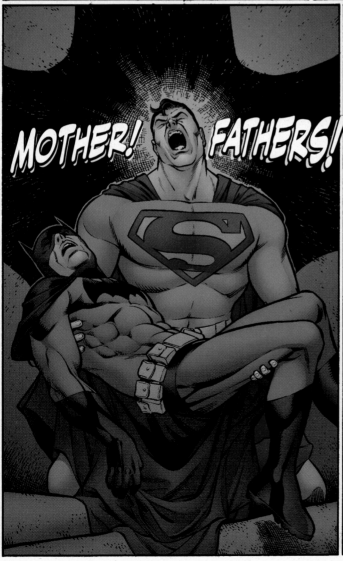

MOTHER! FATHERS!

SAMUEL.

SAMUEL! DON'T GO --

YOU HAVE TO BELIEVE WE'LL WIN THE DAY.

BE CAREFUL, DIANA...

MY... WONDER WOMAN...

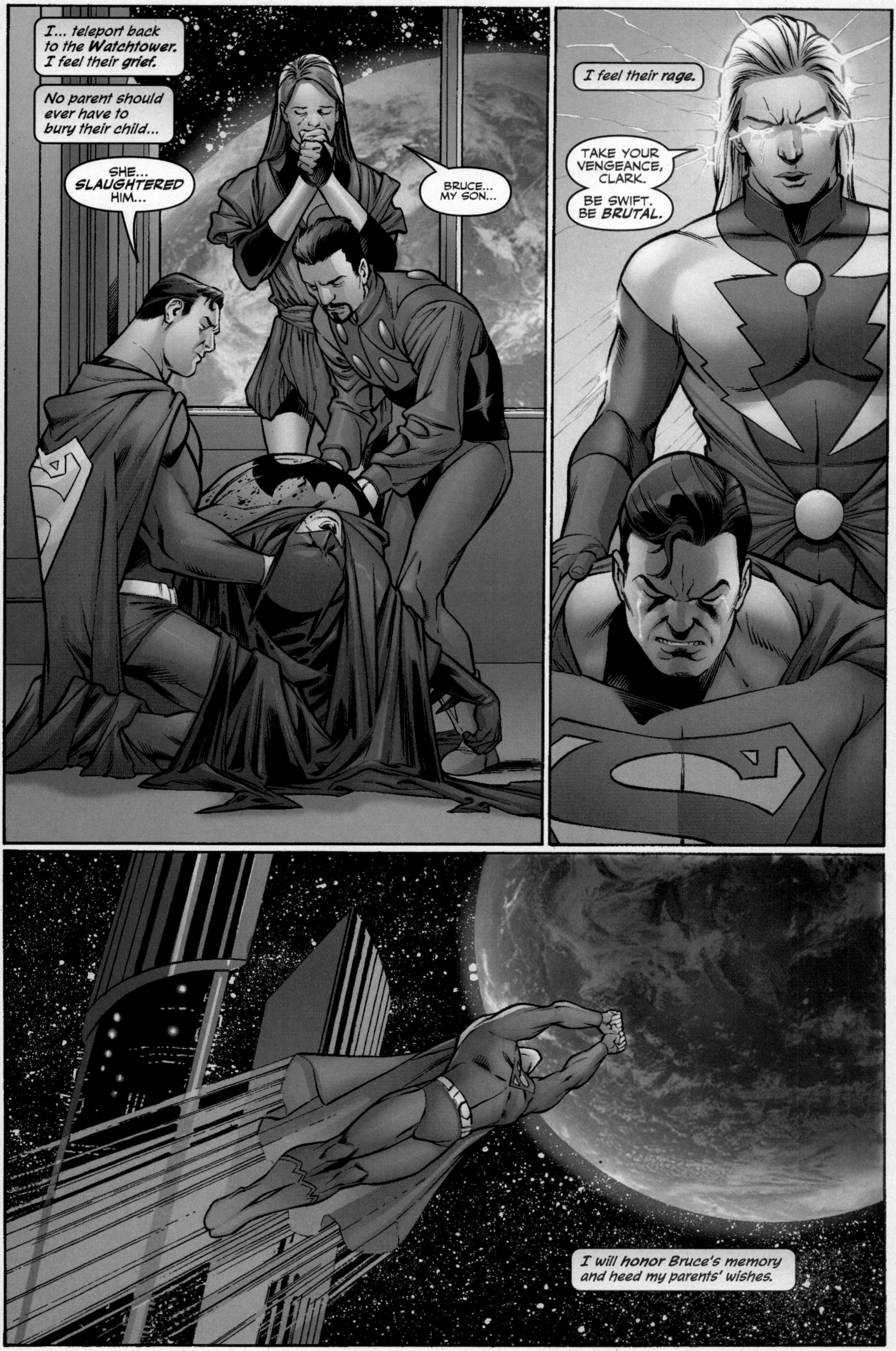
I... teleport back to the Watchtower. I feel their grief.
No parent should ever have to bury their child...
SHE... SLAUGHTERED HIM...
BRUCE... MY SON...
I feel their rage.
TAKE YOUR VENGEANCE, CLARK.
BE SWIFT. BE BRUTAL.
I will honor Bruce's memory and heed my parents' wishes.

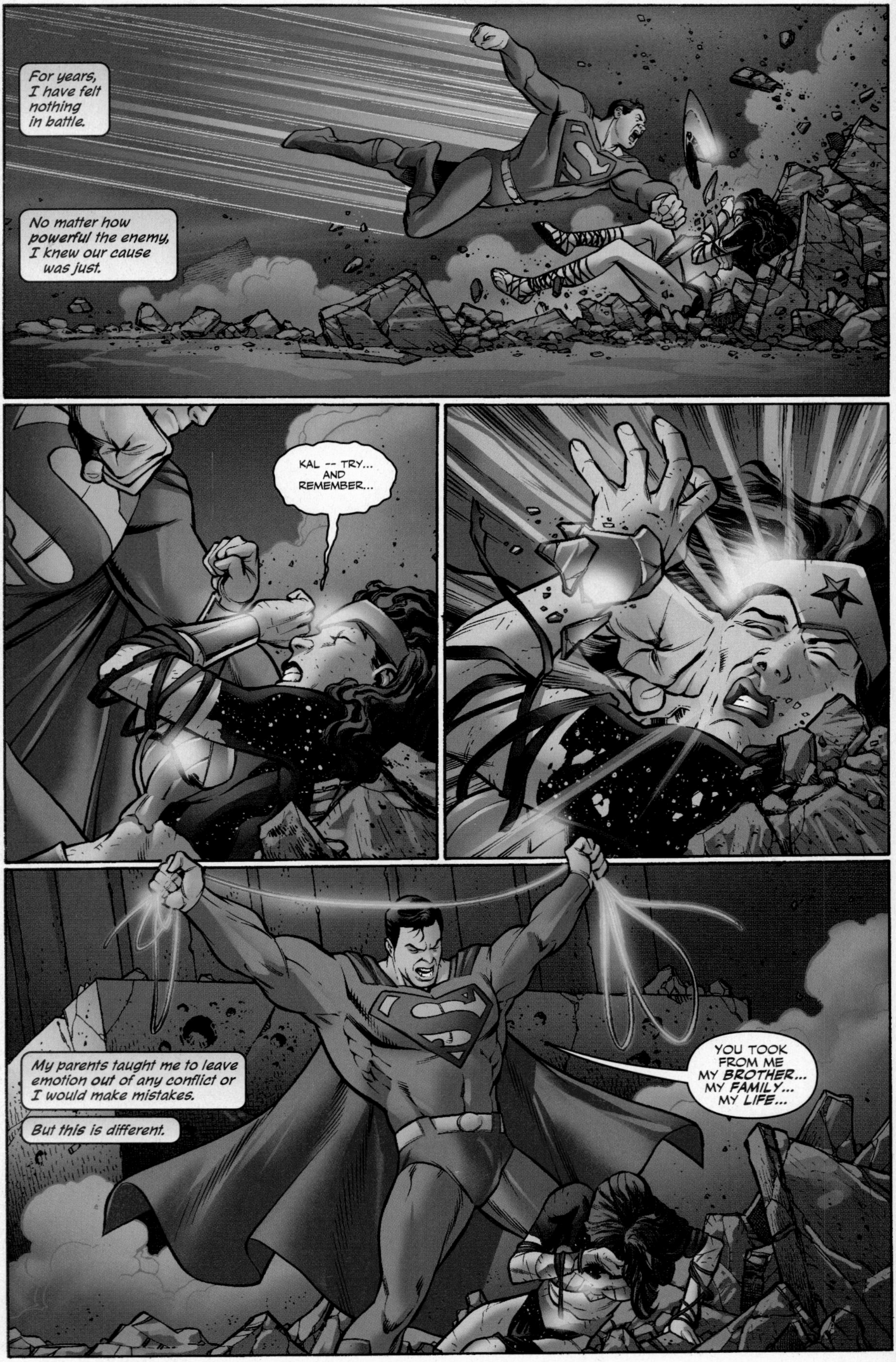

For years, I have felt nothing in battle.
No matter how powerful the enemy, I knew our cause was just.
KAL -- TRY... AND REMEMBER...
My parents taught me to leave emotion out of any conflict or I would make mistakes.
But this is different.
YOU TOOK FROM ME MY BROTHER... MY FAMILY... MY LIFE...

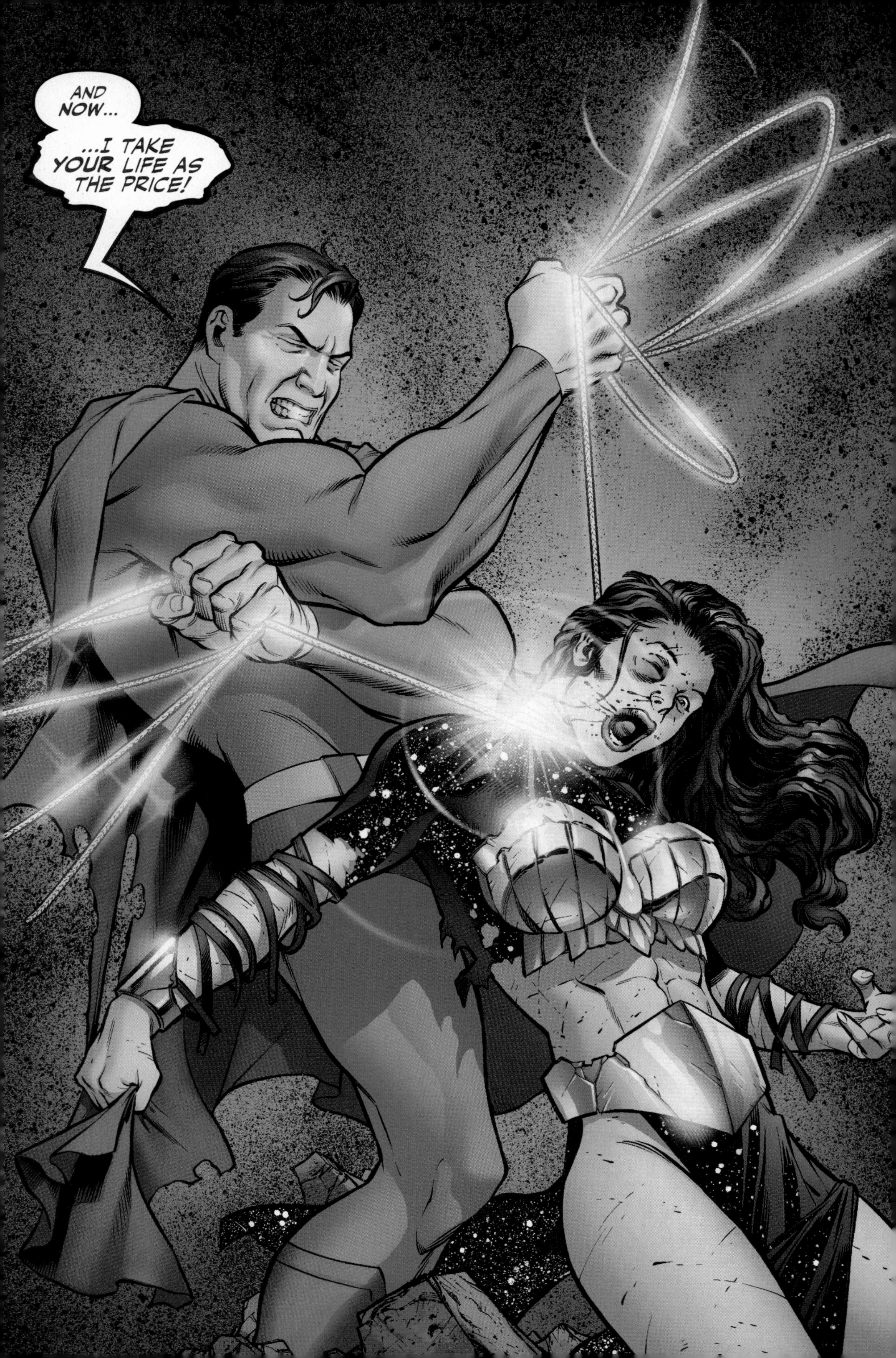
AND NOW...
...I TAKE YOUR LIFE AS THE PRICE!

DIANA SAID WE'D FIND A *TIME MACHINE* --

-- BUT DO YOU THINK IT'LL ACTUALLY WORK?

WITH EVERYBODY WHO *DIED* TODAY, IT'D BETTER.

NEXT STOP, *SMALLVILLE*, KANSAS --

-- IN THE YEAR *NINETEEN HUNDRED* AND --

YOU'RE *NOT* GOING ANYWHERE!

WE *GAVE* YOU A *CHOICE.*

OBEY.

FWOOSH

OR *DIE.*

KRAK

HMMMMMMMMMMMM

THE *TIME BUBBLE* HAS BEEN *ACTIVATED.* YOU DON'T WANT TO MIX MY *ATOMIC ENERGY* WITH --

DON'T TELL ME WHAT I WANT!

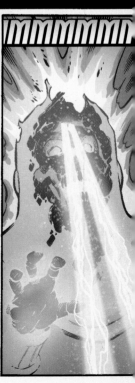

MMMMMMMM

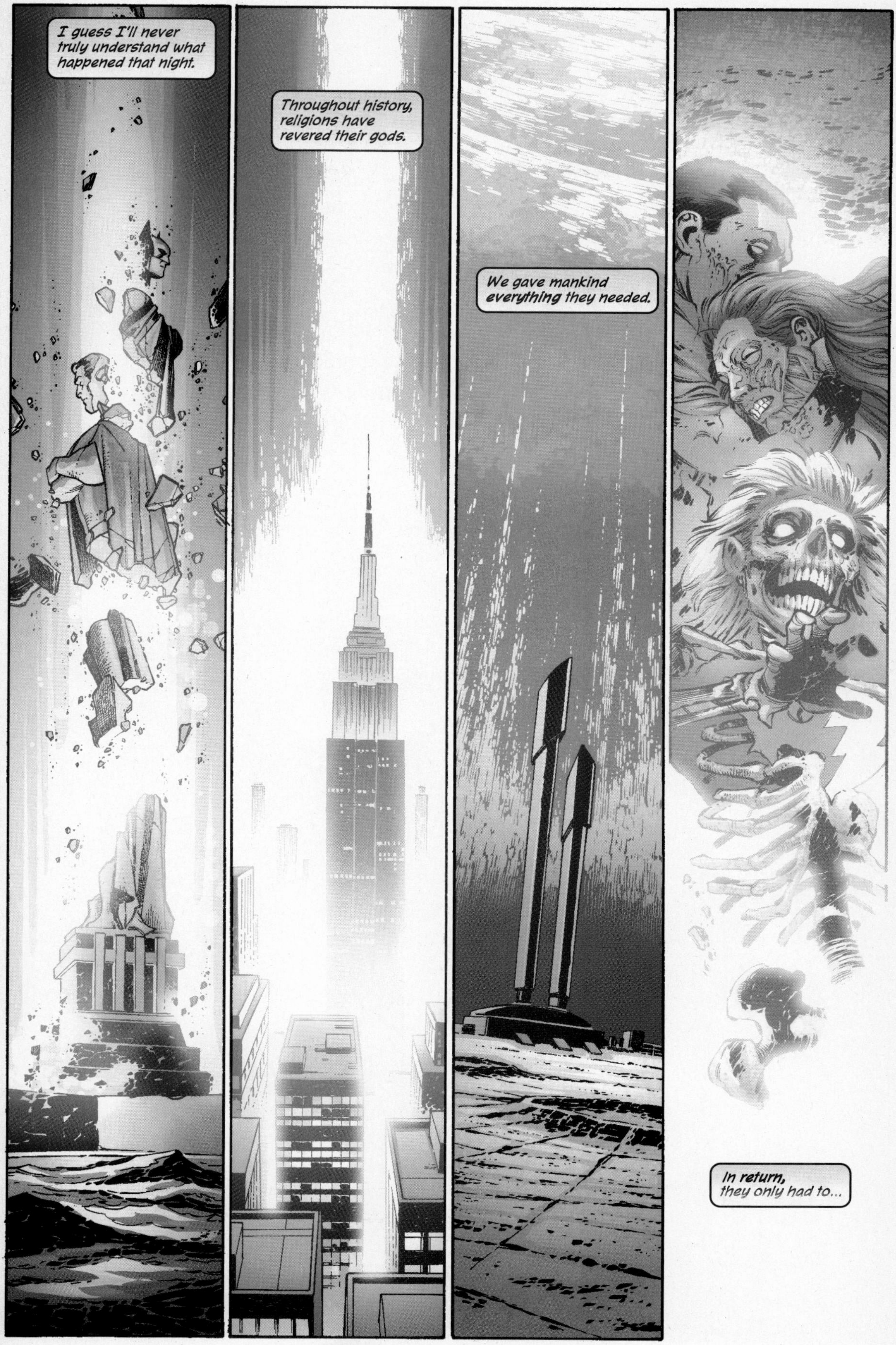

I guess I'll never truly understand what happened that night.
Throughout history, religions have revered their gods.
We gave mankind *everything* they needed.
In return, they only had to...

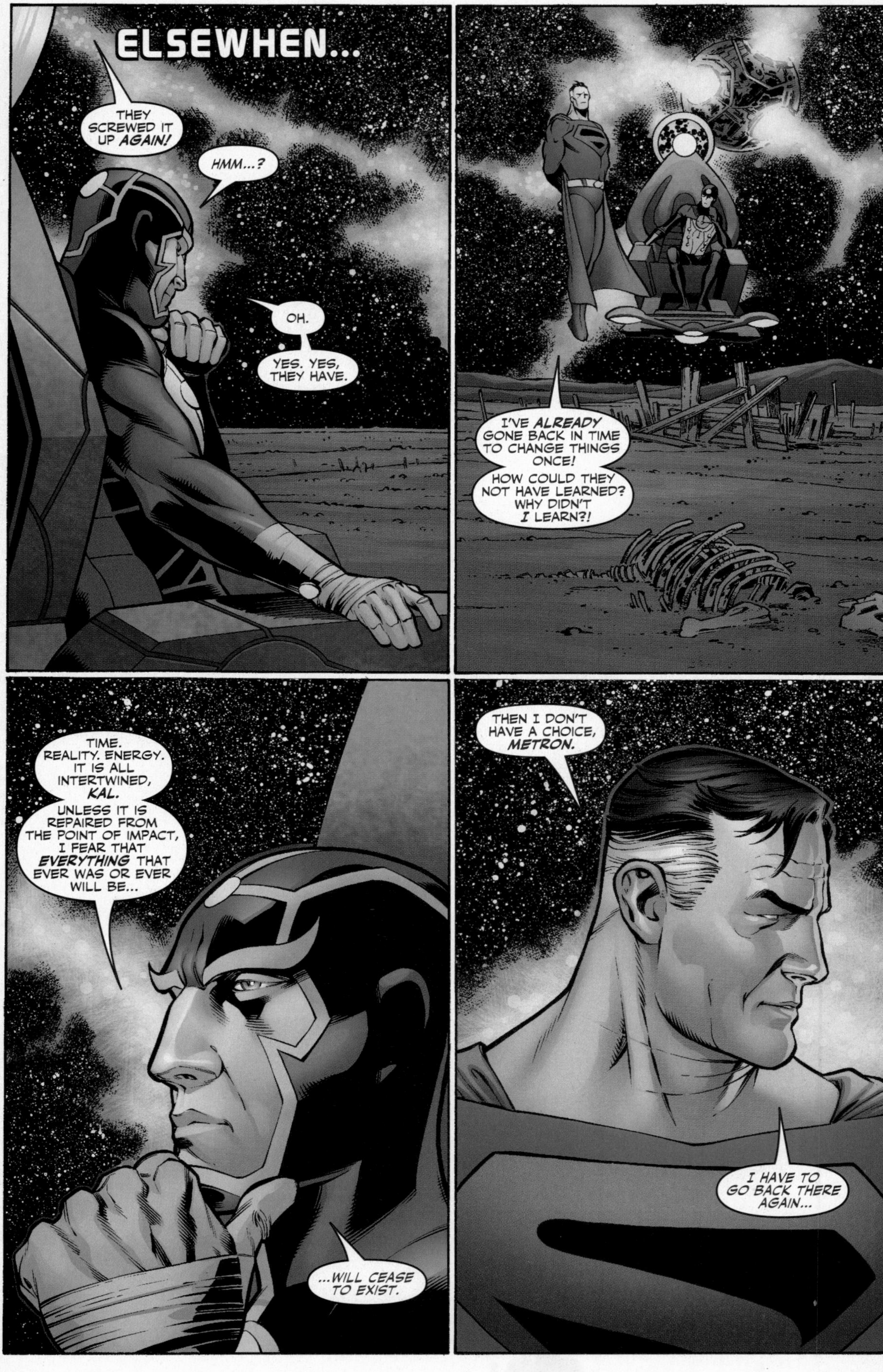
ELSEWHEN...
THEY SCREWED IT UP AGAIN!
HMM...?
OH.
YES. YES, THEY HAVE.
I'VE ALREADY GONE BACK IN TIME TO CHANGE THINGS ONCE!
HOW COULD THEY NOT HAVE LEARNED? WHY DIDN'T I LEARN?!
TIME. REALITY. ENERGY. IT IS ALL INTERTWINED, KAL.
UNLESS IT IS REPAIRED FROM THE POINT OF IMPACT, I FEAR THAT EVERYTHING THAT EVER WAS OR EVER WILL BE...
...WILL CEASE TO EXIST.
THEN I DON'T HAVE A CHOICE, METRON.
I HAVE TO GO BACK THERE AGAIN...

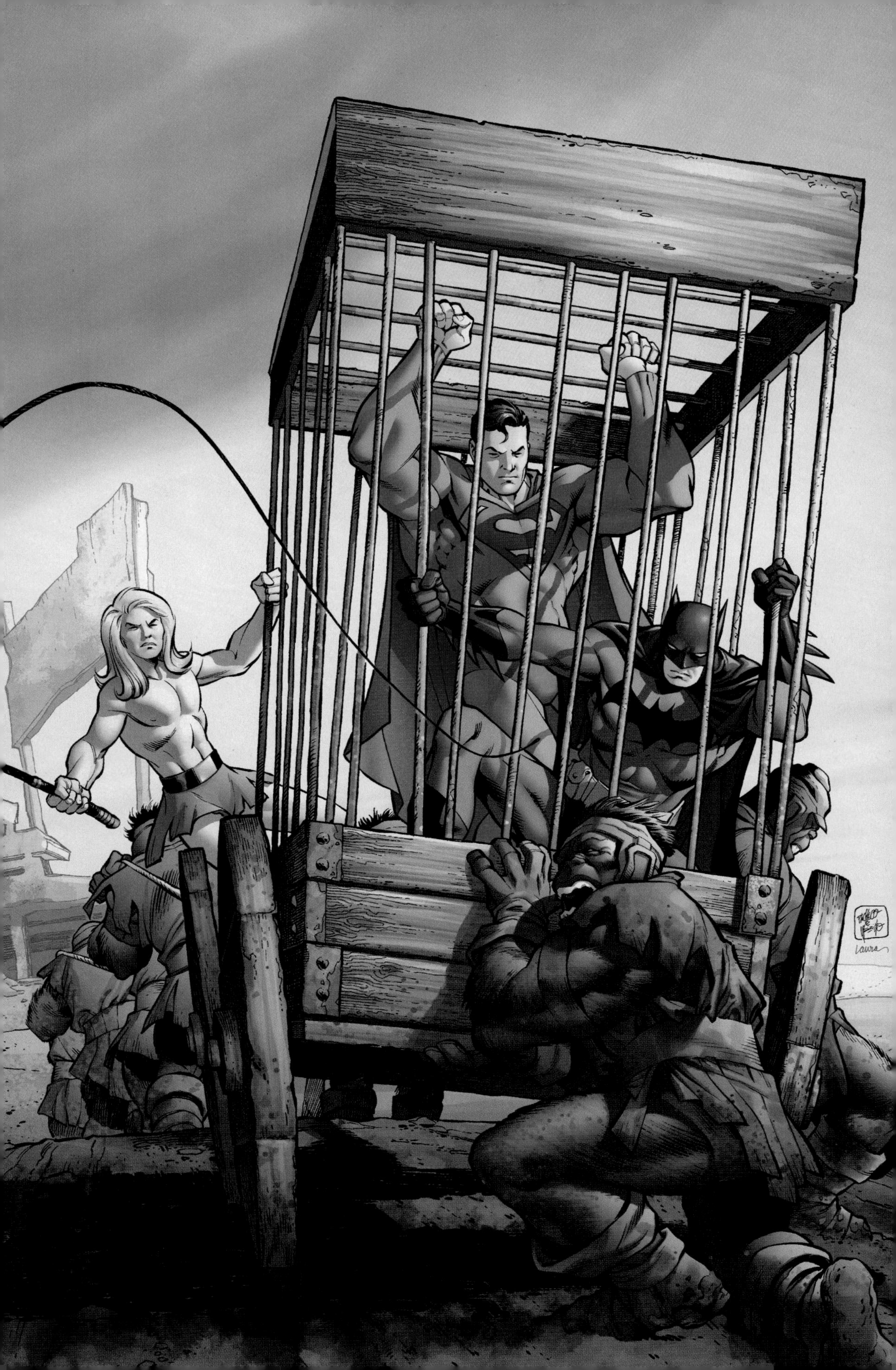

"WHEN TIME GOES ASUNDER..."

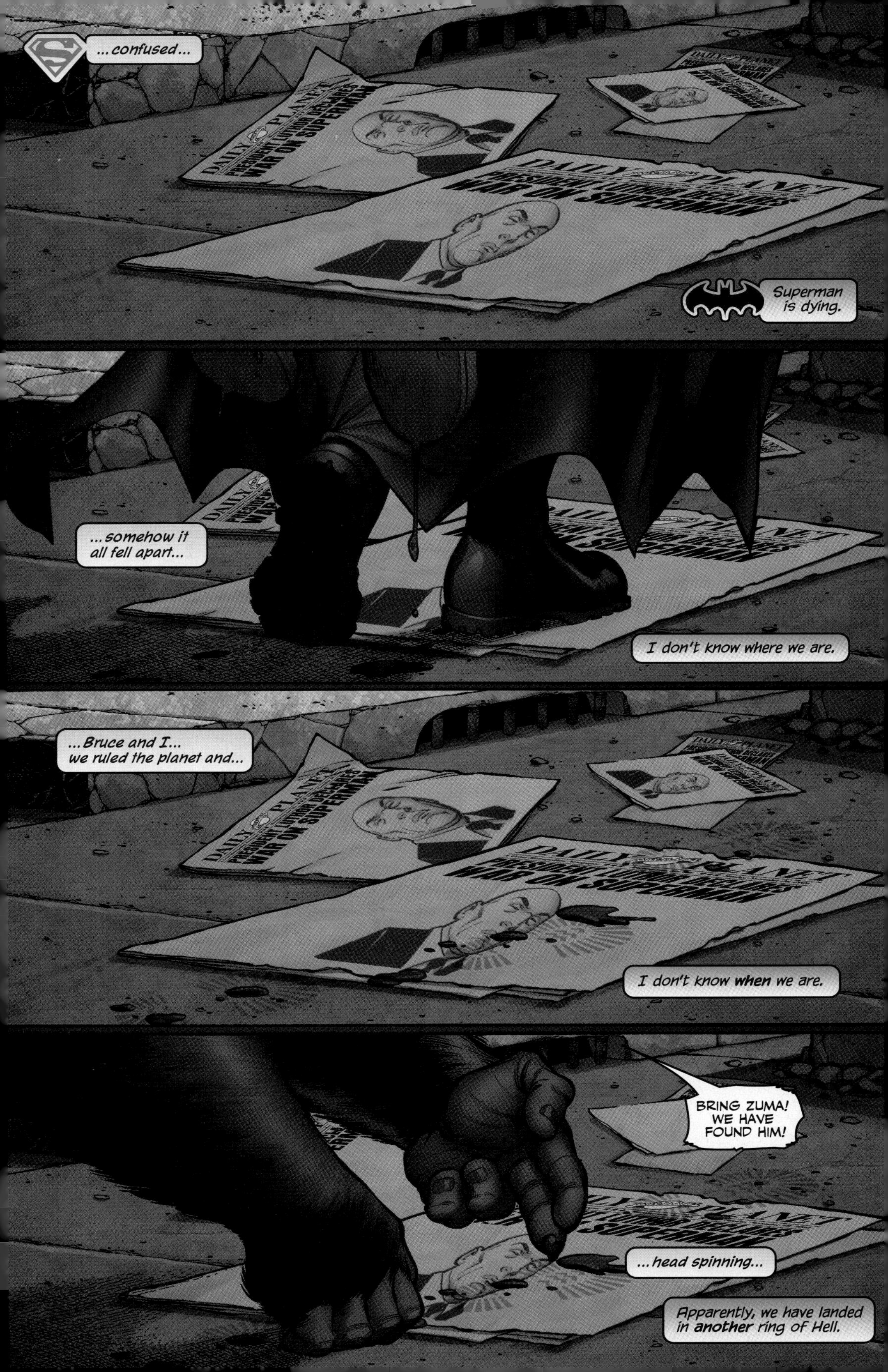

...confused...
DAILY PLANET
PRESIDENT LUTHOR DECLARES
WAR ON SUPERMAN
Superman is dying.
...somehow it all fell apart...
I don't know where we are.
...Bruce and I... we ruled the planet and...
I don't know **when** we are.
BRING ZUMA! WE HAVE FOUND HIM!
...head spinning...
Apparently, we have landed in **another** ring of Hell.

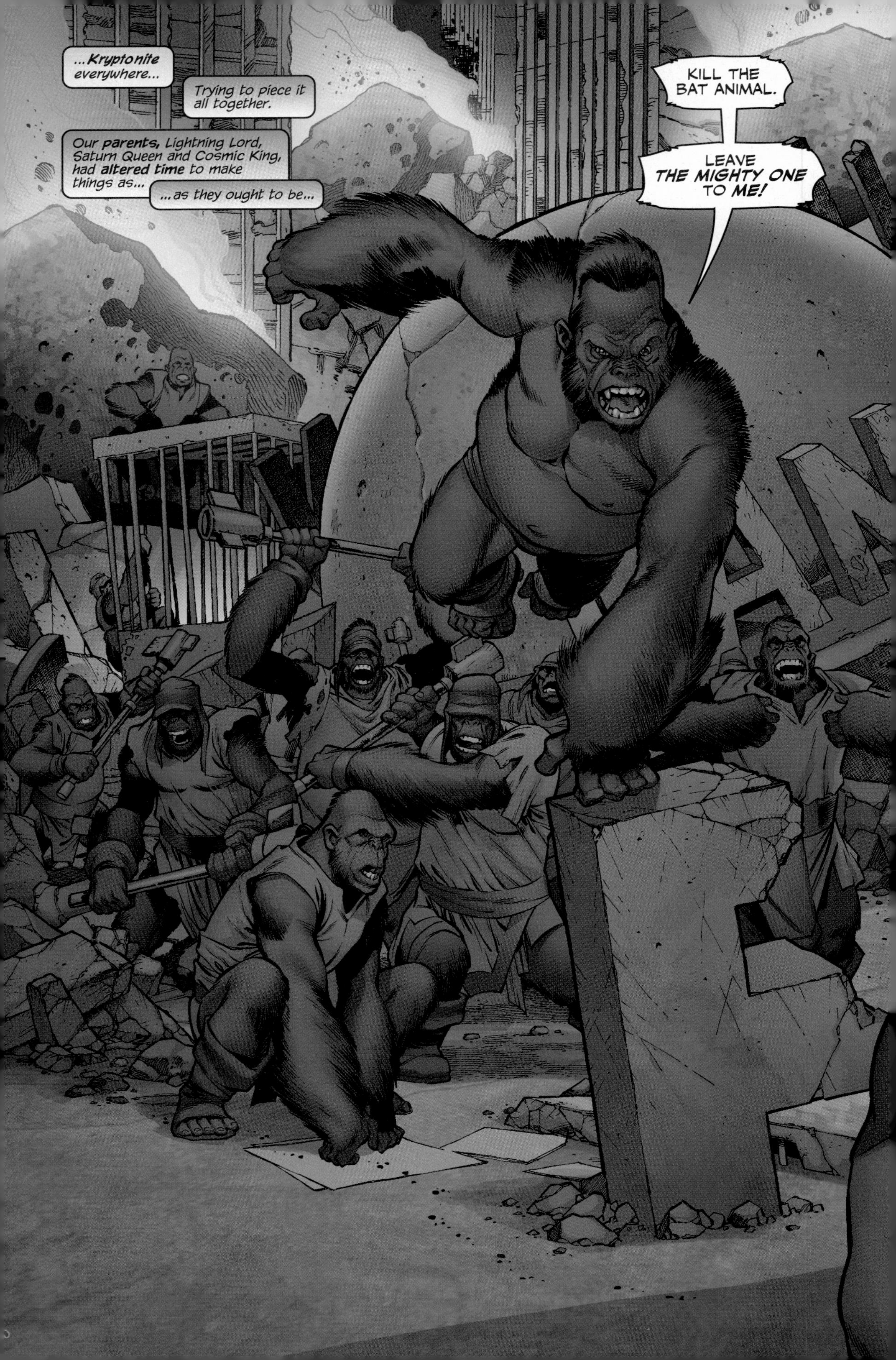

...Kryptonite everywhere...
Trying to piece it all together.
Our parents, Lightning Lord, Saturn Queen and Cosmic King, had altered time to make things as...
...as they ought to be...
KILL THE BAT ANIMAL.
LEAVE THE MIGHTY ONE TO ME!

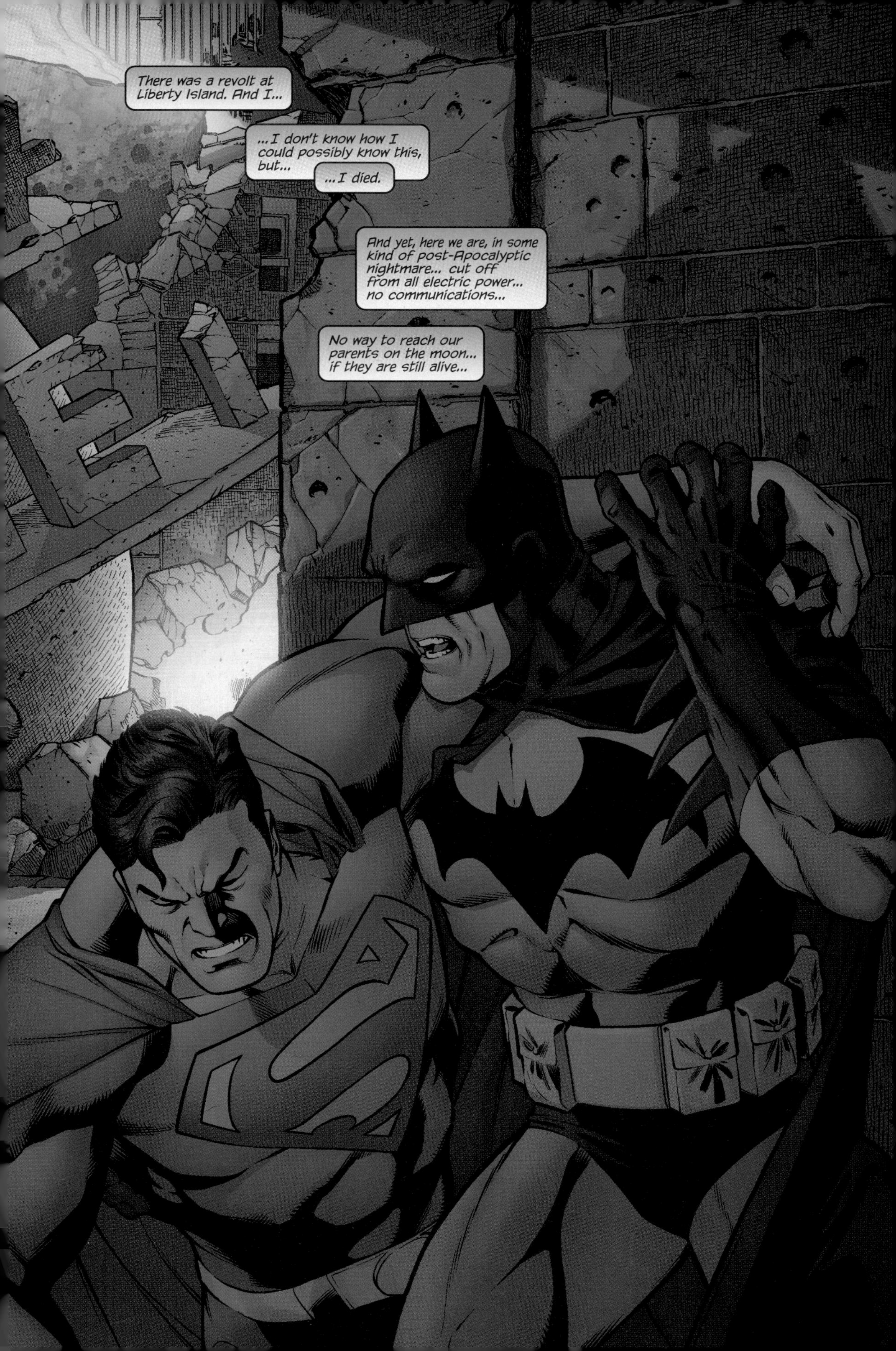
There was a revolt at Liberty Island. And I...
...I don't know how I could possibly know this, but...
...I died.
And yet, here we are, in some kind of post-Apocalyptic nightmare... cut off from all electric power... no communications...
No way to reach our parents on the moon... if they are still alive...

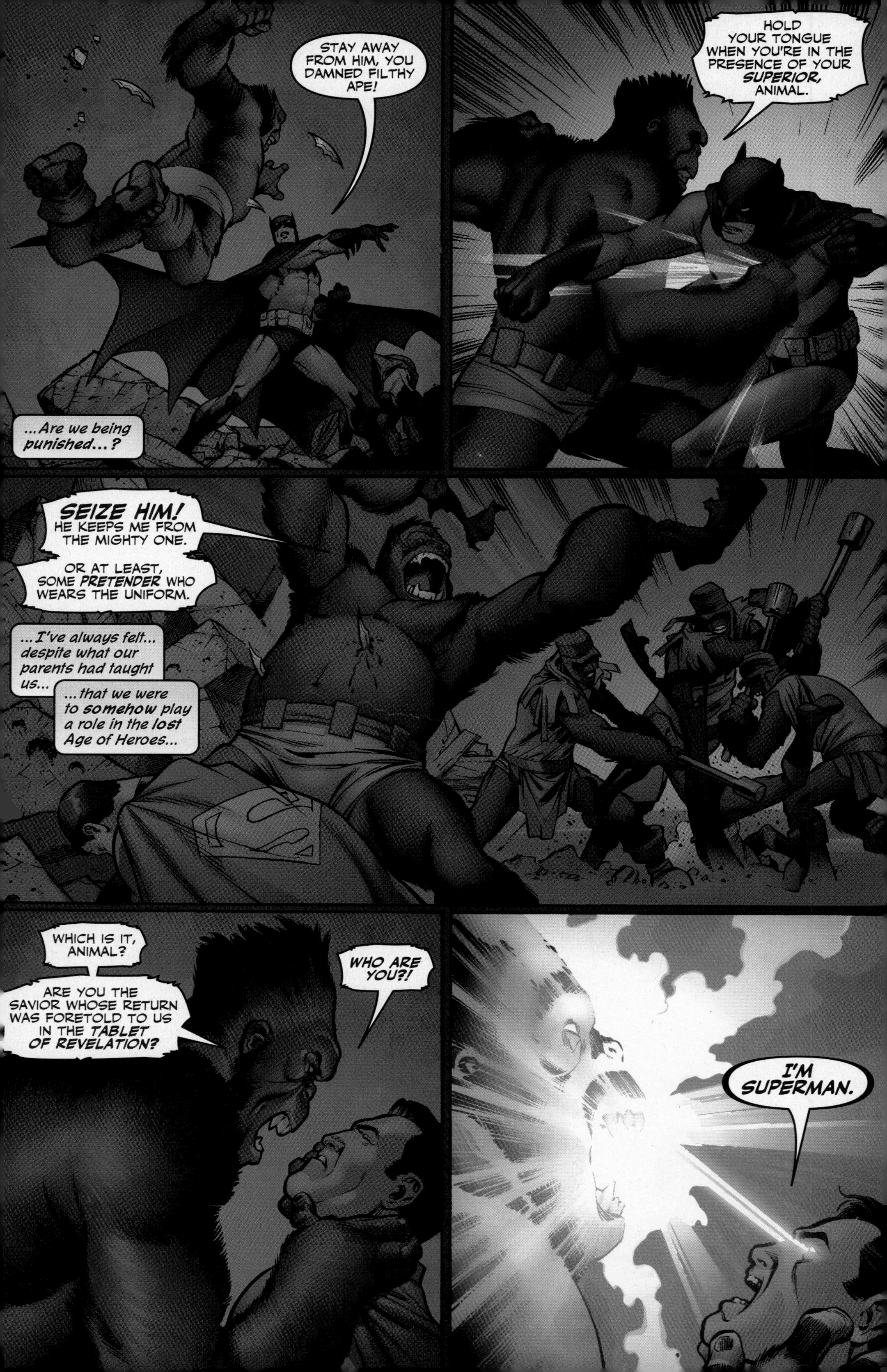
STAY AWAY FROM HIM, YOU DAMNED FILTHY APE!
...Are we being punished...?
HOLD YOUR TONGUE WHEN YOU'RE IN THE PRESENCE OF YOUR SUPERIOR, ANIMAL.
SEIZE HIM! HE KEEPS ME FROM THE MIGHTY ONE.
OR AT LEAST, SOME PRETENDER WHO WEARS THE UNIFORM.
...I've always felt... despite what our parents had taught us...
...that we were to somehow play a role in the lost Age of Heroes...
WHICH IS IT, ANIMAL?
ARE YOU THE SAVIOR WHOSE RETURN WAS FORETOLD TO US IN THE TABLET OF REVELATION?
WHO ARE YOU?!
I'M SUPERMAN.

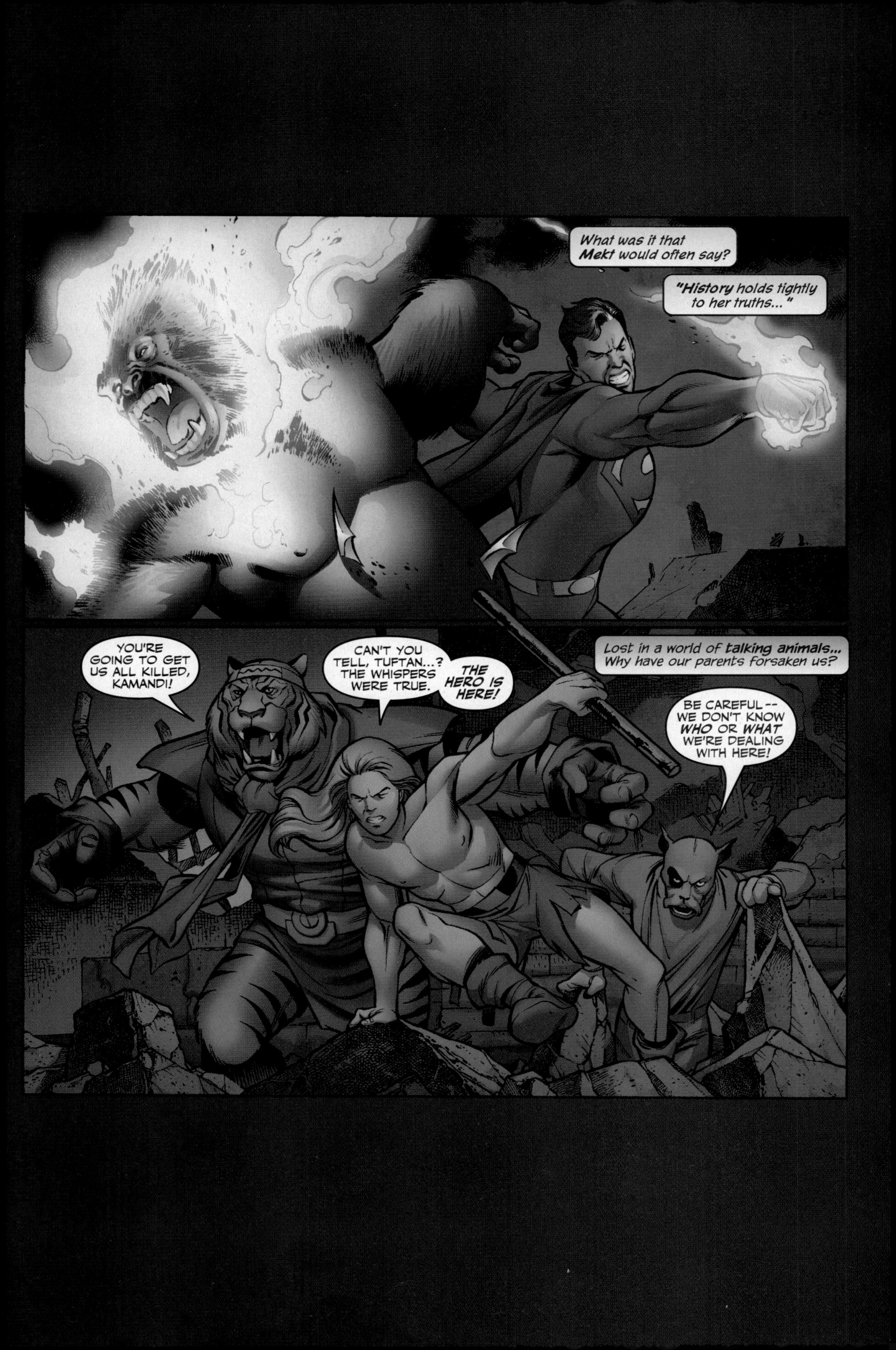
What was it that Mekt would often say?
"History holds tightly to her truths..."
YOU'RE GOING TO GET US ALL KILLED, KAMANDI!
CAN'T YOU TELL, TUFTAN...? THE WHISPERS WERE TRUE.
THE HERO IS HERE!
Lost in a world of talking animals... Why have our parents forsaken us?
BE CAREFUL -- WE DON'T KNOW WHO OR WHAT WE'RE DEALING WITH HERE!

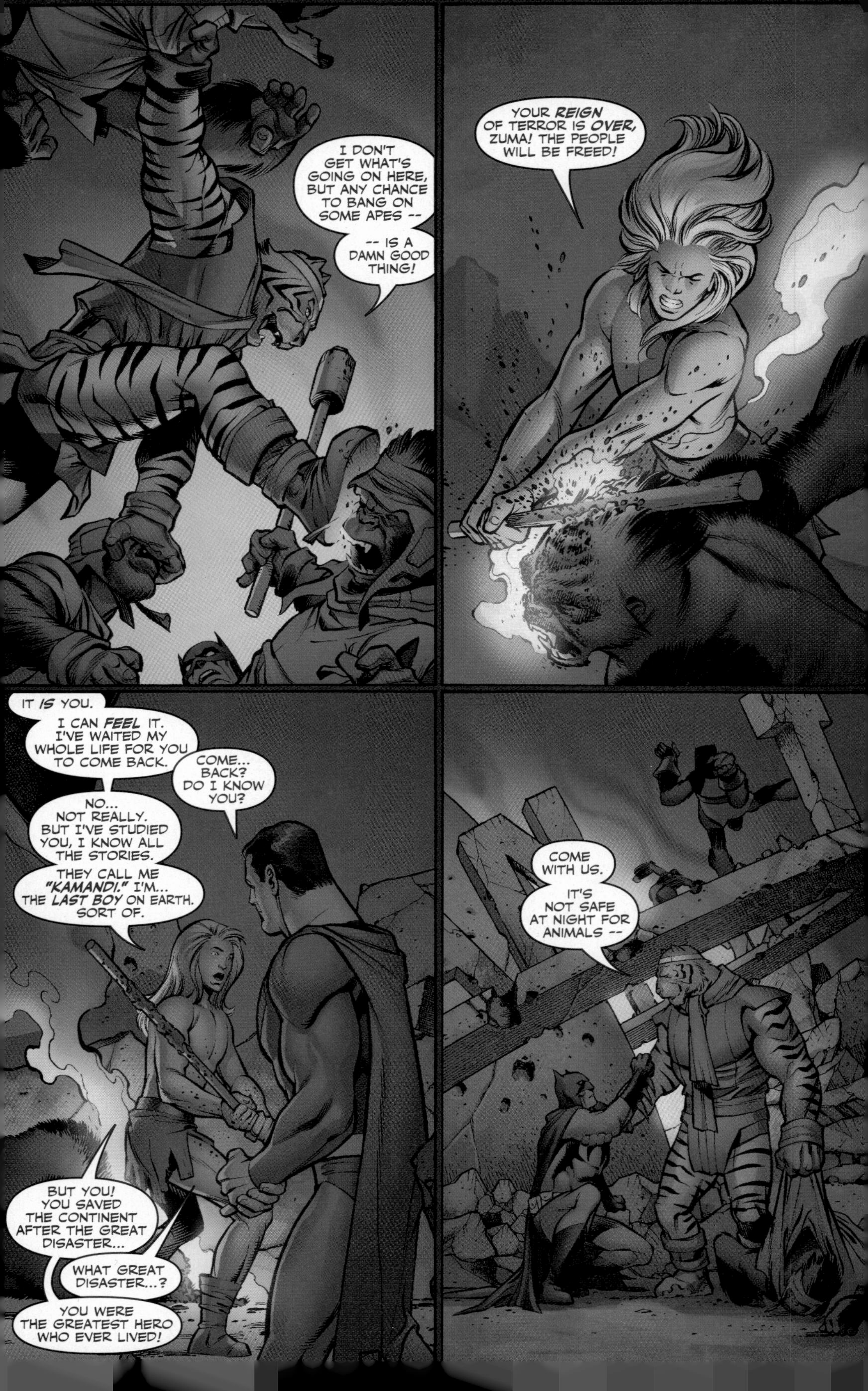
I DON'T GET WHAT'S GOING ON HERE, BUT ANY CHANCE TO BANG ON SOME APES --
-- IS A DAMN GOOD THING!
YOUR REIGN OF TERROR IS OVER, ZUMA! THE PEOPLE WILL BE FREED!
IT IS YOU.
I CAN FEEL IT. I'VE WAITED MY WHOLE LIFE FOR YOU TO COME BACK.
COME... BACK? DO I KNOW YOU?
NO... NOT REALLY. BUT I'VE STUDIED YOU, I KNOW ALL THE STORIES.
THEY CALL ME "KAMANDI." I'M... THE LAST BOY ON EARTH. SORT OF.
BUT YOU! YOU SAVED THE CONTINENT AFTER THE GREAT DISASTER...
WHAT GREAT DISASTER...?
YOU WERE THE GREATEST HERO WHO EVER LIVED!
COME WITH US.
IT'S NOT SAFE AT NIGHT FOR ANIMALS --

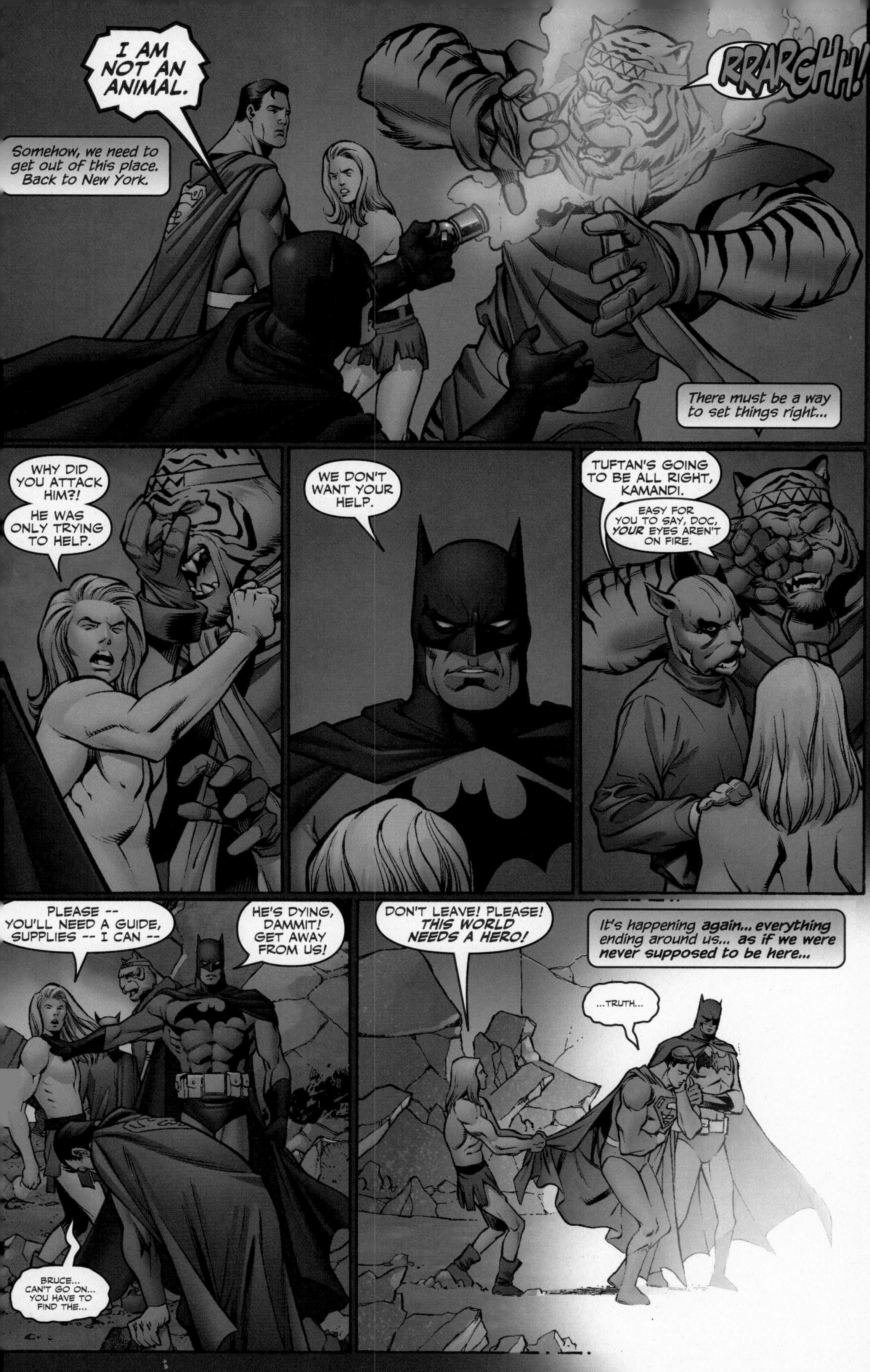
I AM NOT AN ANIMAL.
Somehow, we need to get out of this place. Back to New York.
RRARGHH!
There must be a way to set things right...
WHY DID YOU ATTACK HIM?!
HE WAS ONLY TRYING TO HELP.
WE DON'T WANT YOUR HELP.
TUFTAN'S GOING TO BE ALL RIGHT, KAMANDI.
EASY FOR YOU TO SAY, DOC, YOUR EYES AREN'T ON FIRE.
PLEASE -- YOU'LL NEED A GUIDE, SUPPLIES -- I CAN --
HE'S DYING, DAMMIT! GET AWAY FROM US!
BRUCE... CAN'T GO ON... YOU HAVE TO FIND THE...
DON'T LEAVE! PLEASE! THIS WORLD NEEDS A HERO!
It's happening again... everything ending around us... as if we were never supposed to be here...
...TRUTH...

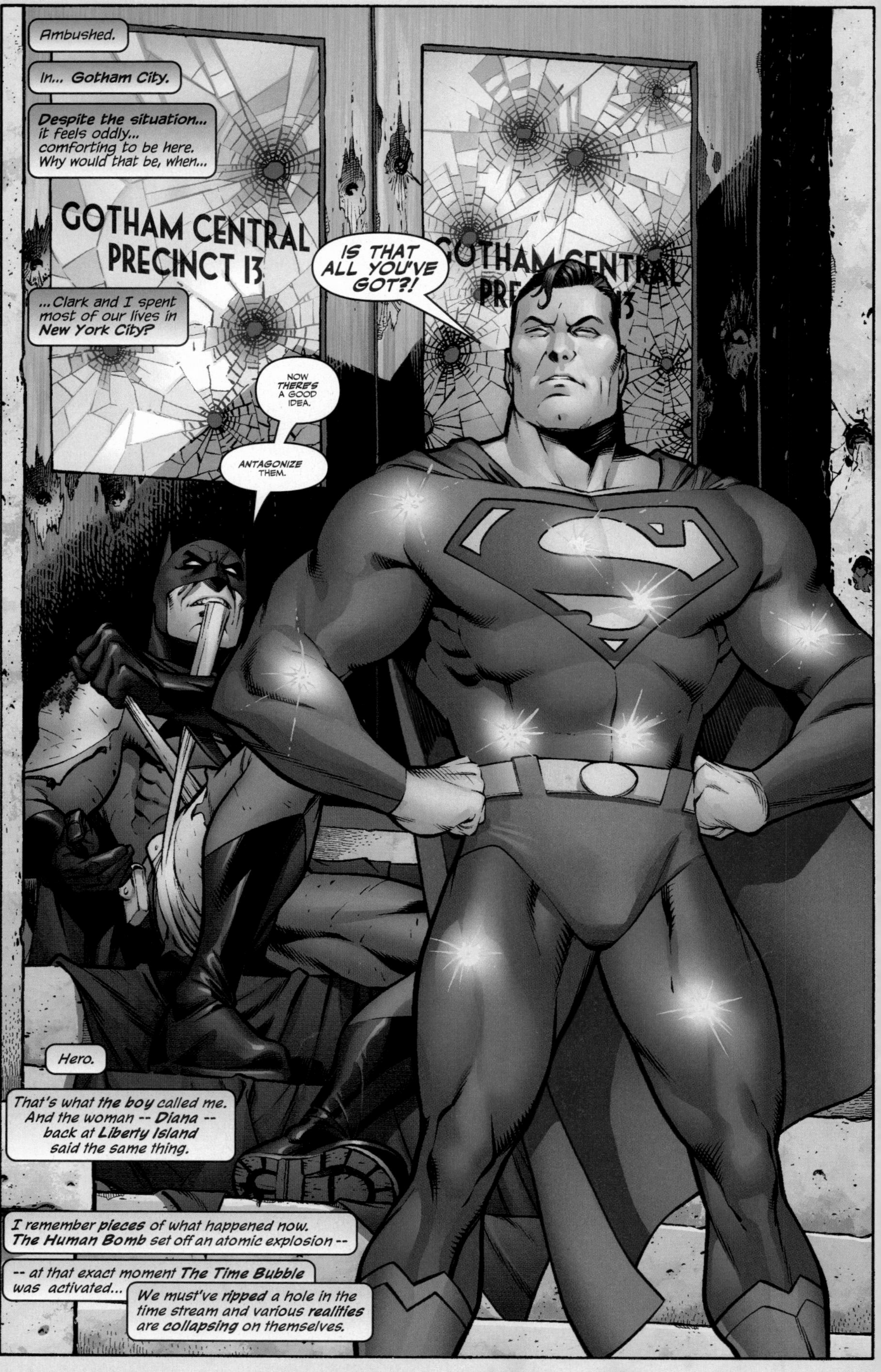
Ambushed.
In... Gotham City.
Despite the situation... it feels oddly... comforting to be here. Why would that be, when...
GOTHAM CENTRAL PRECINCT 13
...Clark and I spent most of our lives in New York City?
IS THAT ALL YOU'VE GOT?!
NOW THERE'S A GOOD IDEA.
ANTAGONIZE THEM.
Hero.
That's what the boy called me. And the woman -- Diana -- back at Liberty Island said the same thing.
I remember pieces of what happened now. The Human Bomb set off an atomic explosion --
-- at that exact moment The Time Bubble was activated...
We must've ripped a hole in the time stream and various realities are collapsing on themselves.

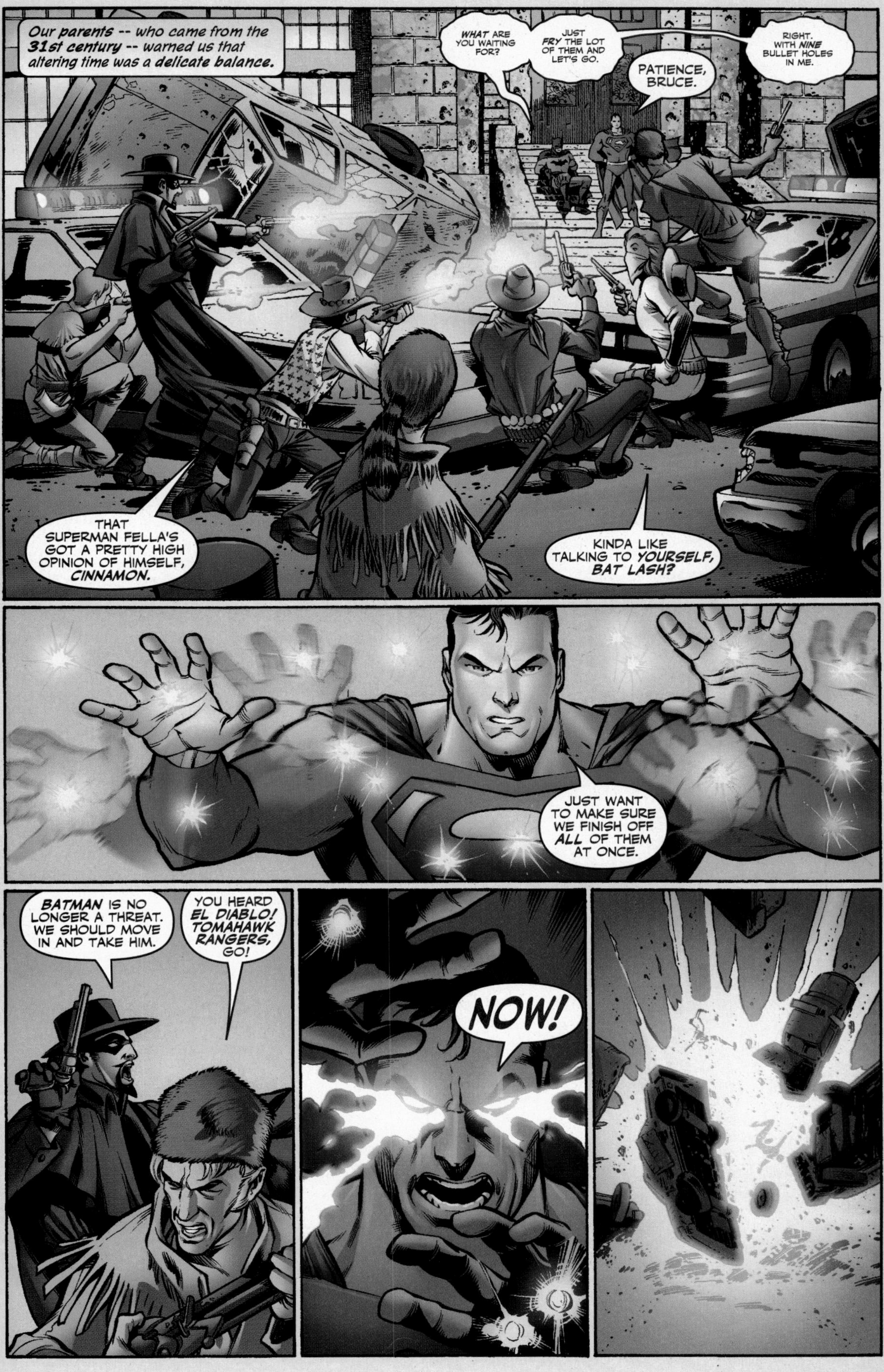
Our parents -- who came from the 31st century -- warned us that altering time was a delicate balance.
WHAT ARE YOU WAITING FOR?
JUST FRY THE LOT OF THEM AND LET'S GO.
PATIENCE, BRUCE.
RIGHT. WITH NINE BULLET HOLES IN ME.
THAT SUPERMAN FELLA'S GOT A PRETTY HIGH OPINION OF HIMSELF, CINNAMON.
KINDA LIKE TALKING TO YOURSELF, BAT LASH?
JUST WANT TO MAKE SURE WE FINISH OFF ALL OF THEM AT ONCE.
BATMAN IS NO LONGER A THREAT. WE SHOULD MOVE IN AND TAKE HIM.
YOU HEARD EL DIABLO! TOMAHAWK RANGERS, GO!
NOW!

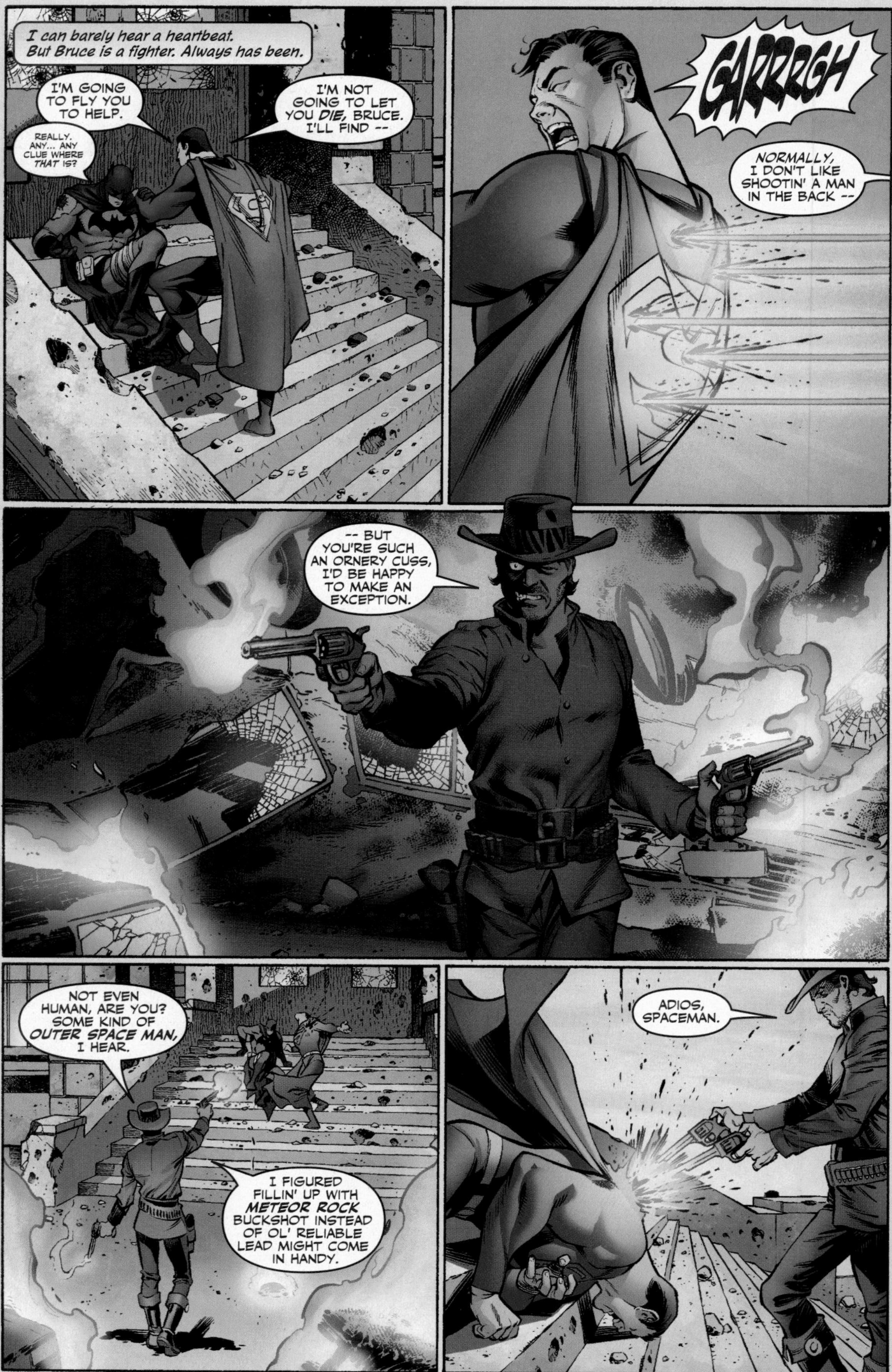
I can barely hear a heartbeat. But Bruce is a fighter. Always has been.
I'M GOING TO FLY YOU TO HELP.
REALLY. ANY... ANY CLUE WHERE THAT IS?
I'M NOT GOING TO LET YOU DIE, BRUCE. I'LL FIND --
GARRRGH
NORMALLY, I DON'T LIKE SHOOTIN' A MAN IN THE BACK --
-- BUT YOU'RE SUCH AN ORNERY CUSS, I'D BE HAPPY TO MAKE AN EXCEPTION.
NOT EVEN HUMAN, ARE YOU? SOME KIND OF OUTER SPACE MAN, I HEAR.
I FIGURED FILLIN' UP WITH METEOR ROCK BUCKSHOT INSTEAD OF OL' RELIABLE LEAD MIGHT COME IN HANDY.
ADIOS, SPACEMAN.

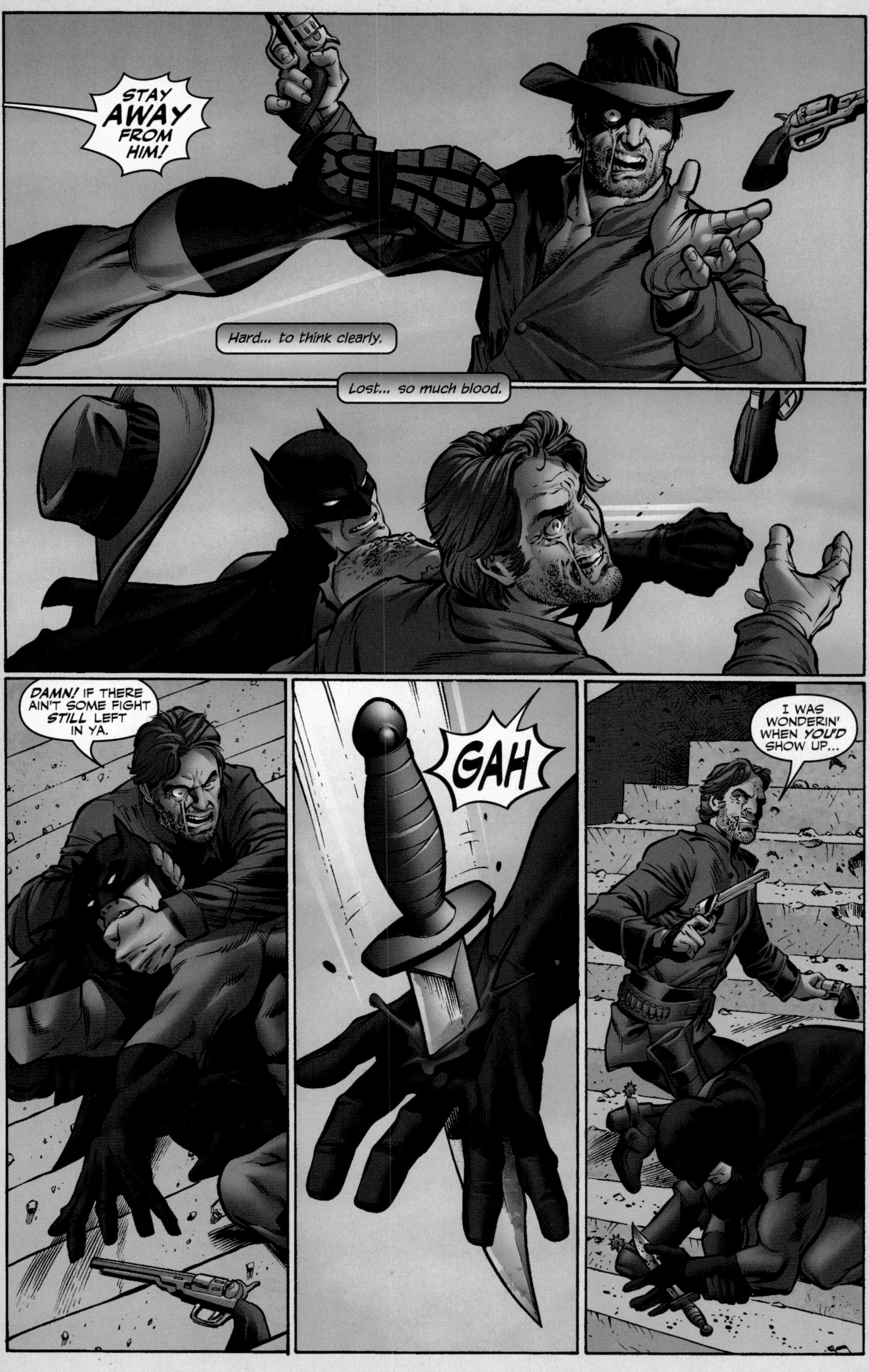
STAY AWAY FROM HIM!
Hard... to think clearly.
Lost... so much blood.
DAMN! IF THERE AIN'T SOME FIGHT STILL LEFT IN YA.
GAH
I WAS WONDERIN' WHEN YOU'D SHOW UP...

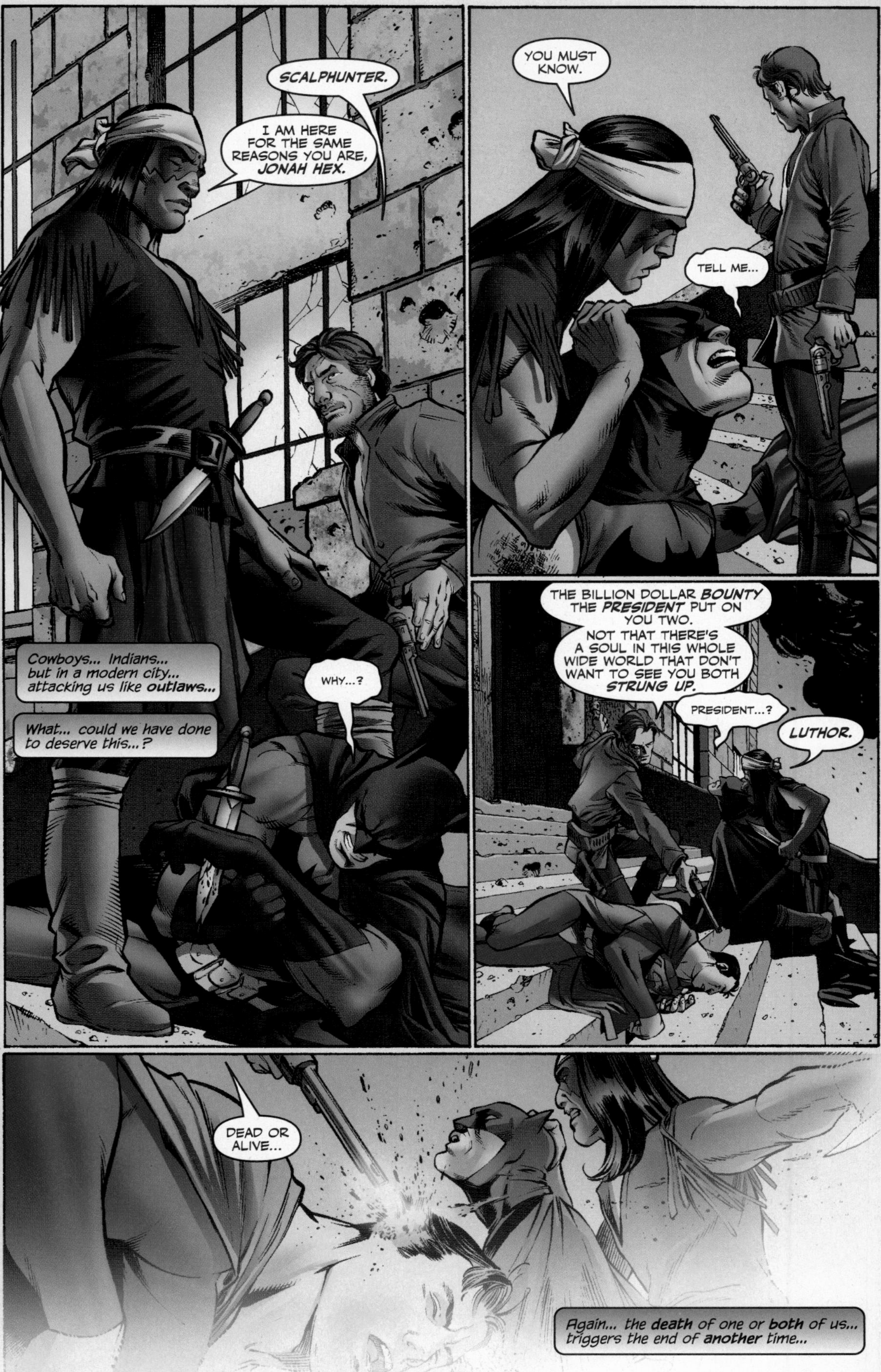
SCALPHUNTER.
I AM HERE FOR THE SAME REASONS YOU ARE, JONAH HEX.
Cowboys... Indians... but in a modern city... attacking us like outlaws...
What... could we have done to deserve this...?
WHY...?
YOU MUST KNOW.
TELL ME...
THE BILLION DOLLAR BOUNTY THE PRESIDENT PUT ON YOU TWO. NOT THAT THERE'S A SOUL IN THIS WHOLE WIDE WORLD THAT DON'T WANT TO SEE YOU BOTH STRUNG UP.
PRESIDENT...?
LUTHOR.
DEAD OR ALIVE...
Again... the death of one or both of us... triggers the end of another time...

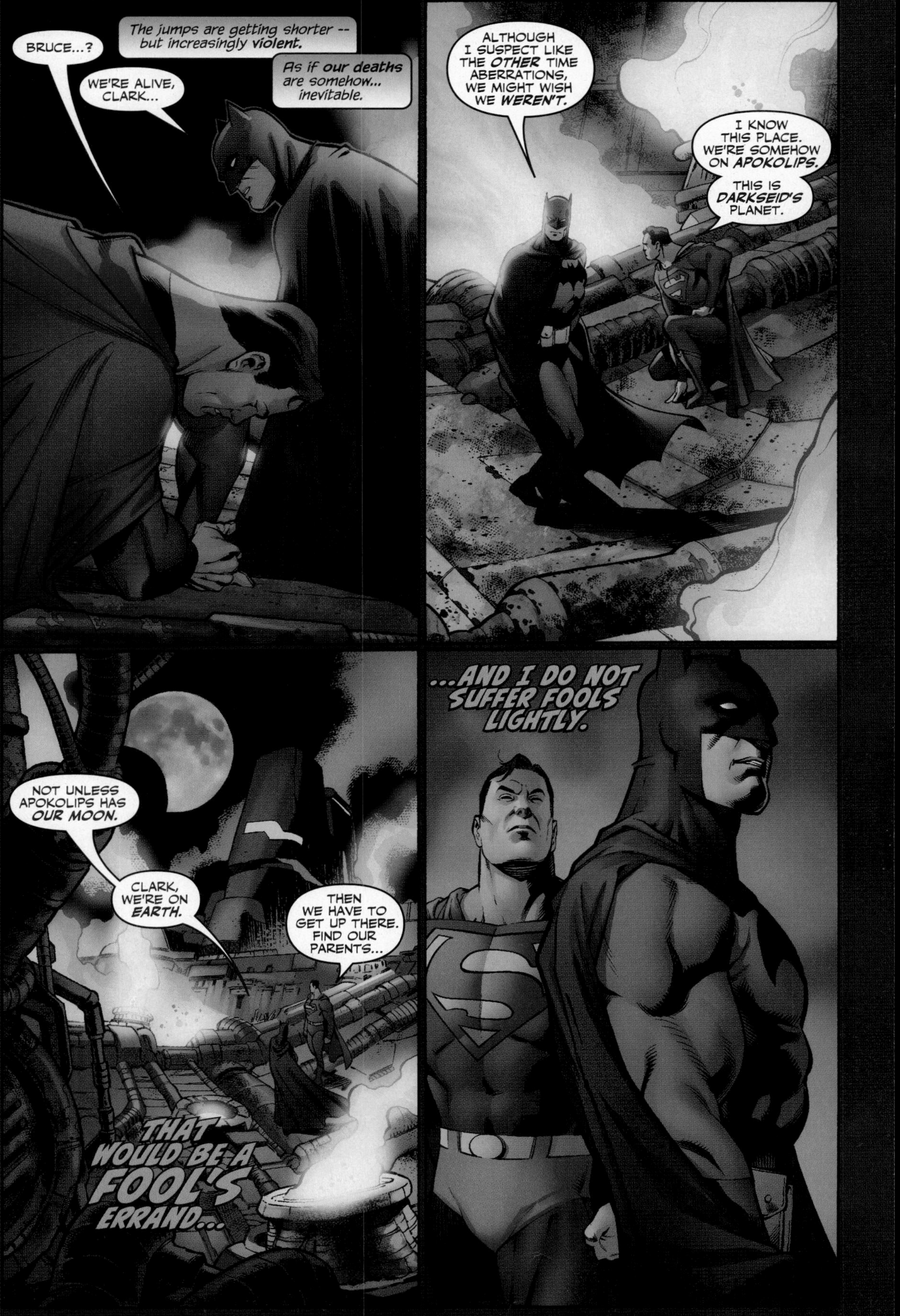
BRUCE...?
The jumps are getting shorter -- but increasingly violent.
WE'RE ALIVE, CLARK...
As if our deaths are somehow... inevitable.
ALTHOUGH I SUSPECT LIKE THE OTHER TIME ABERRATIONS, WE MIGHT WISH WE WEREN'T.
I KNOW THIS PLACE. WE'RE SOMEHOW ON APOKOLIPS.
THIS IS DARKSEID'S PLANET.
NOT UNLESS APOKOLIPS HAS OUR MOON.
CLARK, WE'RE ON EARTH.
THEN WE HAVE TO GET UP THERE. FIND OUR PARENTS...
THAT WOULD BE A FOOL'S ERRAND...
...AND I DO NOT SUFFER FOOLS LIGHTLY.

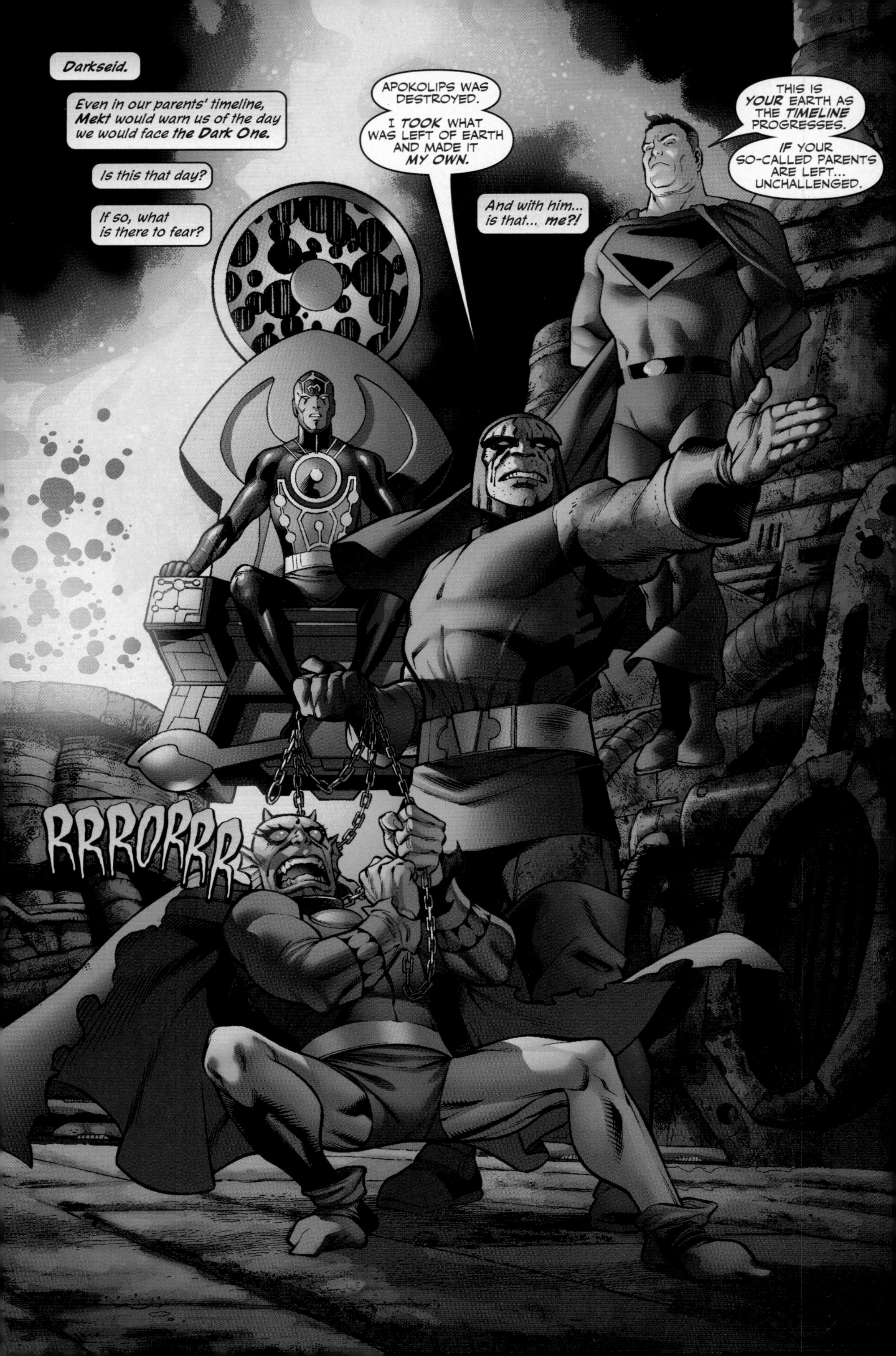
Darkseid.
Even in our parents' timeline, Mekt would warn us of the day we would face the Dark One.
Is this that day?
If so, what is there to fear?
APOKOLIPS WAS DESTROYED.
I TOOK WHAT WAS LEFT OF EARTH AND MADE IT MY OWN.
And with him... is that... me?!
THIS IS YOUR EARTH AS THE TIMELINE PROGRESSES.
IF YOUR SO-CALLED PARENTS ARE LEFT... UNCHALLENGED.
RRRORRR

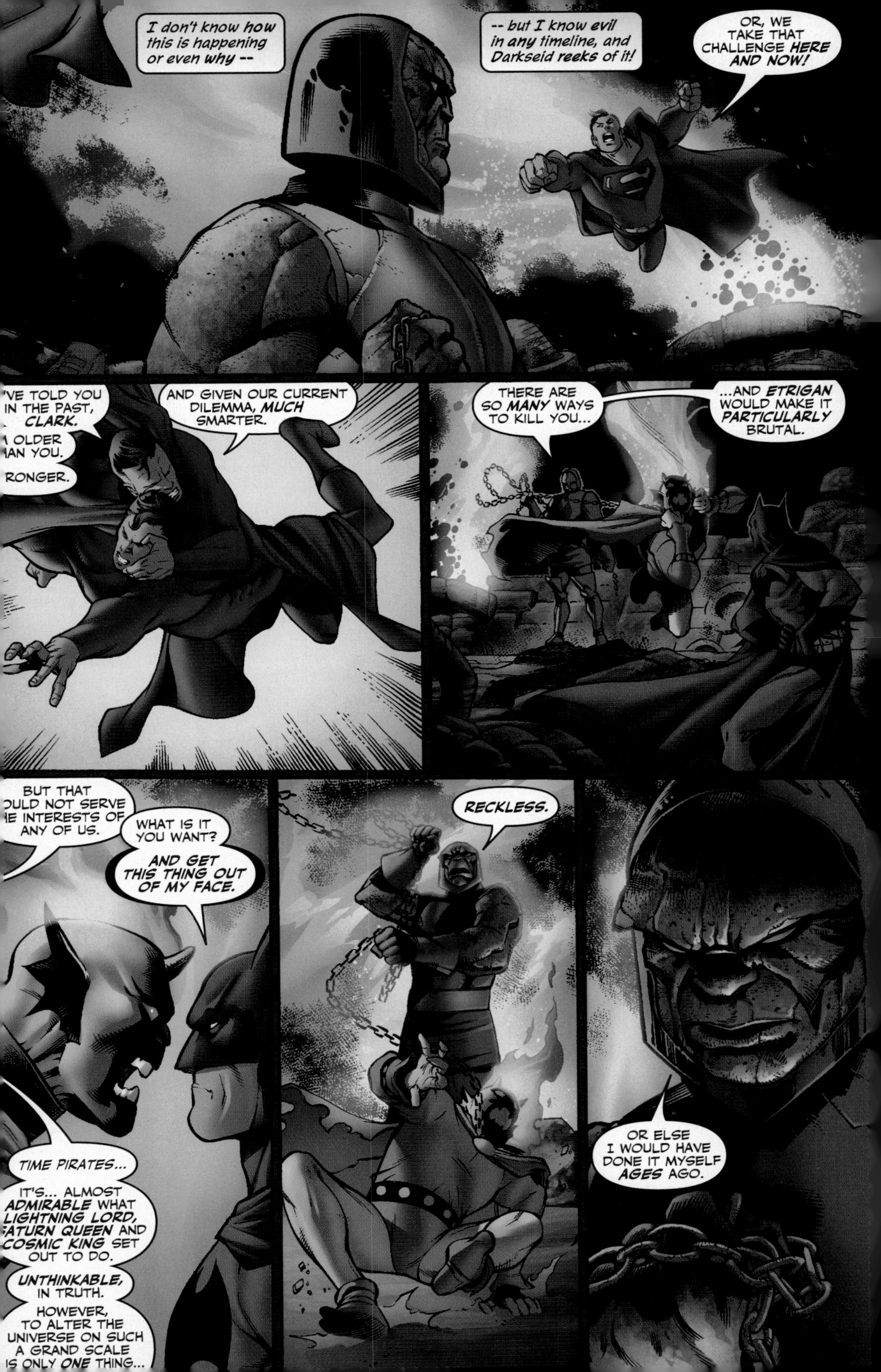

I don't know how this is happening or even why --
-- but I know evil in any timeline, and Darkseid reeks of it!
OR, WE TAKE THAT CHALLENGE HERE AND NOW!
'VE TOLD YOU IN THE PAST, CLARK.
OLDER AN YOU.
RONGER.
AND GIVEN OUR CURRENT DILEMMA, MUCH SMARTER.
THERE ARE SO MANY WAYS TO KILL YOU...
...AND ETRIGAN WOULD MAKE IT PARTICULARLY BRUTAL.
BUT THAT OULD NOT SERVE E INTERESTS OF ANY OF US.
WHAT IS IT YOU WANT?
AND GET THIS THING OUT OF MY FACE.
TIME PIRATES...
IT'S... ALMOST ADMIRABLE WHAT LIGHTNING LORD, ATURN QUEEN AND OSMIC KING SET OUT TO DO.
UNTHINKABLE, IN TRUTH.
HOWEVER, TO ALTER THE UNIVERSE ON SUCH A GRAND SCALE IS ONLY ONE THING...
RECKLESS.
OR ELSE I WOULD HAVE DONE IT MYSELF AGES AGO.

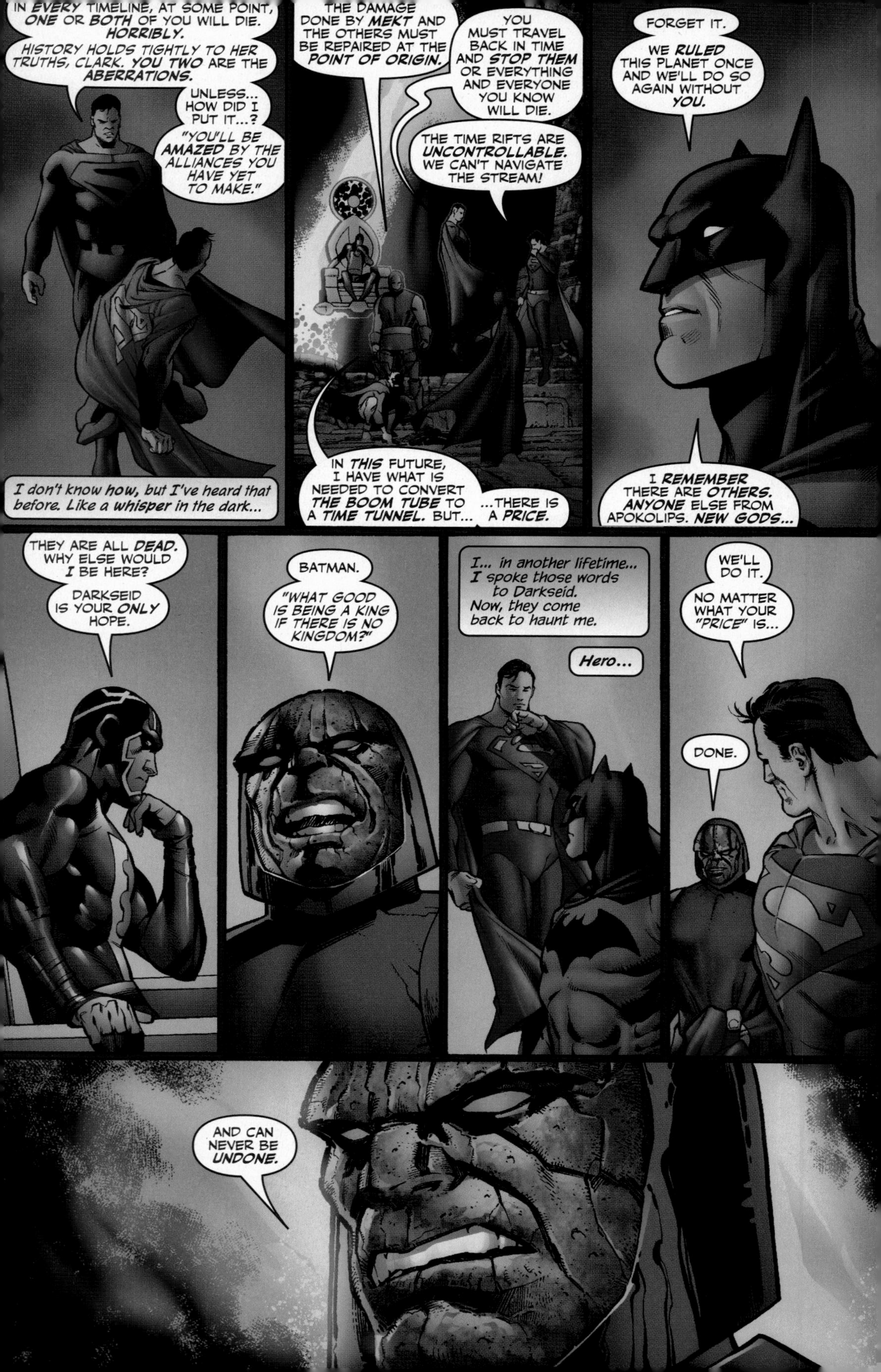
IN EVERY TIMELINE, AT SOME POINT, ONE OR BOTH OF YOU WILL DIE. HORRIBLY.
HISTORY HOLDS TIGHTLY TO HER TRUTHS, CLARK. YOU TWO ARE THE ABERRATIONS.
UNLESS... HOW DID I PUT IT...?
"YOU'LL BE AMAZED BY THE ALLIANCES YOU HAVE YET TO MAKE."
I don't know how, but I've heard that before. Like a whisper in the dark...
THE DAMAGE DONE BY MEKT AND THE OTHERS MUST BE REPAIRED AT THE POINT OF ORIGIN.
YOU MUST TRAVEL BACK IN TIME AND STOP THEM OR EVERYTHING AND EVERYONE YOU KNOW WILL DIE.
THE TIME RIFTS ARE UNCONTROLLABLE. WE CAN'T NAVIGATE THE STREAM!
IN THIS FUTURE, I HAVE WHAT IS NEEDED TO CONVERT THE BOOM TUBE TO A TIME TUNNEL. BUT...
...THERE IS A PRICE.
FORGET IT.
WE RULED THIS PLANET ONCE AND WE'LL DO SO AGAIN WITHOUT YOU.
I REMEMBER THERE ARE OTHERS. ANYONE ELSE FROM APOKOLIPS. NEW GODS...
THEY ARE ALL DEAD. WHY ELSE WOULD I BE HERE?
DARKSEID IS YOUR ONLY HOPE.
BATMAN.
"WHAT GOOD IS BEING A KING IF THERE IS NO KINGDOM?"
I... in another lifetime... I spoke those words to Darkseid. Now, they come back to haunt me.
Hero...
WE'LL DO IT.
NO MATTER WHAT YOUR "PRICE" IS...
DONE.
AND CAN NEVER BE UNDONE.

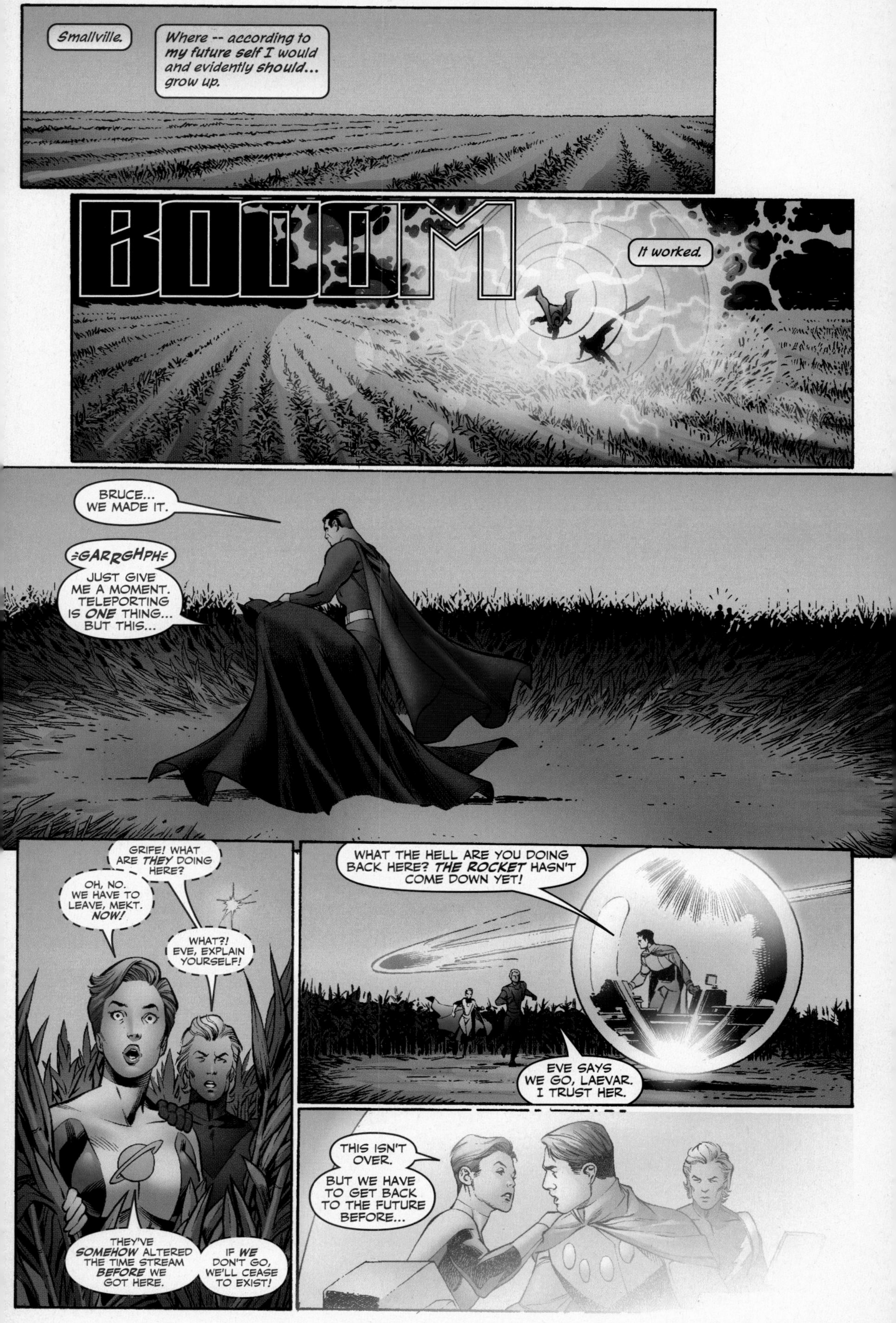

Smallville.
Where -- according to my future self I would and evidently should... grow up.
BOOM
It worked.
BRUCE... WE MADE IT.
GARRGHPH
JUST GIVE ME A MOMENT. TELEPORTING IS ONE THING... BUT THIS...
GRIFE! WHAT ARE THEY DOING HERE?
OH, NO. WE HAVE TO LEAVE, MEKT. NOW!
WHAT?! EVE, EXPLAIN YOURSELF!
THEY'VE SOMEHOW ALTERED THE TIME STREAM BEFORE WE GOT HERE.
IF WE DON'T GO, WE'LL CEASE TO EXIST!
WHAT THE HELL ARE YOU DOING BACK HERE? THE ROCKET HASN'T COME DOWN YET!
EVE SAYS WE GO, LAEVAR. I TRUST HER.
THIS ISN'T OVER.
BUT WE HAVE TO GET BACK TO THE FUTURE BEFORE...

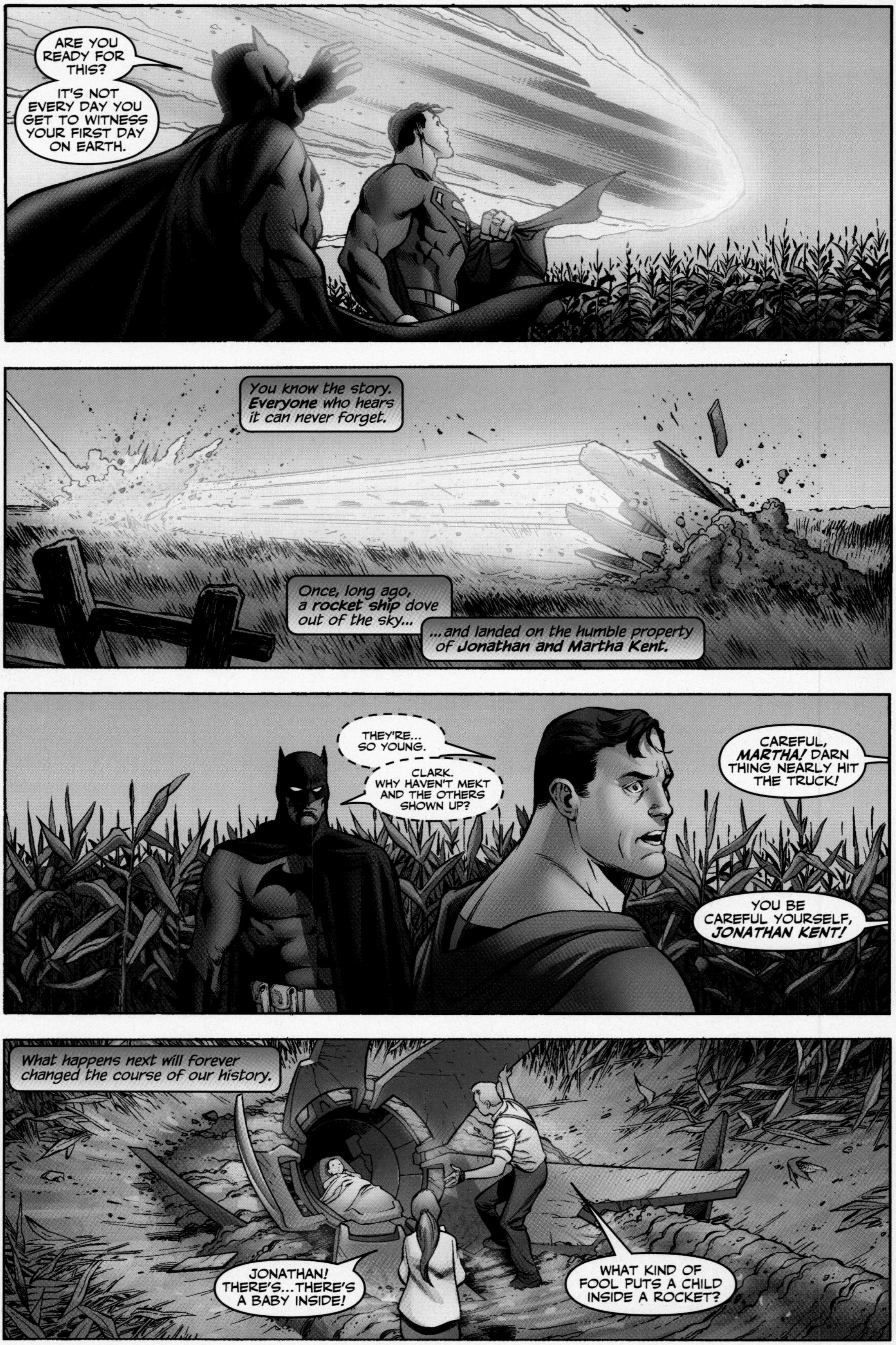
ARE YOU READY FOR THIS?
IT'S NOT EVERY DAY YOU GET TO WITNESS YOUR FIRST DAY ON EARTH.
You know the story. Everyone who hears it can never forget.
Once, long ago, a rocket ship dove out of the sky...
...and landed on the humble property of Jonathan and Martha Kent.
THEY'RE... SO YOUNG.
CLARK. WHY HAVEN'T MEKT AND THE OTHERS SHOWN UP?
CAREFUL, MARTHA! DARN THING NEARLY HIT THE TRUCK!
YOU BE CAREFUL YOURSELF, JONATHAN KENT!
What happens next will forever changed the course of our history.
JONATHAN! THERE'S...THERE'S A BABY INSIDE!
WHAT KIND OF FOOL PUTS A CHILD INSIDE A ROCKET?

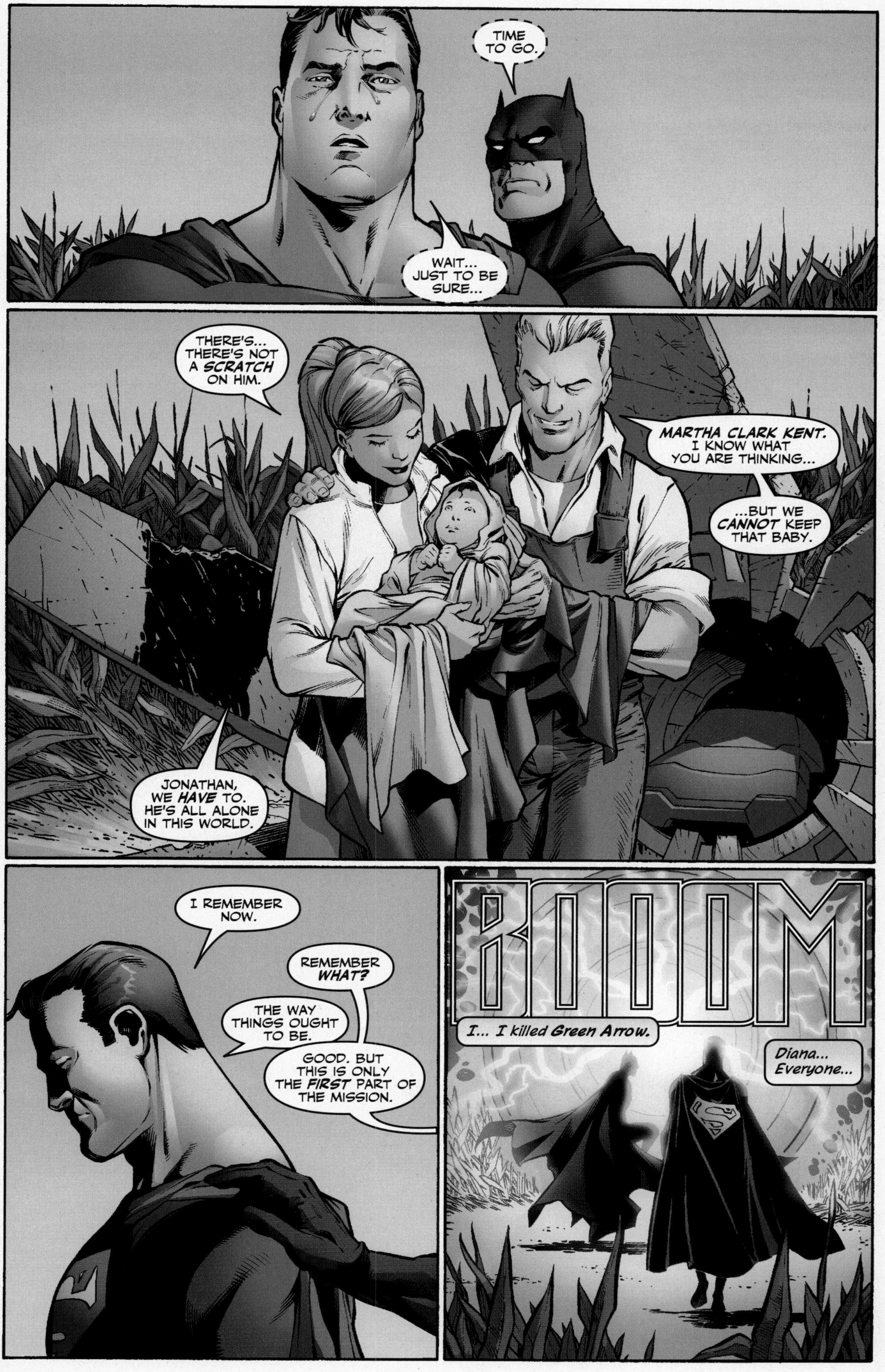
TIME TO GO.
WAIT... JUST TO BE SURE...
THERE'S... THERE'S NOT A *SCRATCH* ON HIM.
MARTHA CLARK KENT. I KNOW WHAT YOU ARE THINKING...
...BUT WE *CANNOT* KEEP THAT BABY.
JONATHAN, WE *HAVE* TO. HE'S ALL ALONE IN THIS WORLD.
I REMEMBER NOW.
REMEMBER *WHAT?*
THE WAY THINGS OUGHT TO BE.
GOOD. BUT THIS IS ONLY THE *FIRST* PART OF THE MISSION.
BOOOM
I... I killed Green Arrow.
Diana... Everyone...

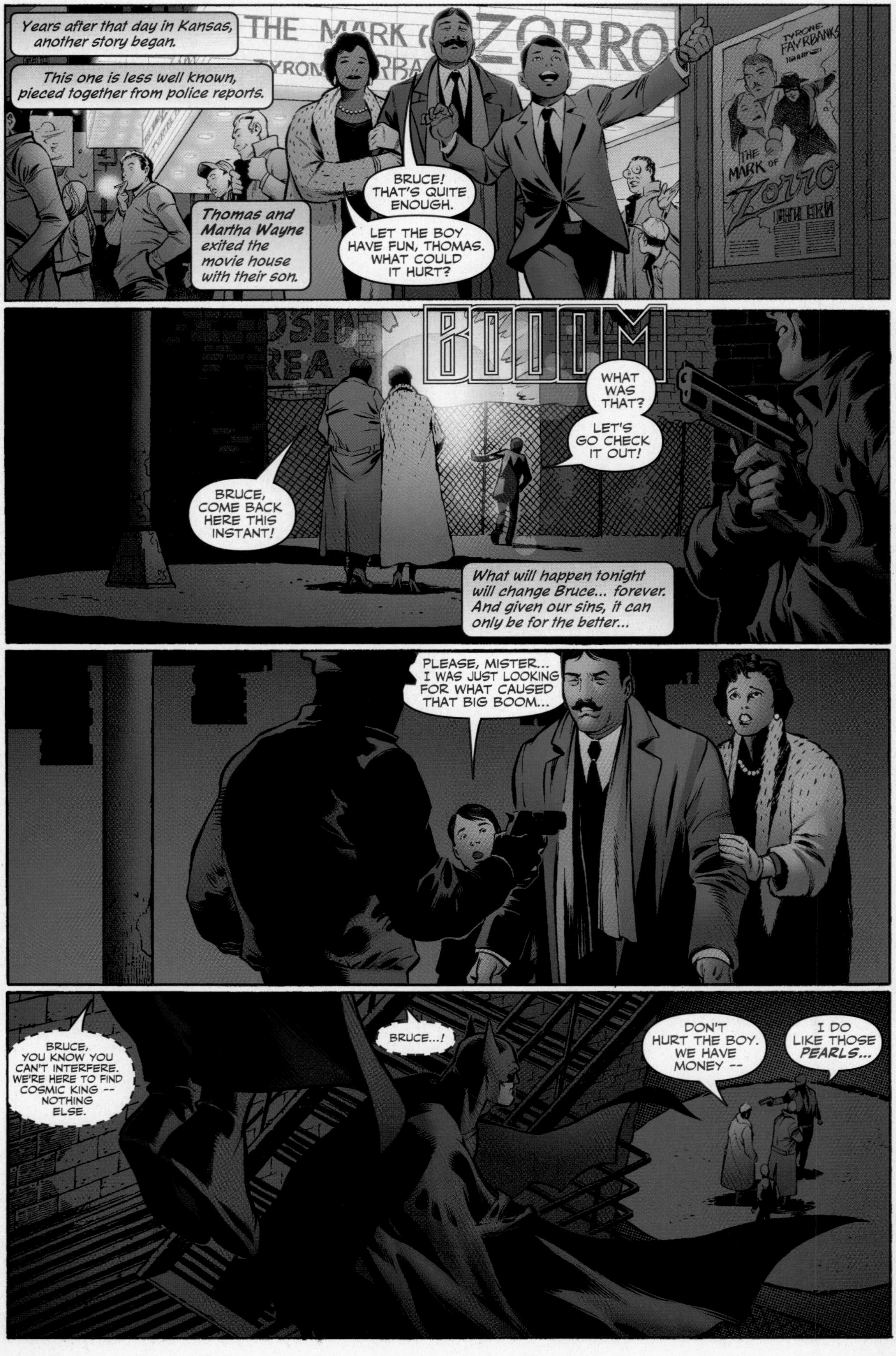
Years after that day in Kansas, another story began.
This one is less well known, pieced together from police reports.
THE MARK OF ZORRO
BRUCE! THAT'S QUITE ENOUGH.
LET THE BOY HAVE FUN, THOMAS. WHAT COULD IT HURT?
Thomas and Martha Wayne exited the movie house with their son.
TYRONE FAYRBANKS
THE MARK OF Zorro
BOOOM
WHAT WAS THAT?
LET'S GO CHECK IT OUT!
BRUCE, COME BACK HERE THIS INSTANT!
What will happen tonight will change Bruce... forever. And given our sins, it can only be for the better...
PLEASE, MISTER... I WAS JUST LOOKING FOR WHAT CAUSED THAT BIG BOOM...
BRUCE, YOU KNOW YOU CAN'T INTERFERE. WE'RE HERE TO FIND COSMIC KING -- NOTHING ELSE.
BRUCE...!
DON'T HURT THE BOY. WE HAVE MONEY --
I DO LIKE THOSE PEARLS...

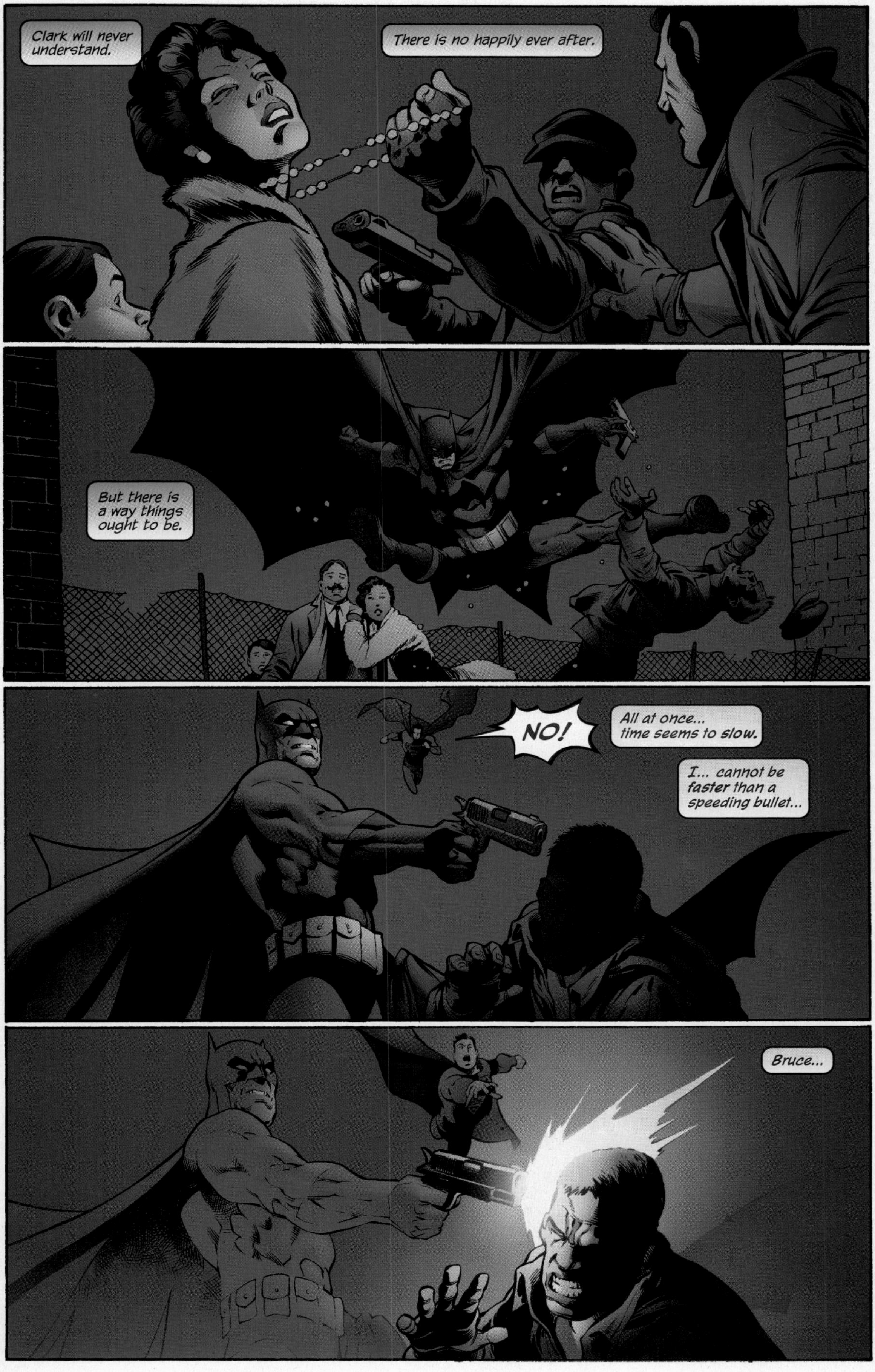
Clark will never understand.
There is no happily ever after.
But there is a way things ought to be.
NO!
All at once... time seems to slow.
I... cannot be faster than a speeding bullet...
Bruce...

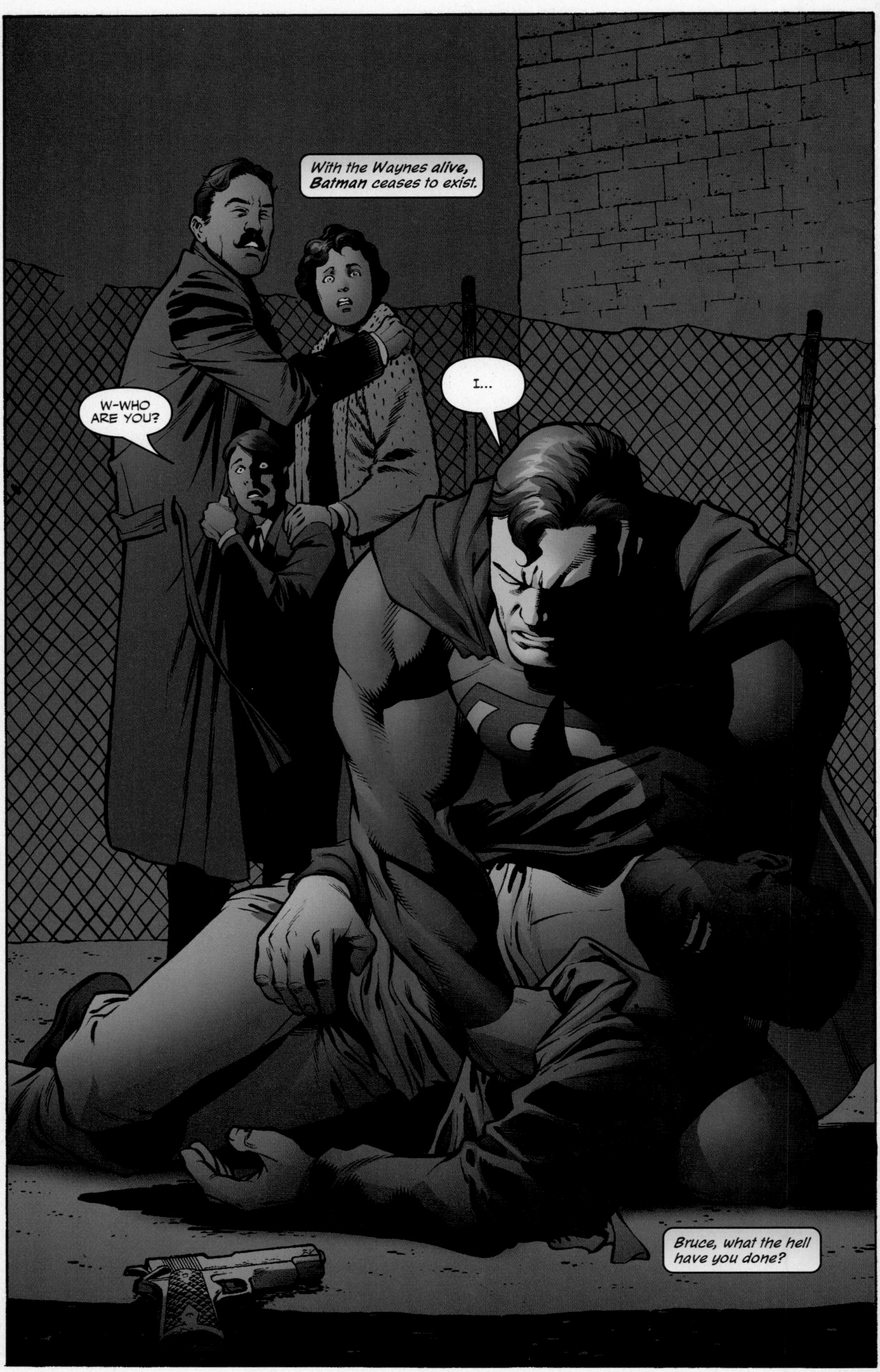

With the Waynes alive, Batman ceases to exist.
W-WHO ARE YOU?
I...
Bruce, what the hell have you done?

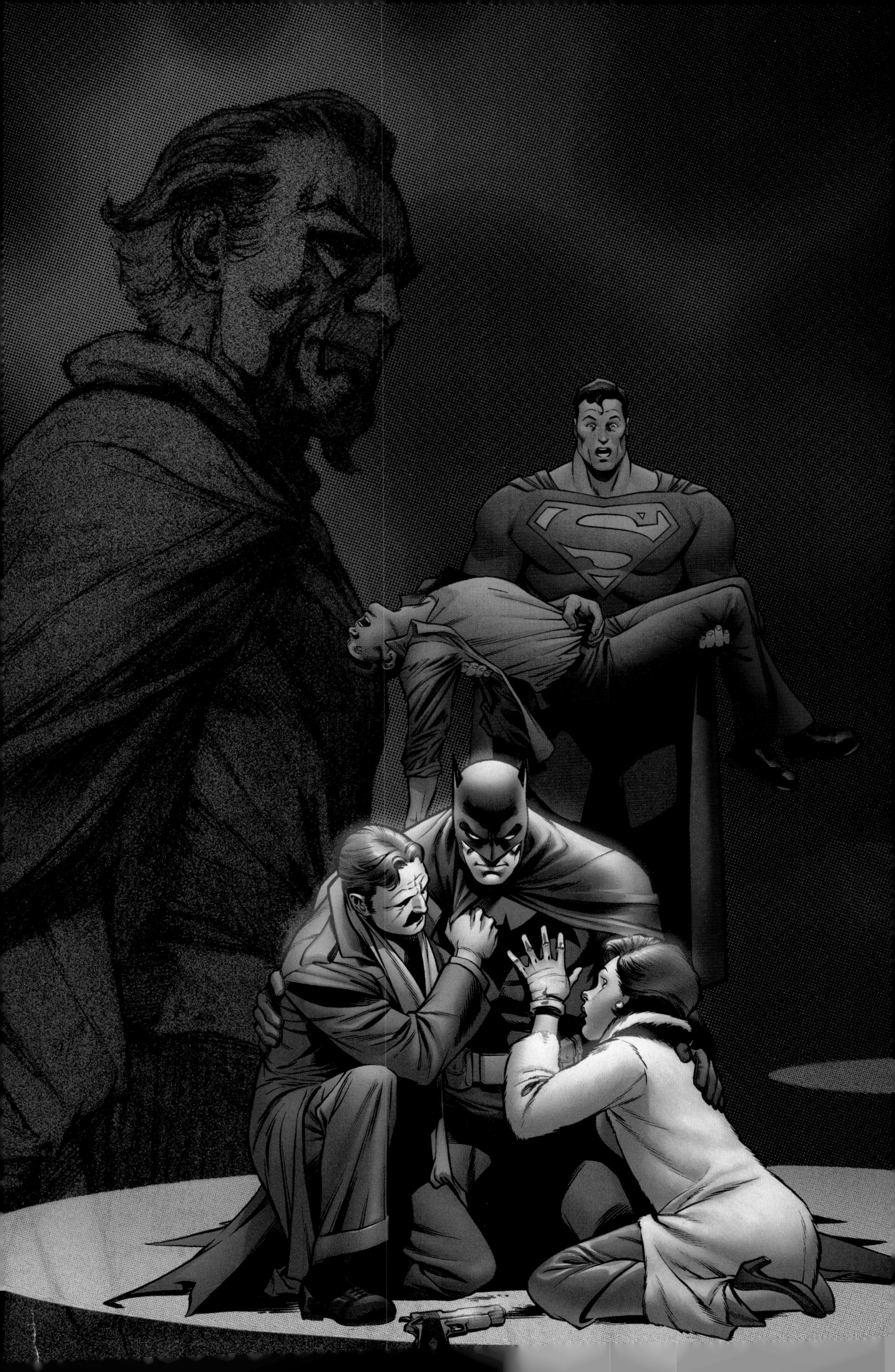

"A WORLD WITHOUT BATMAN..."

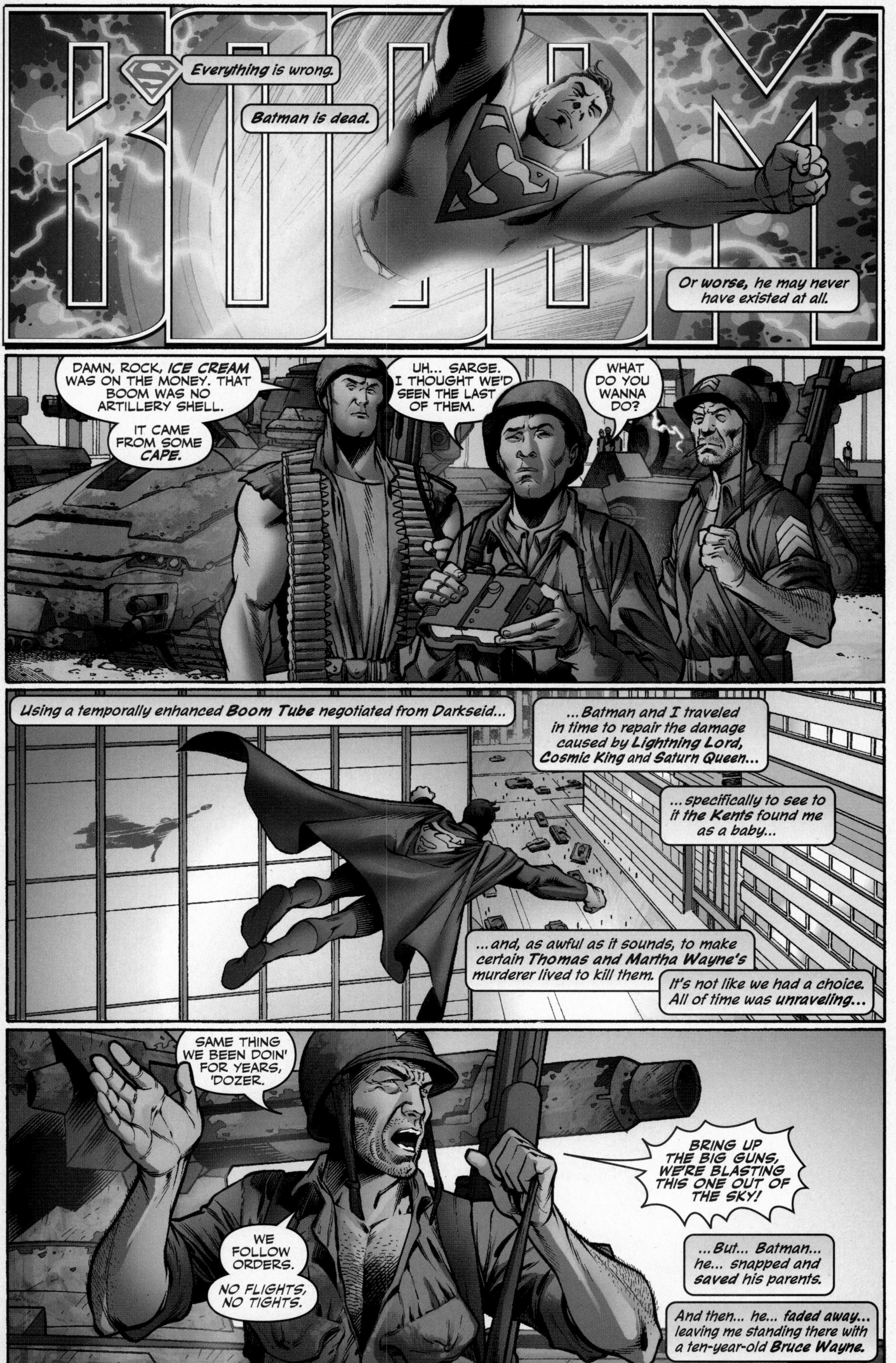
BOOM
Everything is wrong.
Batman is dead.
Or worse, he may never have existed at all.
DAMN, ROCK, ICE CREAM WAS ON THE MONEY. THAT BOOM WAS NO ARTILLERY SHELL.
IT CAME FROM SOME CAPE.
UH... SARGE. I THOUGHT WE'D SEEN THE LAST OF THEM.
WHAT DO YOU WANNA DO?
Using a temporally enhanced Boom Tube negotiated from Darkseid...
...Batman and I traveled in time to repair the damage caused by Lightning Lord, Cosmic King and Saturn Queen...
...specifically to see to it the Kents found me as a baby...
...and, as awful as it sounds, to make certain Thomas and Martha Wayne's murderer lived to kill them.
It's not like we had a choice. All of time was unraveling...
SAME THING WE BEEN DOIN' FOR YEARS, 'DOZER.
WE FOLLOW ORDERS.
NO FLIGHTS, NO TIGHTS.
BRING UP THE BIG GUNS, WE'RE BLASTING THIS ONE OUT OF THE SKY!
...But... Batman... he... snapped and saved his parents.
And then... he... faded away... leaving me standing there with a ten-year-old Bruce Wayne.

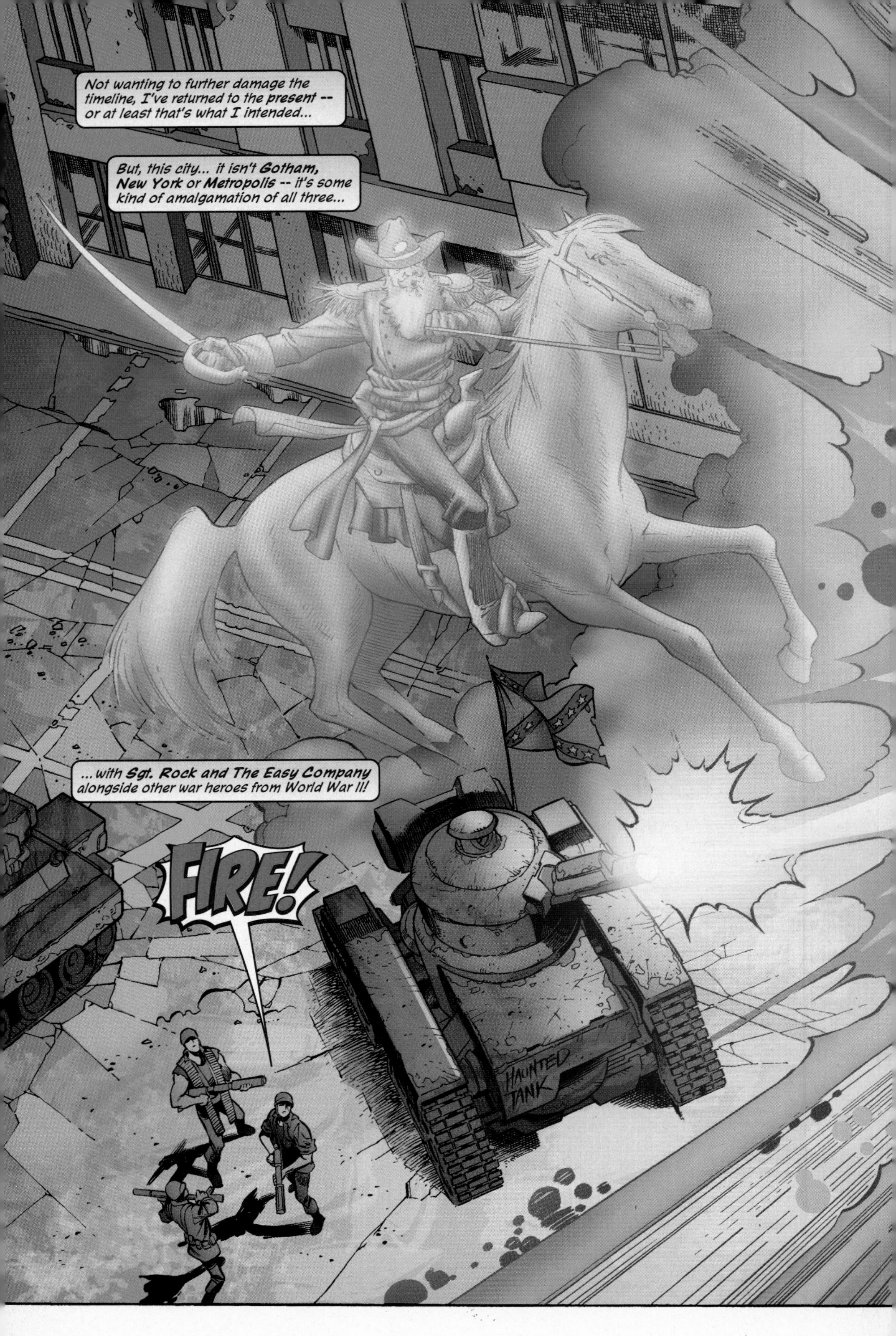

Not wanting to further damage the timeline, I've returned to the present -- or at least that's what I intended...
But, this city... it isn't Gotham, New York or Metropolis -- it's some kind of amalgamation of all three...
...with Sgt. Rock and The Easy Company alongside other war heroes from World War II!
FIRE!
HAUNTED TANK

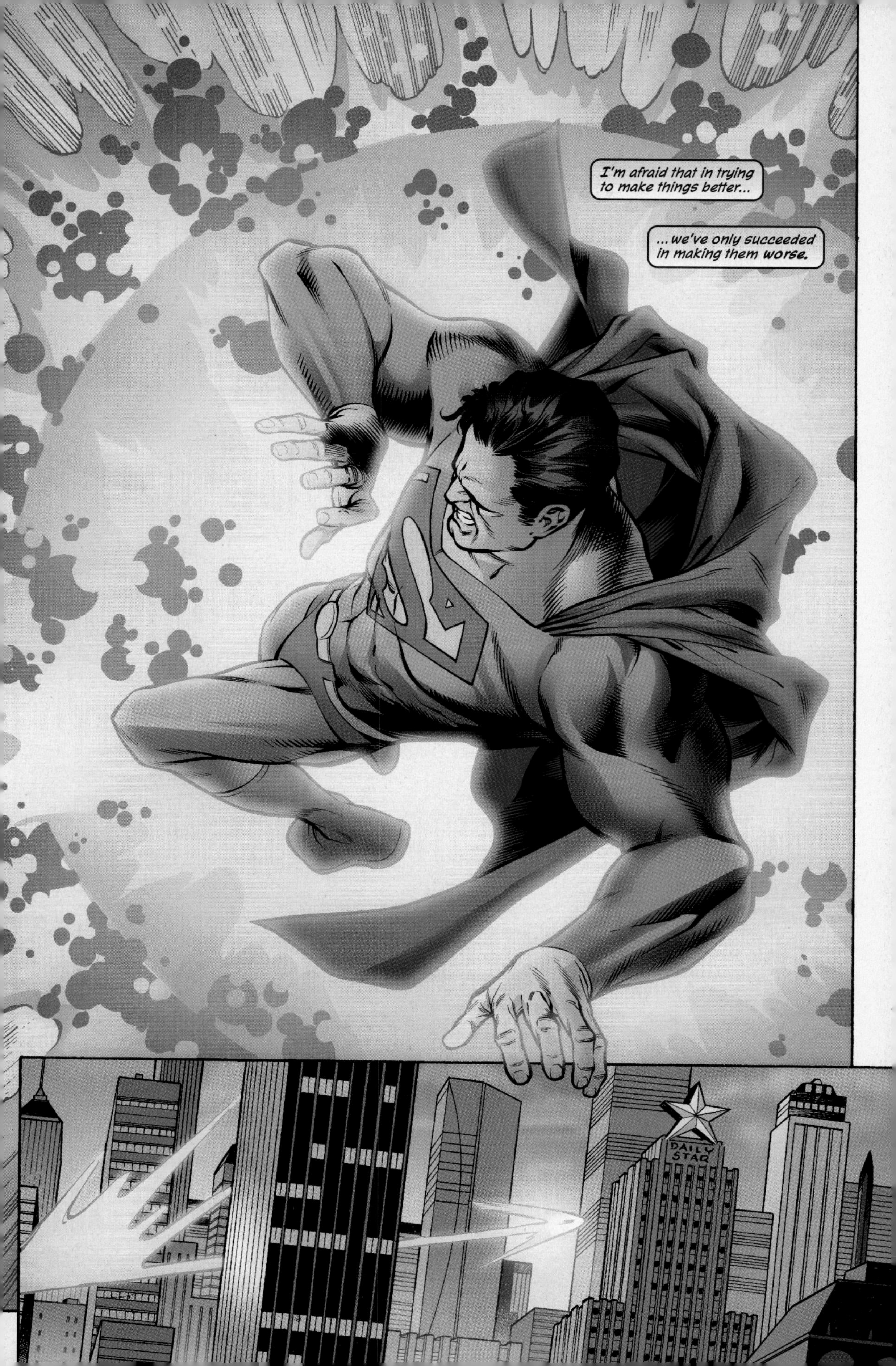
I'm afraid that in trying to make things better...
...we've only succeeded in making them worse.
DAILY STAR

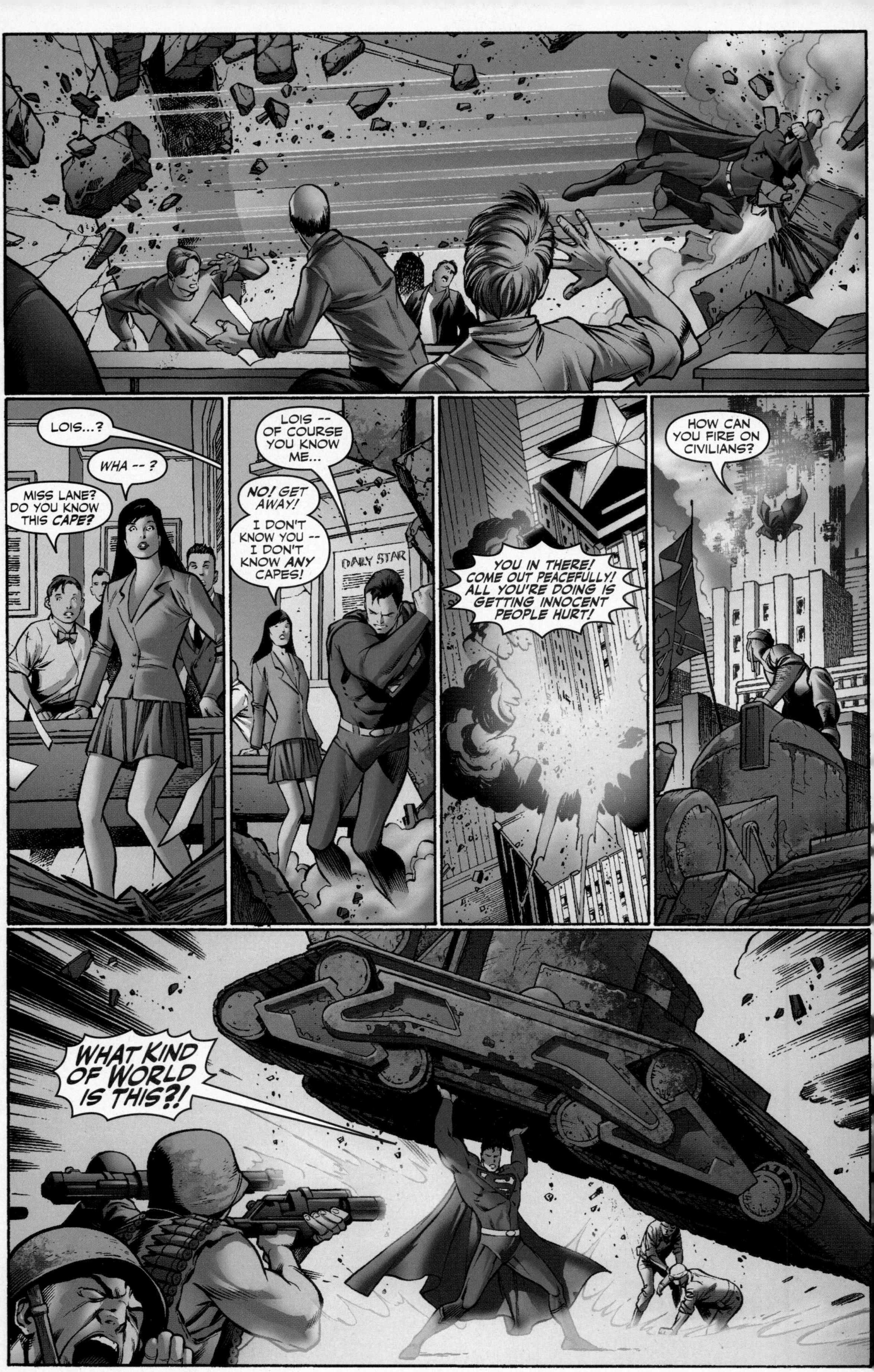

LOIS...?
WHA -- ?
MISS LANE? DO YOU KNOW THIS CAPE?
LOIS -- OF COURSE YOU KNOW ME...
NO! GET AWAY!
I DON'T KNOW YOU -- I DON'T KNOW ANY CAPES!
DAILY STAR
YOU IN THERE! COME OUT PEACEFULLY! ALL YOU'RE DOING IS GETTING INNOCENT PEOPLE HURT!
HOW CAN YOU FIRE ON CIVILIANS?
WHAT KIND OF WORLD IS THIS?!

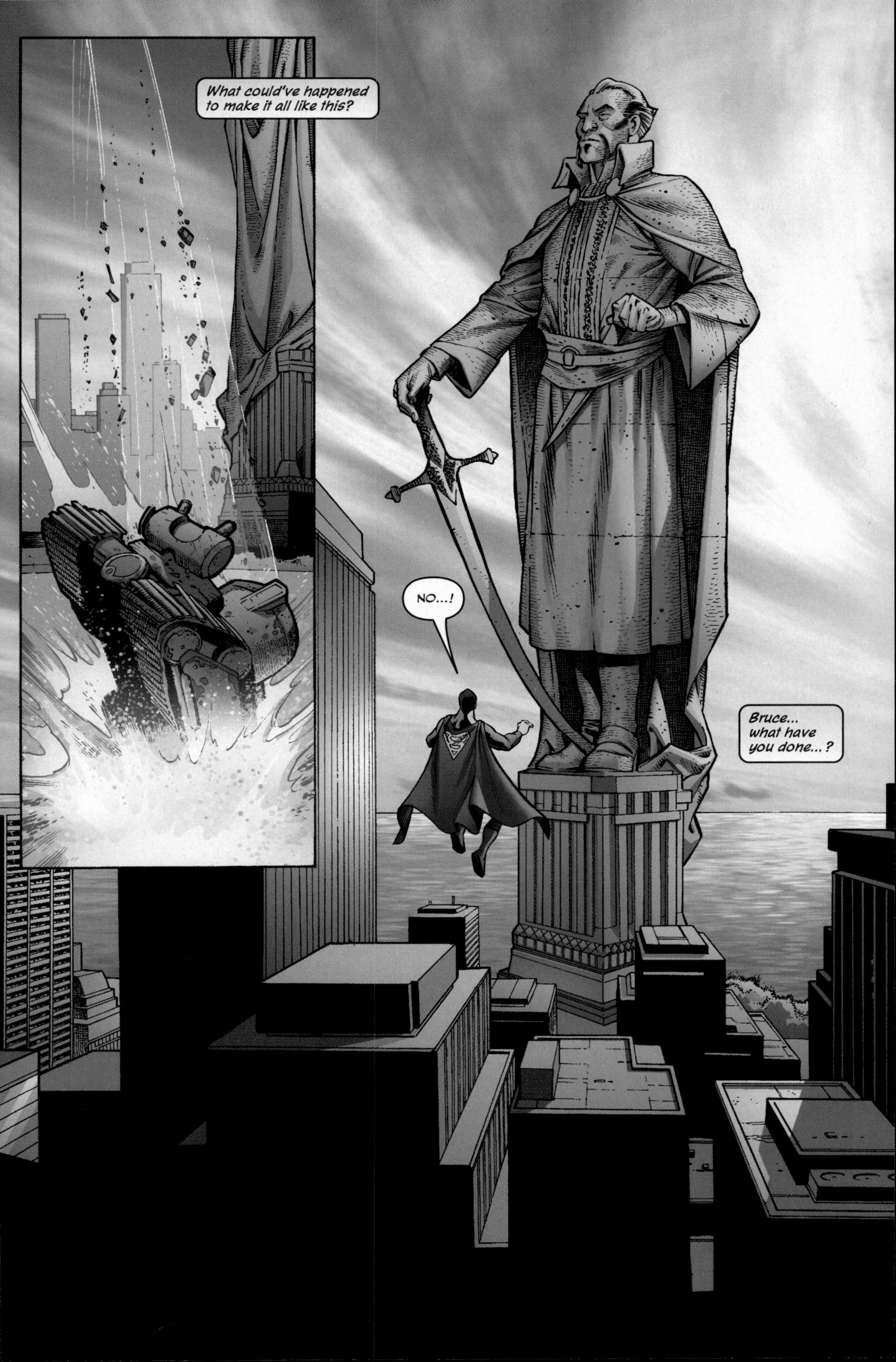
What could've happened to make it all like this?
NO...!
Bruce... what have you done...?

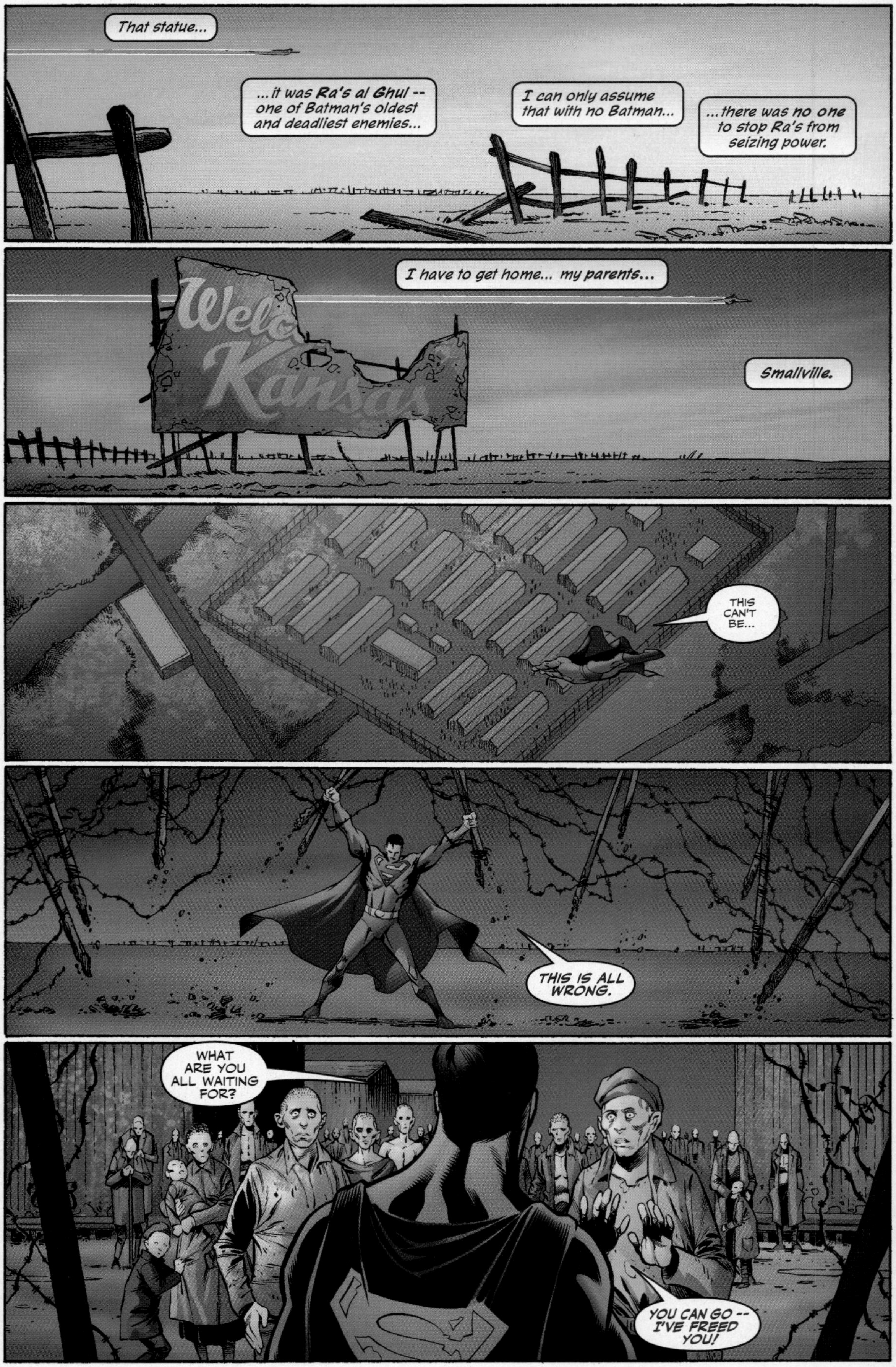
That statue...
...it was Ra's al Ghul -- one of Batman's oldest and deadliest enemies...
I can only assume that with no Batman...
...there was no one to stop Ra's from seizing power.
I have to get home... my parents...
Smallville.
THIS CAN'T BE...
THIS IS ALL WRONG.
WHAT ARE YOU ALL WAITING FOR?
YOU CAN GO -- I'VE FREED YOU!

YOU. ON THE GROUND. REMAIN WHERE YOU ARE.

THE HELL I WILL!

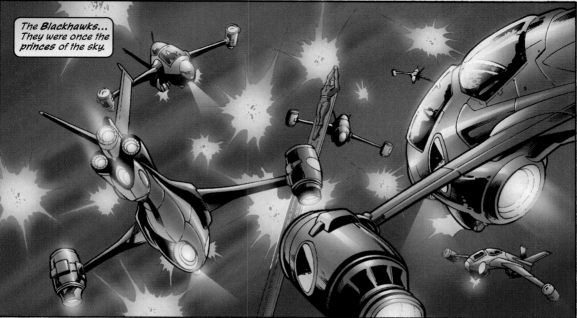

The *Blackhawks...* They were once the *princes* of the sky.

DO WE HAVE ANY *INTEL* ON THIS CAPE, *LADY B?* HE FIGHTS LIKE NOBODY'S BUSINESS.

NONE WHATSOEVER, *BLACKHAWK.* JUST THAT REPORT FROM GOTHAM CITY...

...LIFTING UP A *TANK...*

AND HERE I THOUGHT WE'D GOTTEN RID OF ALL OF THEM IN THE PURGE...

This is insanity. All I'm going to do is get someone killed.

There has to be a way to set things right again.

But I can't do that without...

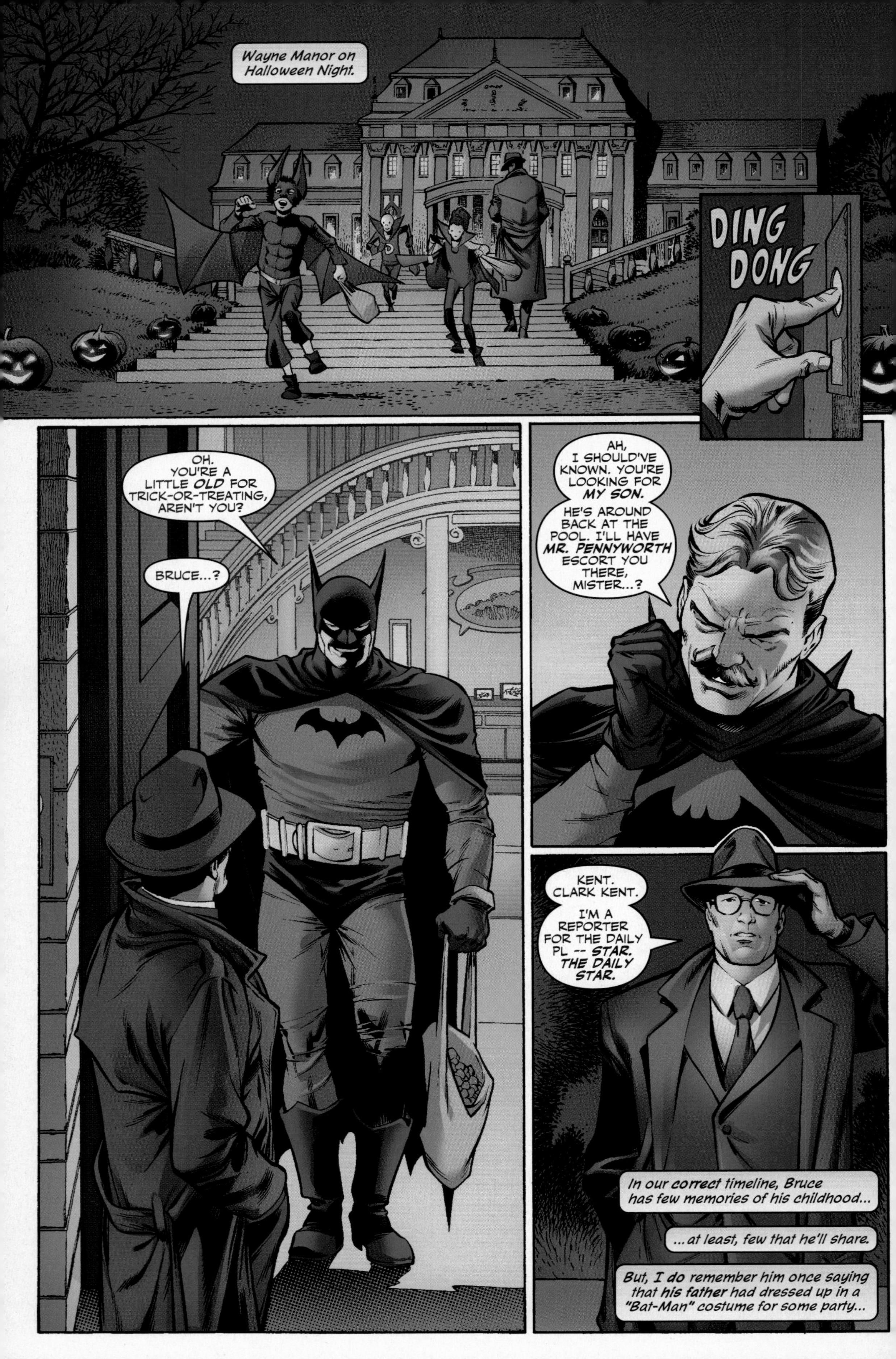
Wayne Manor on Halloween Night.
DING DONG
OH. YOU'RE A LITTLE OLD FOR TRICK-OR-TREATING, AREN'T YOU?
BRUCE...?
AH, I SHOULD'VE KNOWN. YOU'RE LOOKING FOR MY SON.
HE'S AROUND BACK AT THE POOL. I'LL HAVE MR. PENNYWORTH ESCORT YOU THERE, MISTER...?
KENT. CLARK KENT.
I'M A REPORTER FOR THE DAILY PL -- STAR. THE DAILY STAR.
In our correct timeline, Bruce has few memories of his childhood...
...at least, few that he'll share.
But, I do remember him once saying that his father had dressed up in a "Bat-Man" costume for some party...

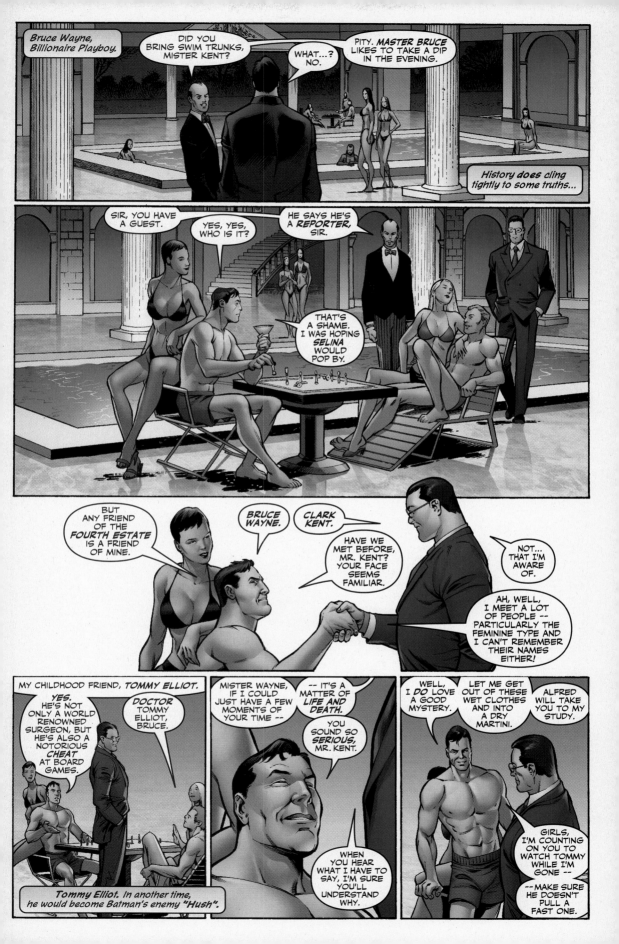

Bruce Wayne, Billionaire Playboy.

DID YOU BRING SWIM TRUNKS, MISTER KENT?

WHAT...? NO.

PITY. *MASTER BRUCE* LIKES TO TAKE A DIP IN THE EVENING.

History does cling tightly to some truths...

SIR, YOU HAVE A GUEST.

YES, YES, WHO IS IT?

HE SAYS HE'S A *REPORTER*, SIR.

THAT'S A SHAME. I WAS HOPING *SELINA* WOULD POP BY.

BUT ANY FRIEND OF THE *FOURTH ESTATE* IS A FRIEND OF MINE.

BRUCE WAYNE.

CLARK KENT.

HAVE WE MET BEFORE, MR. KENT? YOUR FACE SEEMS FAMILIAR.

NOT... THAT I'M AWARE OF.

AH, WELL, I MEET A LOT OF PEOPLE -- PARTICULARLY THE FEMININE TYPE AND I CAN'T REMEMBER THEIR NAMES EITHER!

MY CHILDHOOD FRIEND, *TOMMY ELLIOT.*

YES. HE'S NOT ONLY A WORLD RENOWNED SURGEON, BUT HE'S ALSO A NOTORIOUS *CHEAT* AT BOARD GAMES.

DOCTOR TOMMY ELLIOT, BRUCE.

MISTER WAYNE, IF I COULD JUST HAVE A FEW MOMENTS OF YOUR TIME --

-- IT'S A MATTER OF *LIFE AND DEATH.*

YOU SOUND SO *SERIOUS,* MR. KENT.

WHEN YOU HEAR WHAT I HAVE TO SAY, I'M SURE YOU'LL UNDERSTAND WHY.

Tommy Elliot. In another time, he would become Batman's enemy "Hush".

WELL, I *DO* LOVE A GOOD MYSTERY.

LET ME GET OUT OF THESE WET CLOTHES AND INTO A DRY MARTINI.

ALFRED WILL TAKE YOU TO MY STUDY.

GIRLS, I'M COUNTING ON YOU TO WATCH TOMMY WHILE I'M GONE --

-- MAKE SURE HE DOESN'T PULL A FAST ONE.

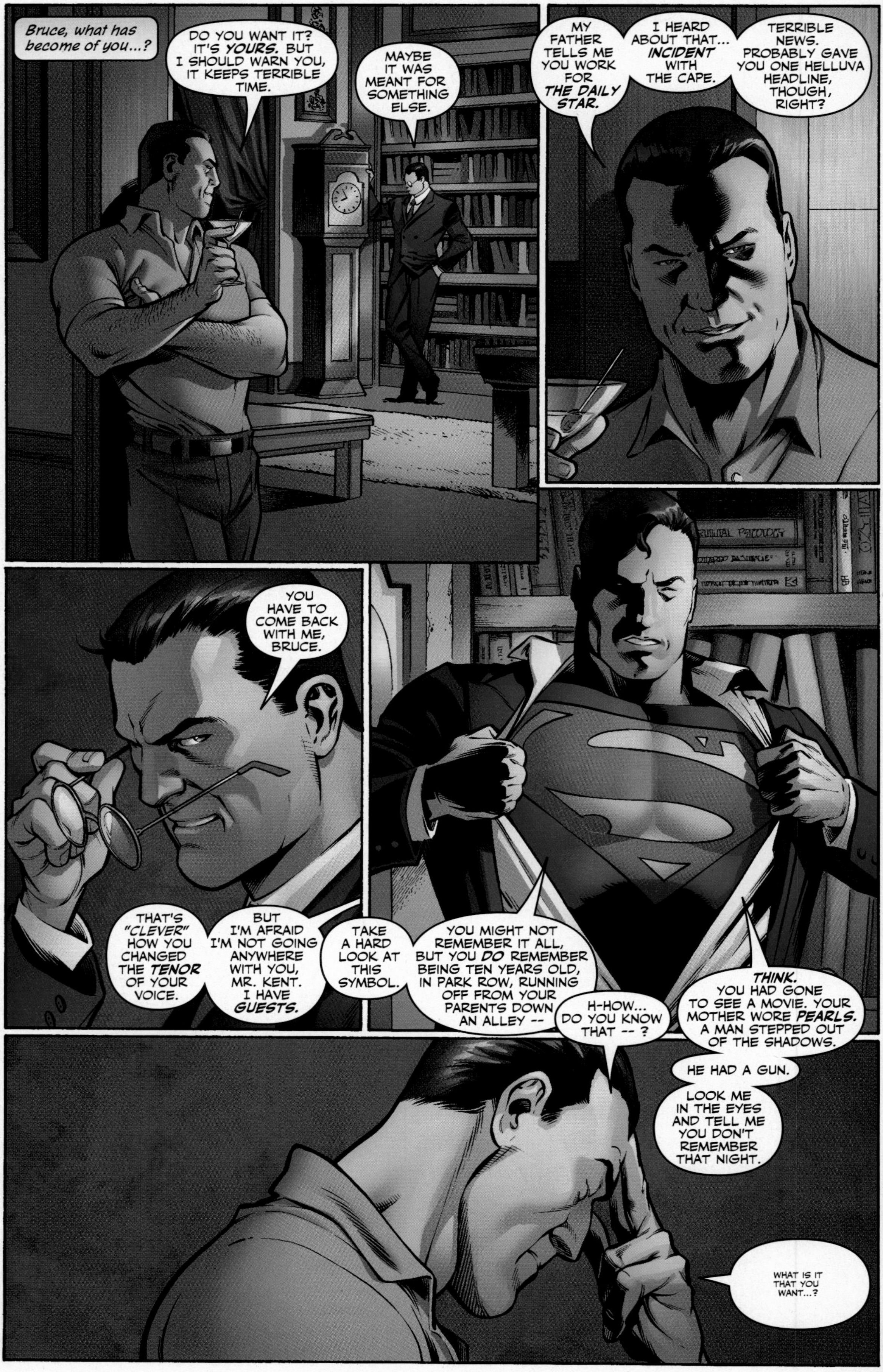
Bruce, what has become of you...?
DO YOU WANT IT? IT'S YOURS. BUT I SHOULD WARN YOU, IT KEEPS TERRIBLE TIME.
MAYBE IT WAS MEANT FOR SOMETHING ELSE.
MY FATHER TELLS ME YOU WORK FOR THE DAILY STAR.
I HEARD ABOUT THAT... INCIDENT WITH THE CAPE.
TERRIBLE NEWS. PROBABLY GAVE YOU ONE HELLUVA HEADLINE, THOUGH, RIGHT?
YOU HAVE TO COME BACK WITH ME, BRUCE.
THAT'S "CLEVER" HOW YOU CHANGED THE TENOR OF YOUR VOICE.
BUT I'M AFRAID I'M NOT GOING ANYWHERE WITH YOU, MR. KENT. I HAVE GUESTS.
TAKE A HARD LOOK AT THIS SYMBOL.
YOU MIGHT NOT REMEMBER IT ALL, BUT YOU DO REMEMBER BEING TEN YEARS OLD, IN PARK ROW, RUNNING OFF FROM YOUR PARENTS DOWN AN ALLEY --
H-HOW... DO YOU KNOW THAT -- ?
THINK. YOU HAD GONE TO SEE A MOVIE. YOUR MOTHER WORE PEARLS. A MAN STEPPED OUT OF THE SHADOWS.
HE HAD A GUN.
LOOK ME IN THE EYES AND TELL ME YOU DON'T REMEMBER THAT NIGHT.
WHAT IS IT THAT YOU WANT...?

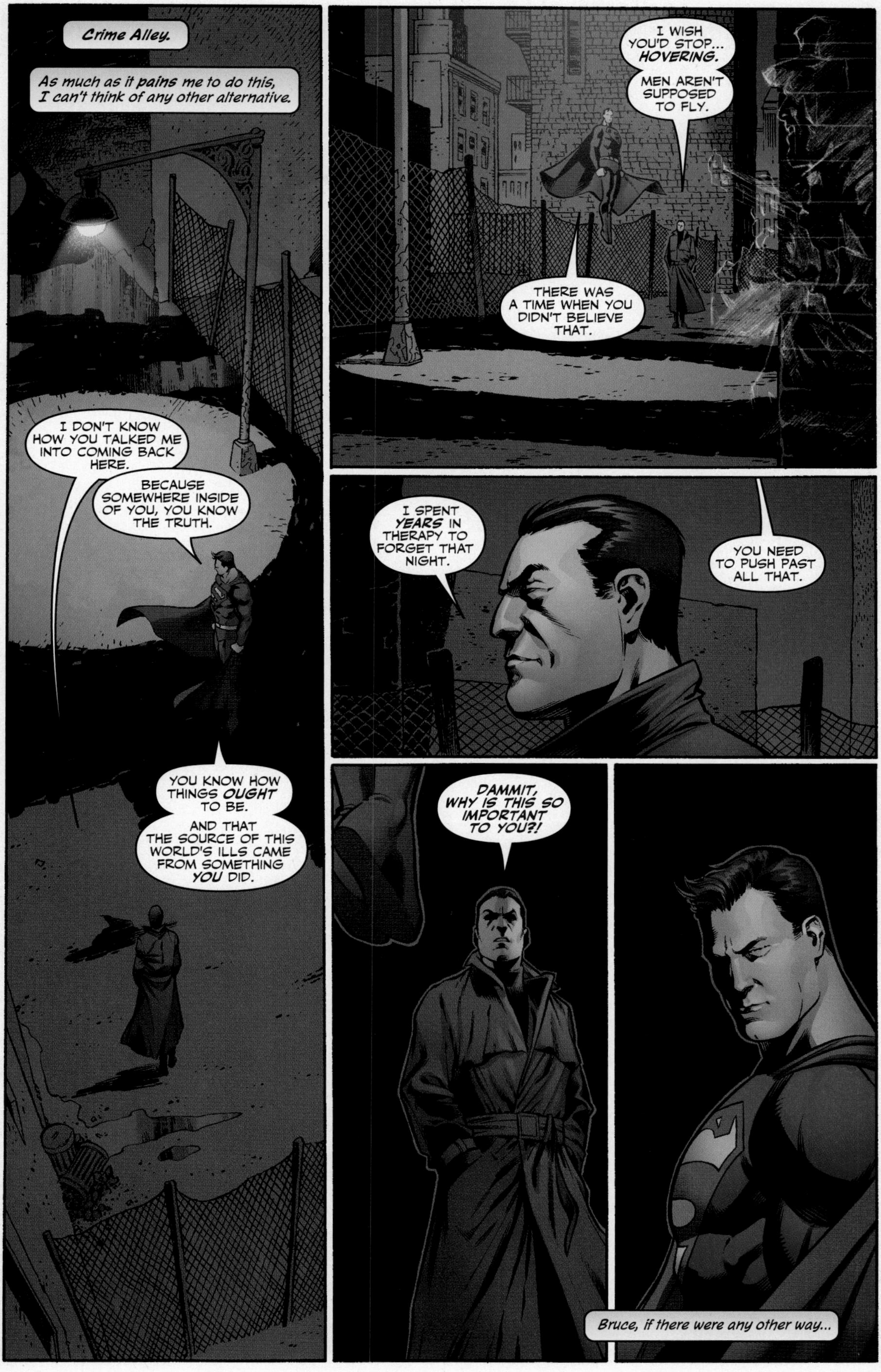
Crime Alley.
As much as it pains me to do this, I can't think of any other alternative.
I WISH YOU'D STOP... HOVERING.
MEN AREN'T SUPPOSED TO FLY.
THERE WAS A TIME WHEN YOU DIDN'T BELIEVE THAT.
I DON'T KNOW HOW YOU TALKED ME INTO COMING BACK HERE.
BECAUSE SOMEWHERE INSIDE OF YOU, YOU KNOW THE TRUTH.
I SPENT YEARS IN THERAPY TO FORGET THAT NIGHT.
YOU NEED TO PUSH PAST ALL THAT.
YOU KNOW HOW THINGS OUGHT TO BE.
AND THAT THE SOURCE OF THIS WORLD'S ILLS CAME FROM SOMETHING YOU DID.
DAMMIT, WHY IS THIS SO IMPORTANT TO YOU?!
Bruce, if there were any other way...

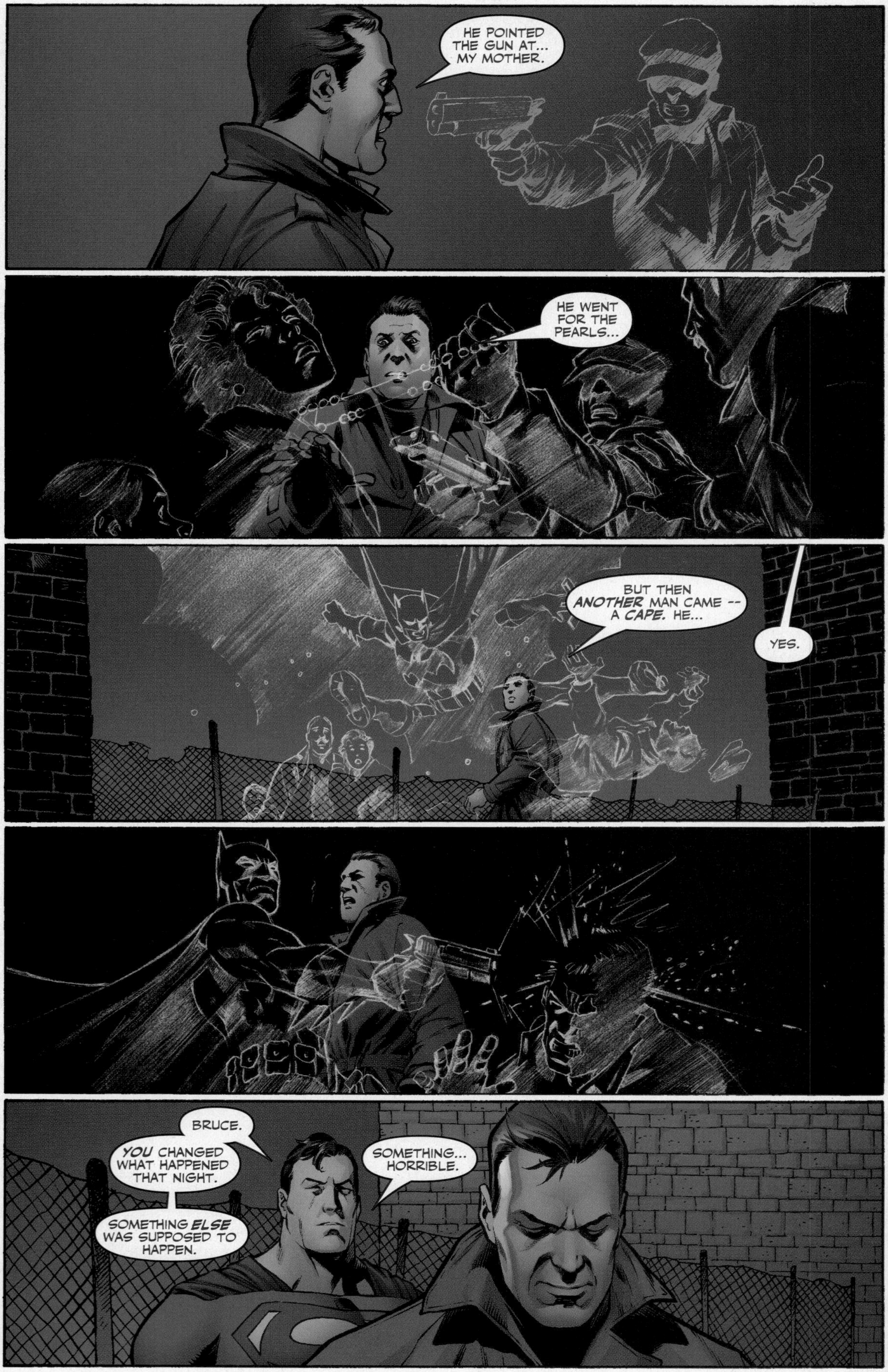
HE POINTED THE GUN AT... MY MOTHER.
HE WENT FOR THE PEARLS...
BUT THEN ANOTHER MAN CAME -- A CAPE. HE...
YES.
BRUCE.
YOU CHANGED WHAT HAPPENED THAT NIGHT.
SOMETHING ELSE WAS SUPPOSED TO HAPPEN.
SOMETHING... HORRIBLE.

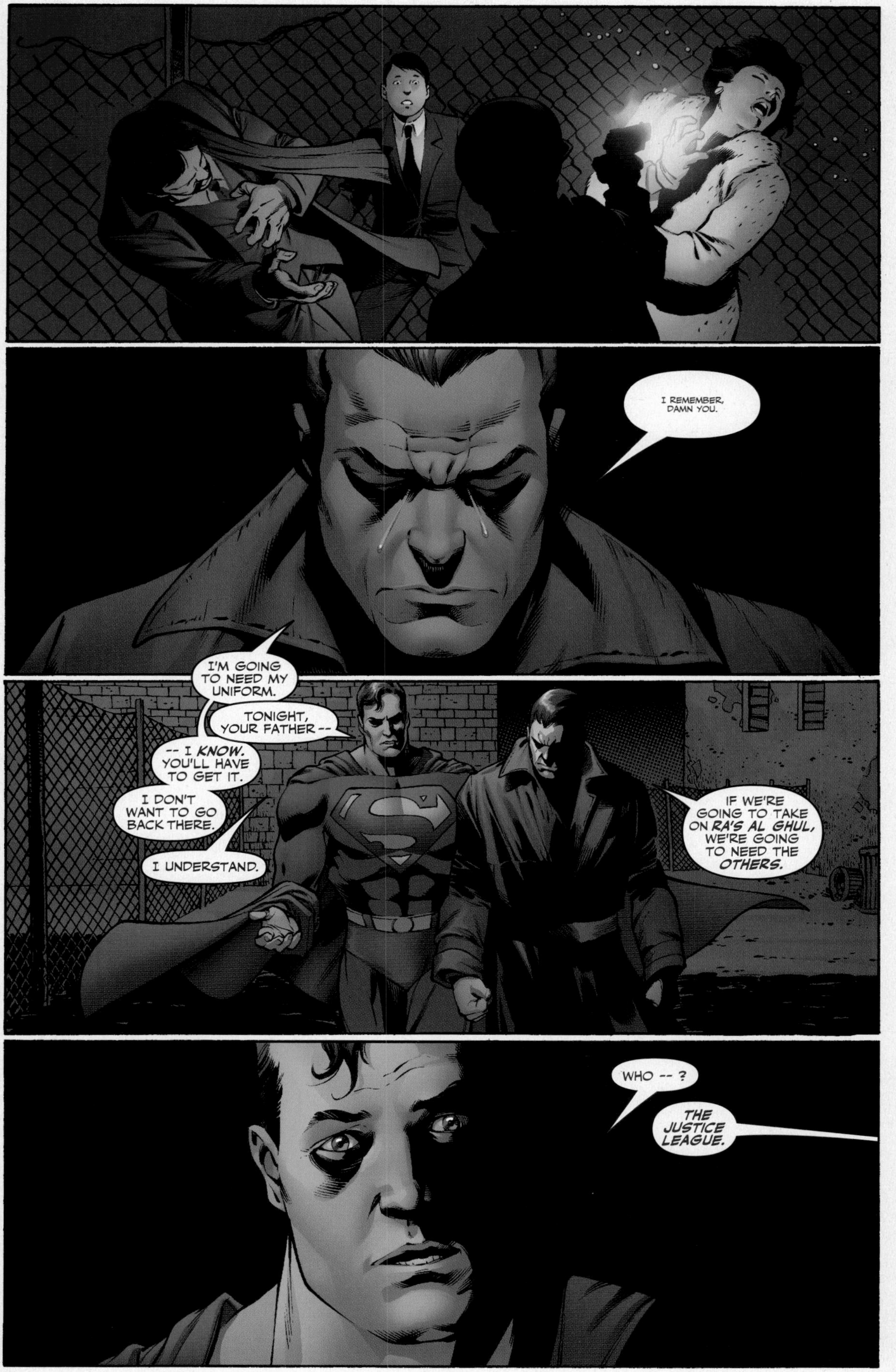
I REMEMBER, DAMN YOU.
I'M GOING TO NEED MY UNIFORM.
TONIGHT, YOUR FATHER --
-- I *KNOW.* YOU'LL HAVE TO GET IT.
I DON'T WANT TO GO BACK THERE.
I UNDERSTAND.
IF WE'RE GOING TO TAKE ON *RA'S AL GHUL,* WE'RE GOING TO NEED THE *OTHERS.*
WHO -- ?
THE JUSTICE LEAGUE.

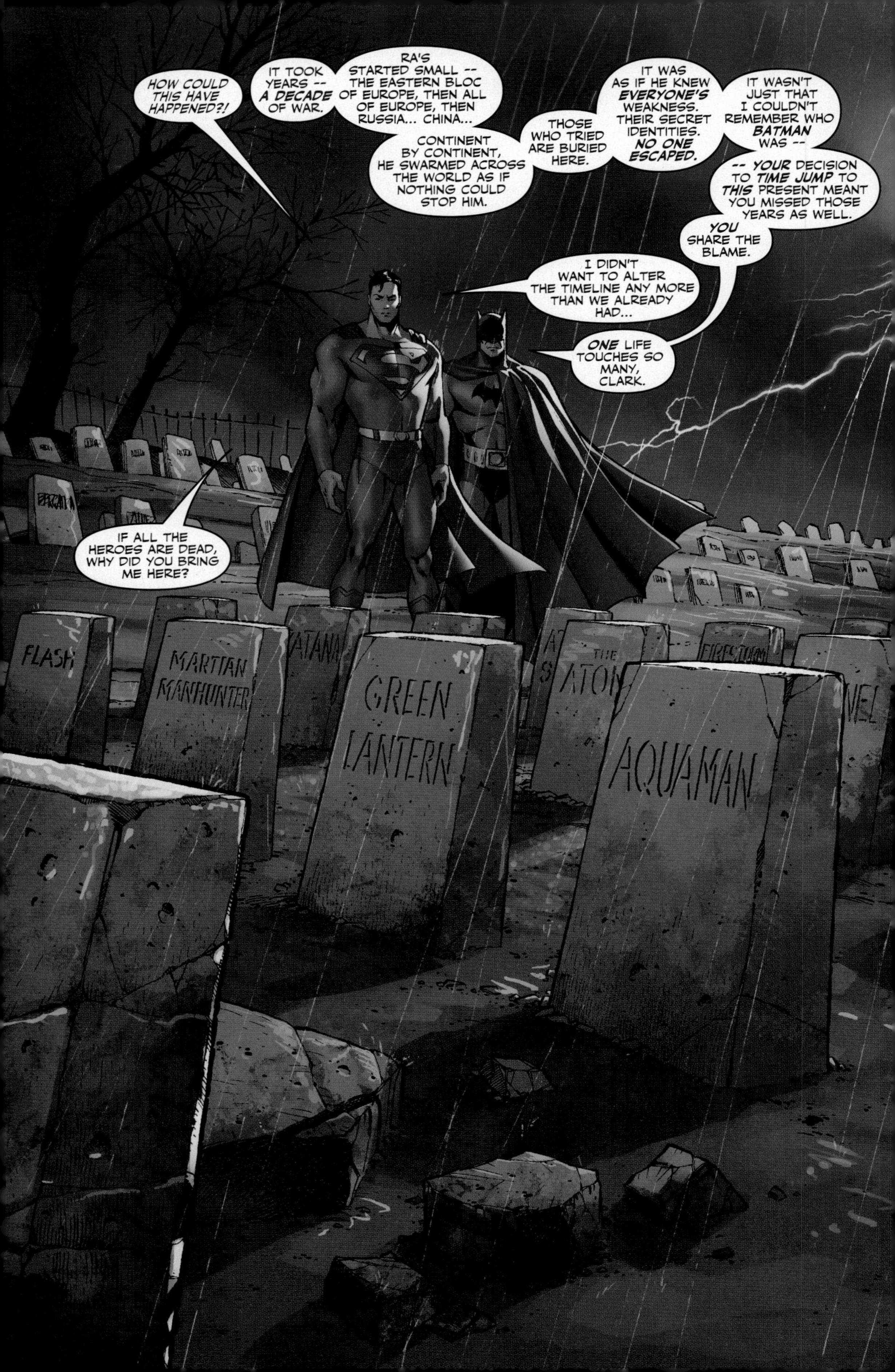
HOW COULD THIS HAVE HAPPENED?!
IT TOOK YEARS -- *A DECADE* OF WAR.
RA'S STARTED SMALL -- THE EASTERN BLOC OF EUROPE, THEN ALL OF EUROPE, THEN RUSSIA... CHINA...
CONTINENT BY CONTINENT, HE SWARMED ACROSS THE WORLD AS IF NOTHING COULD STOP HIM.
THOSE WHO TRIED ARE BURIED HERE.
IT WAS AS IF HE KNEW *EVERYONE'S* WEAKNESS. THEIR SECRET IDENTITIES. *NO ONE ESCAPED.*
IT WASN'T JUST THAT I COULDN'T REMEMBER WHO *BATMAN* WAS --
-- YOUR DECISION TO *TIME JUMP* TO *THIS* PRESENT MEANT YOU MISSED THOSE YEARS AS WELL.
YOU SHARE THE BLAME.
I DIDN'T WANT TO ALTER THE TIMELINE ANY MORE THAN WE ALREADY HAD...
ONE LIFE TOUCHES SO MANY, CLARK.
IF ALL THE HEROES ARE DEAD, WHY DID YOU BRING ME HERE?
FLASH
MARTIAN MANHUNTER
GREEN LANTERN
FIRESTORM
AQUAMAN

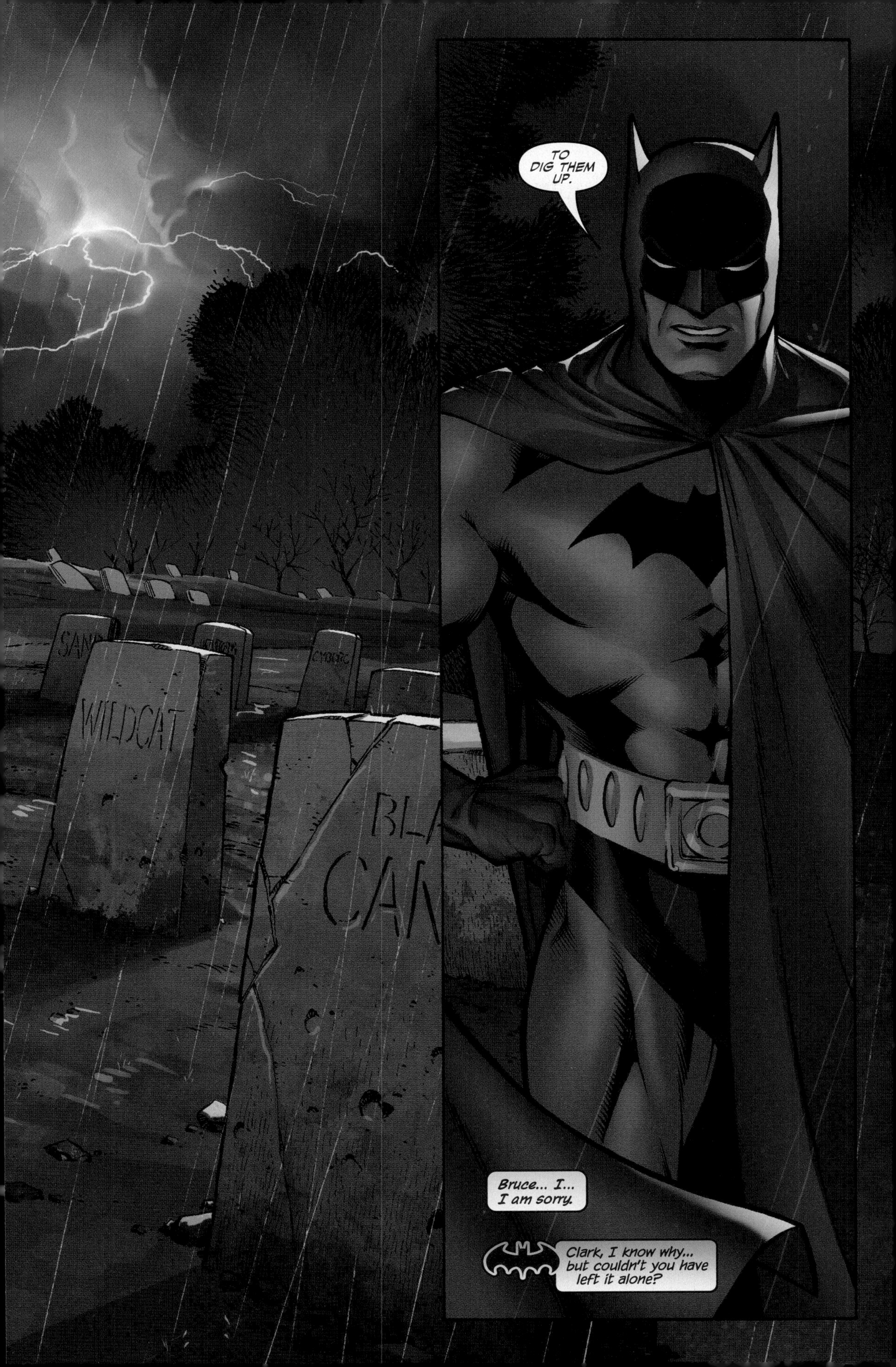

TO DIG THEM UP.
WILDCAT
CYBORG
Bruce... I... I am sorry.
Clark, I know why... but couldn't you have left it alone?

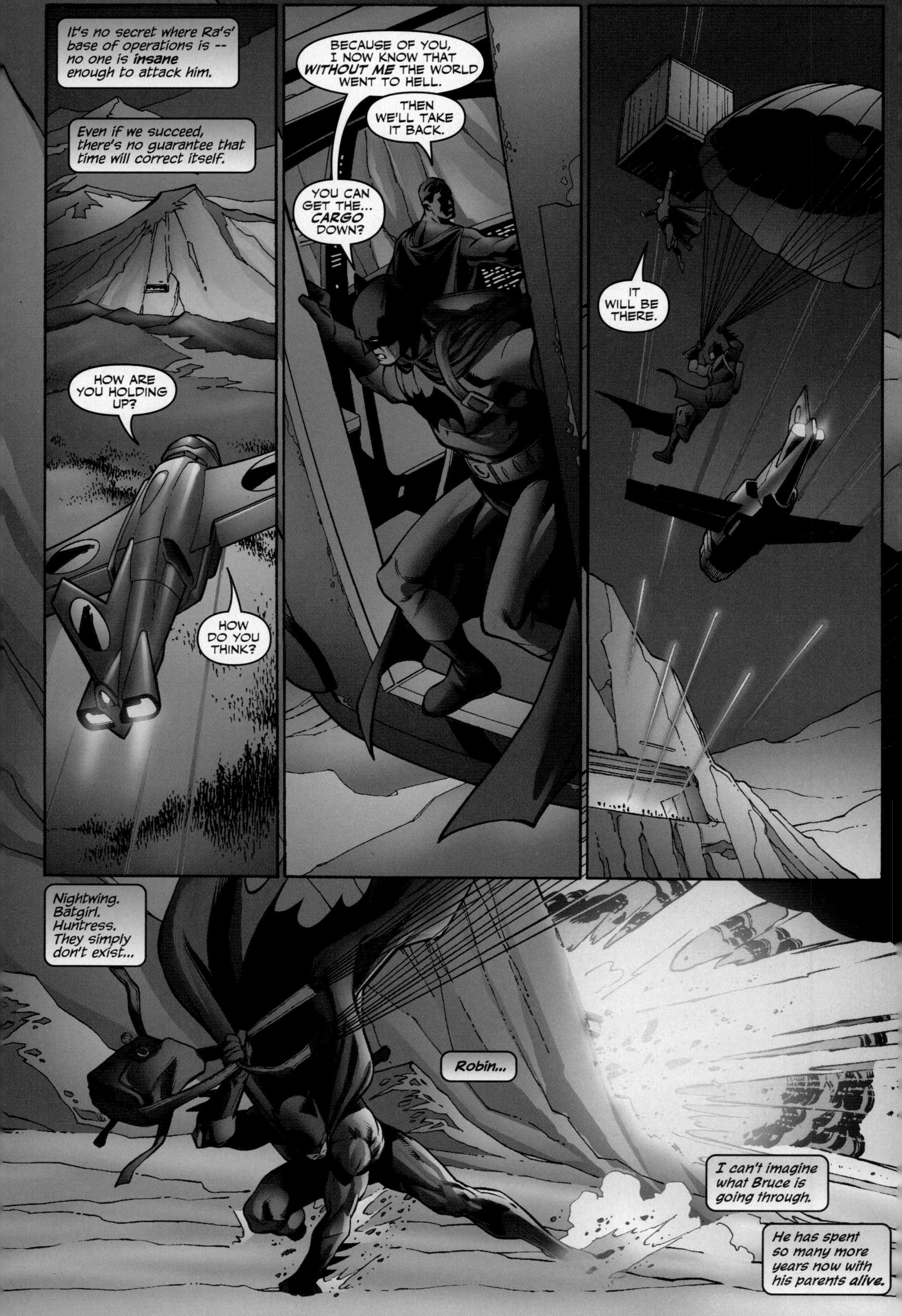
It's no secret where Ra's' base of operations is -- no one is **insane** enough to attack him.
Even if we succeed, there's no guarantee that time will correct itself.
HOW ARE YOU HOLDING UP?
HOW DO YOU THINK?
BECAUSE OF YOU, I NOW KNOW THAT **WITHOUT ME** THE WORLD WENT TO HELL.
THEN WE'LL TAKE IT BACK.
YOU CAN GET THE... **CARGO** DOWN?
IT WILL BE THERE.
Nightwing. Batgirl. Huntress. They simply don't exist...
Robin...
I can't imagine what Bruce is going through.
He has spent so many more years now with his parents alive.

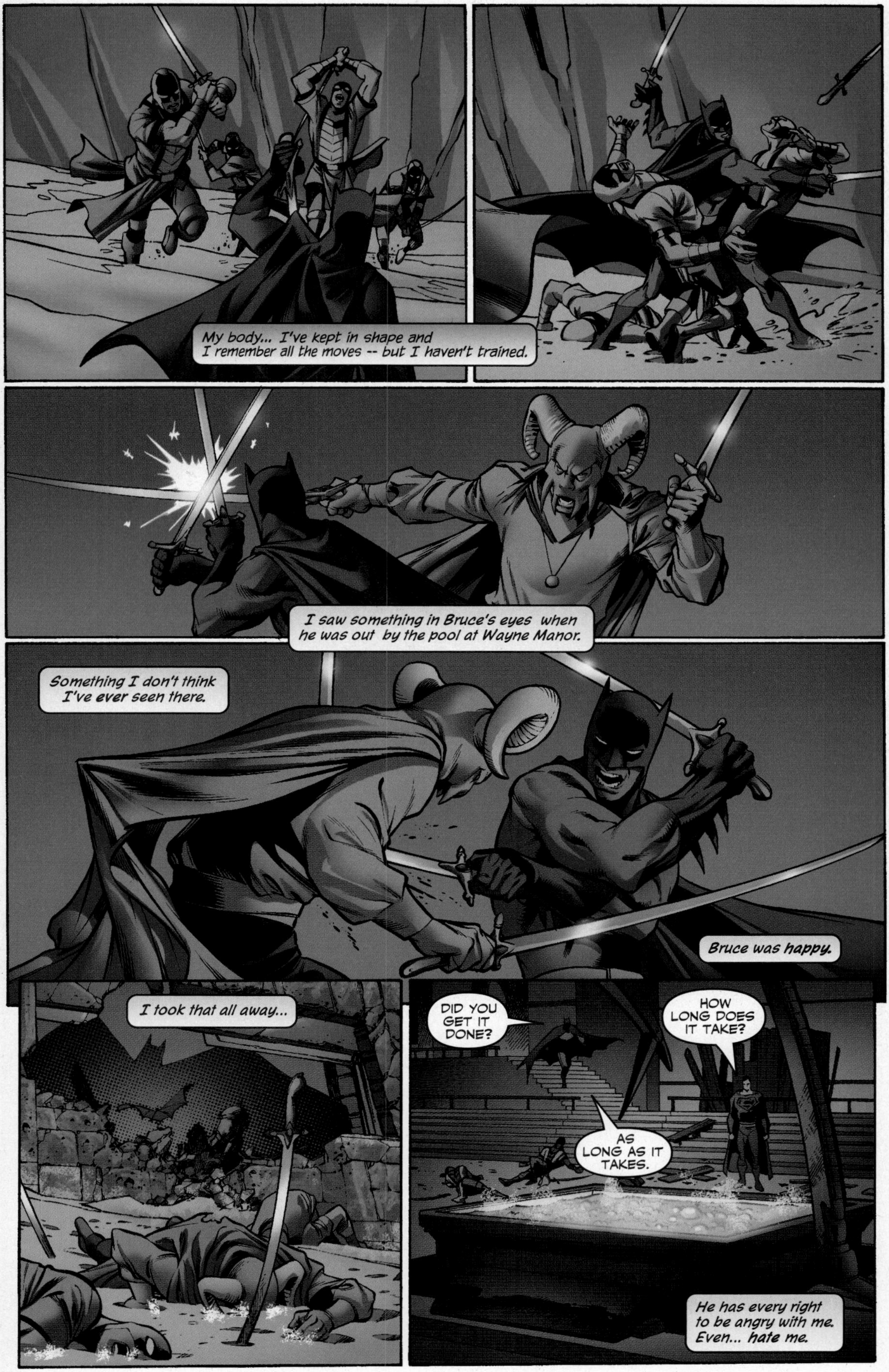

My body... I've kept in shape and I remember all the moves -- but I haven't trained.
I saw something in Bruce's eyes when he was out by the pool at Wayne Manor.
Something I don't think I've ever seen there.
Bruce was happy.
I took that all away...
DID YOU GET IT DONE?
HOW LONG DOES IT TAKE?
AS LONG AS IT TAKES.
He has every right to be angry with me. Even... hate me.

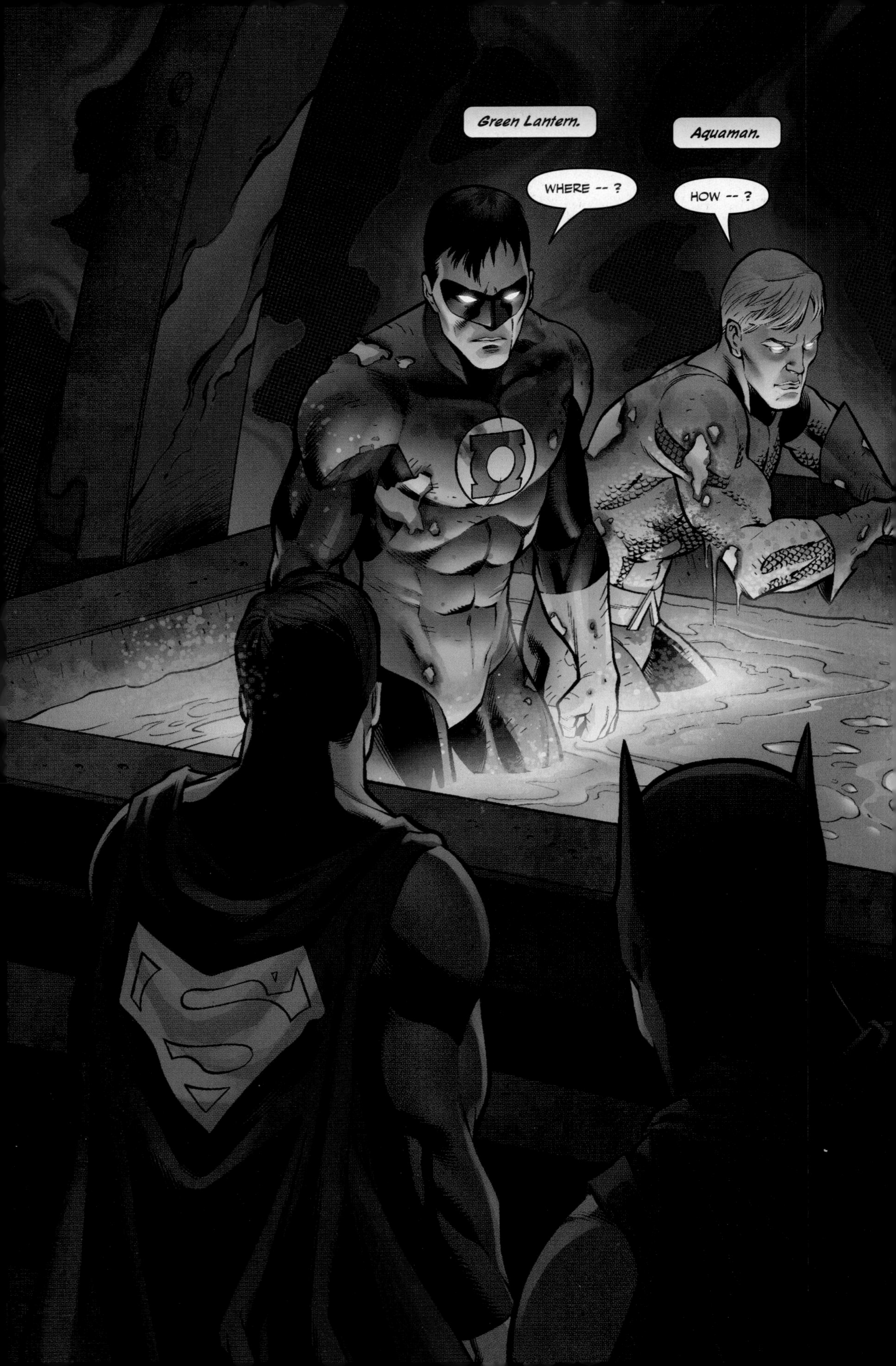
Green Lantern.
WHERE -- ?
Aquaman.
HOW -- ?

Flash.
FEELS LIKE WE'VE BEEN GONE FOR SUCH A LONG TIME.
The Martian Manhunter...
Seeing them again... even in this horrific condition... it can only bring about --
-- Hope.
WHATEVER YOU REMEMBER, YOU ALL KNOW THIS --
-- RA'S AL GHUL TOOK YOUR WORLD FROM EACH OF YOU.
HE STOLE IT FROM ALL OF HUMANITY.
Ra's' Lazarus Pit. It restores life to the dying. Or to the recently dead.
But... all of them. It has been so long.
We won't have much time before they... all die again forever.
WE WERE LOST IN DARKNESS... WHO ARE YOU?
FRIENDS.

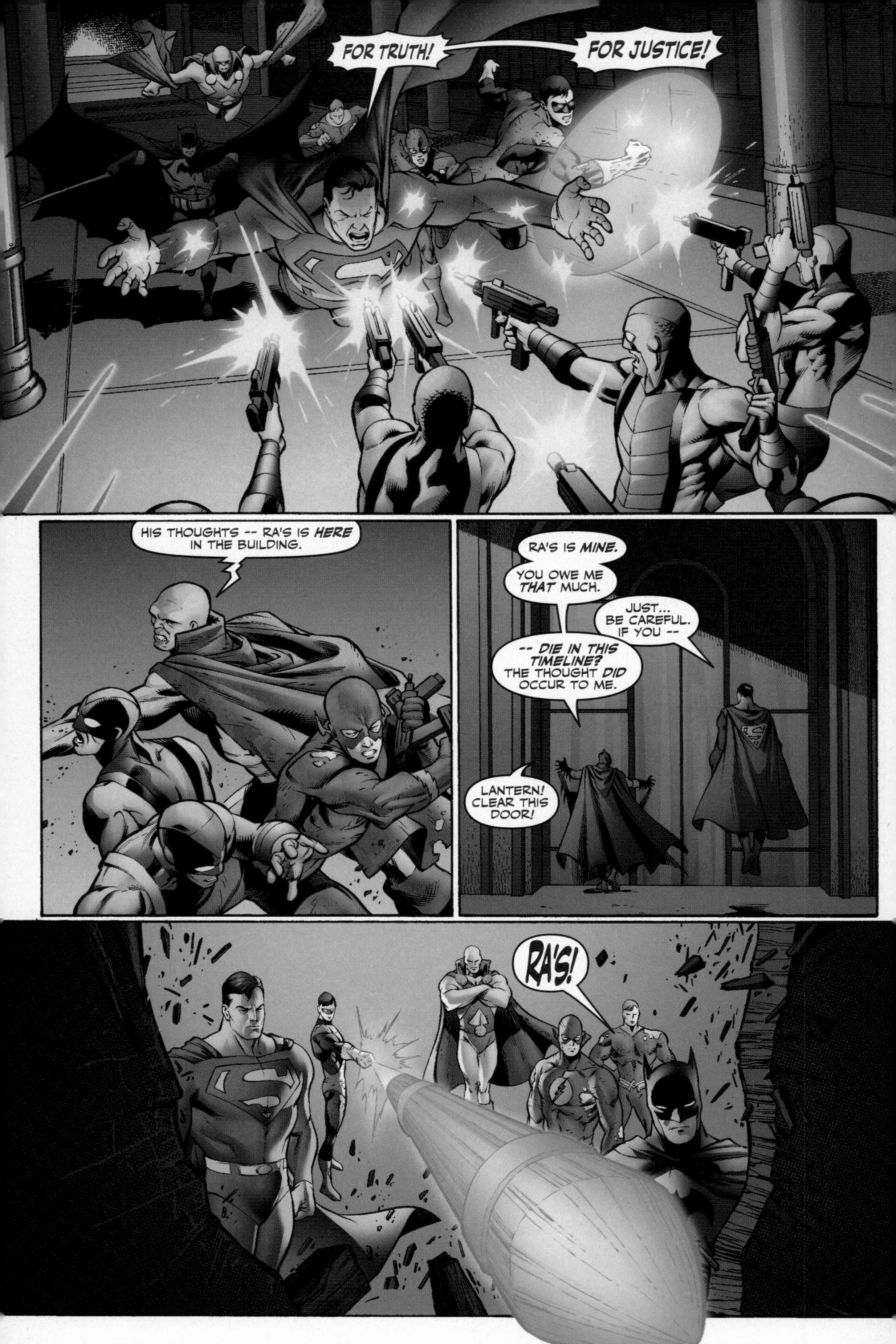
FOR TRUTH!
FOR JUSTICE!
HIS THOUGHTS -- RA'S IS HERE IN THE BUILDING.
RA'S IS MINE.
YOU OWE ME THAT MUCH.
JUST... BE CAREFUL. IF YOU --
-- DIE IN THIS TIMELINE? THE THOUGHT DID OCCUR TO ME.
LANTERN! CLEAR THIS DOOR!
RA'S!

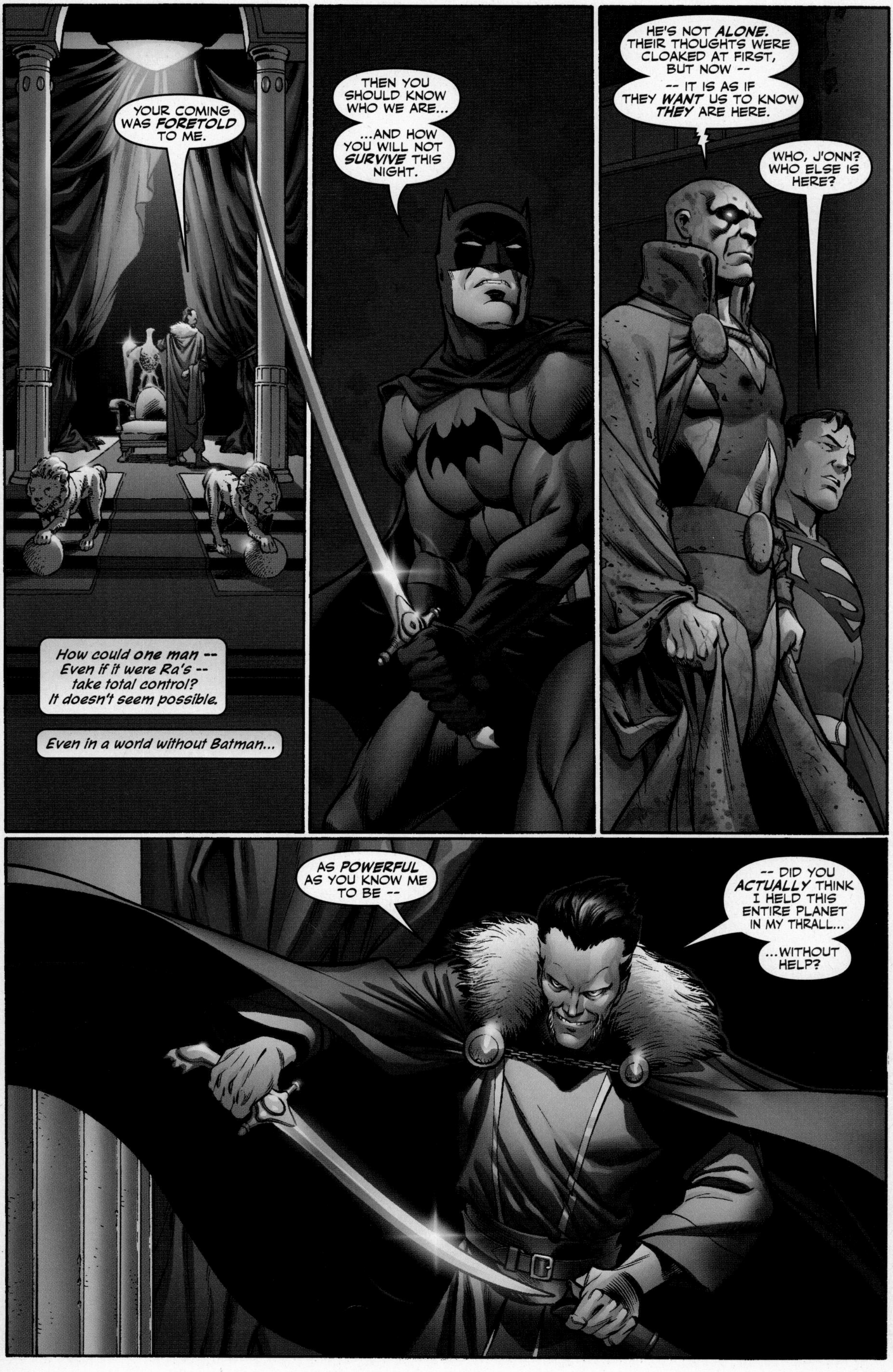

YOUR COMING WAS FORETOLD TO ME.
How could one man -- Even if it were Ra's -- take total control? It doesn't seem possible.
Even in a world without Batman...
THEN YOU SHOULD KNOW WHO WE ARE...
...AND HOW YOU WILL NOT SURVIVE THIS NIGHT.
HE'S NOT ALONE. THEIR THOUGHTS WERE CLOAKED AT FIRST, BUT NOW --
-- IT IS AS IF THEY WANT US TO KNOW THEY ARE HERE.
WHO, J'ONN? WHO ELSE IS HERE?
AS POWERFUL AS YOU KNOW ME TO BE --
-- DID YOU ACTUALLY THINK I HELD THIS ENTIRE PLANET IN MY THRALL...
...WITHOUT HELP?

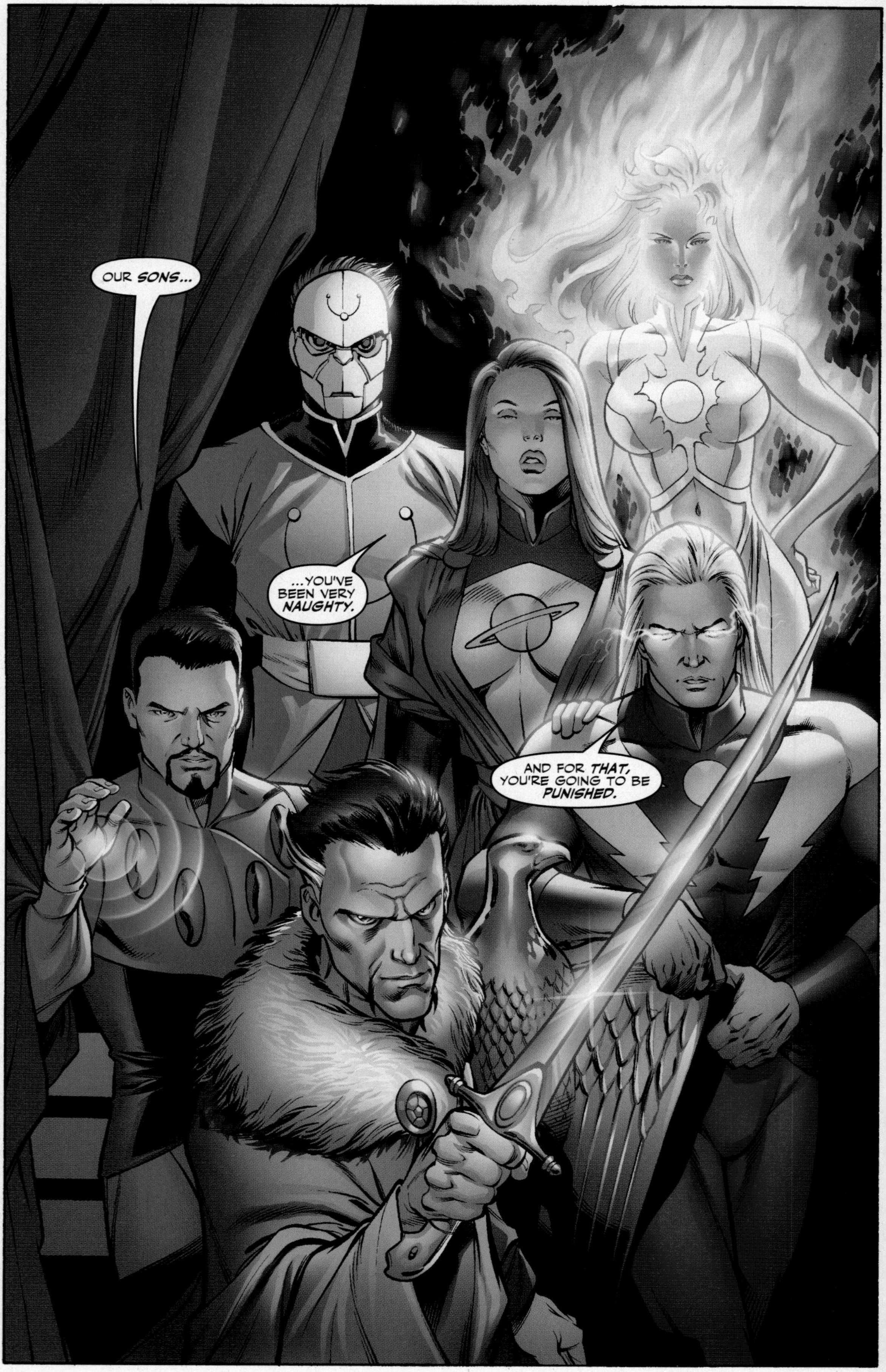
OUR SONS...
...YOU'VE BEEN VERY NAUGHTY.
AND FOR THAT, YOU'RE GOING TO BE PUNISHED.

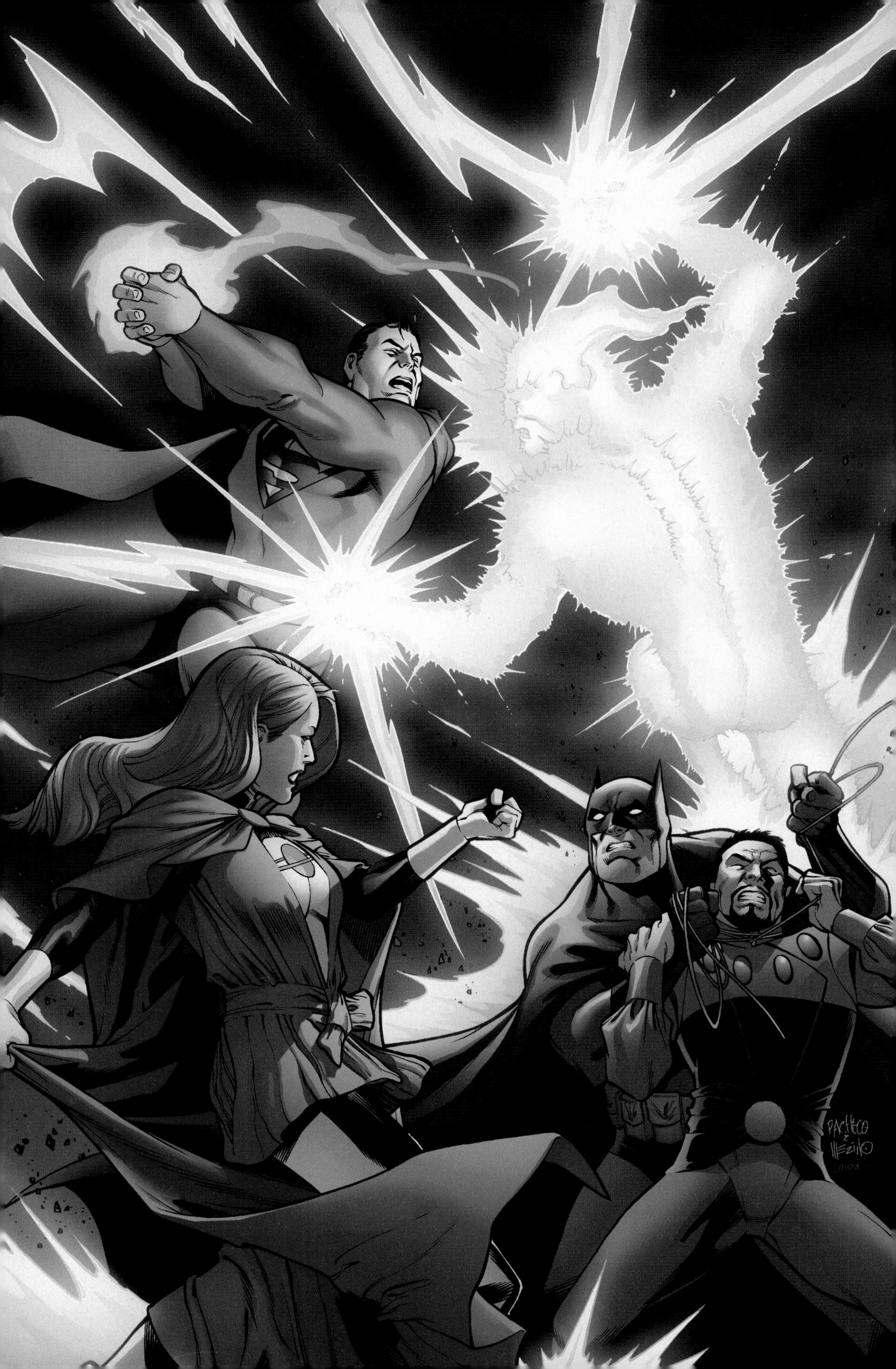

"THY WILL BE DONE..."

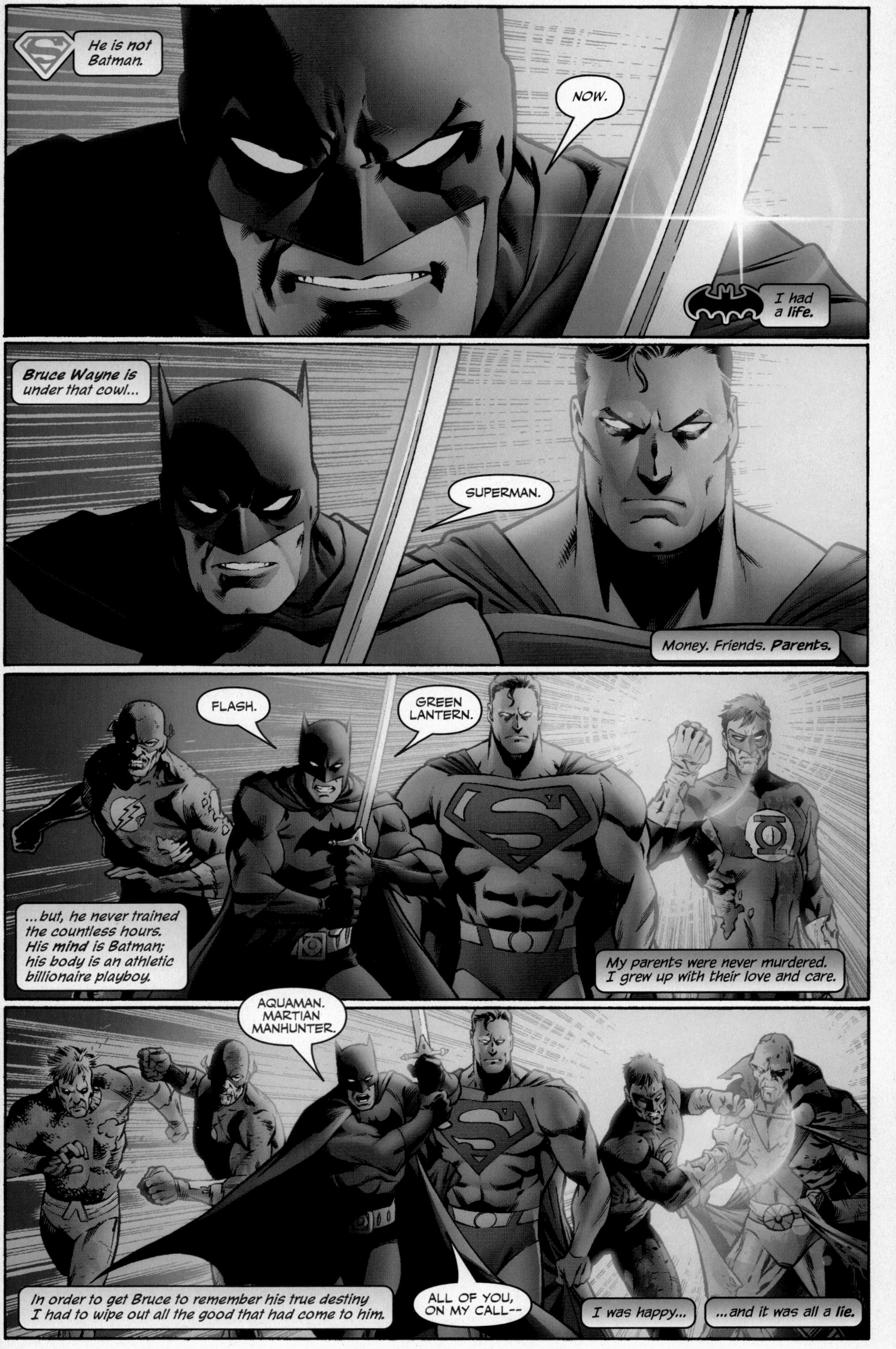

He is not Batman.
NOW.
I had a life.
Bruce Wayne is under that cowl...
SUPERMAN.
Money. Friends. Parents.
FLASH.
GREEN LANTERN.
...but, he never trained the countless hours. His mind is Batman; his body is an athletic billionaire playboy.
My parents were never murdered. I grew up with their love and care.
AQUAMAN. MARTIAN MANHUNTER.
In order to get Bruce to remember his true destiny I had to wipe out all the good that had come to him.
ALL OF YOU, ON MY CALL--
I was happy...
...and it was all a lie.

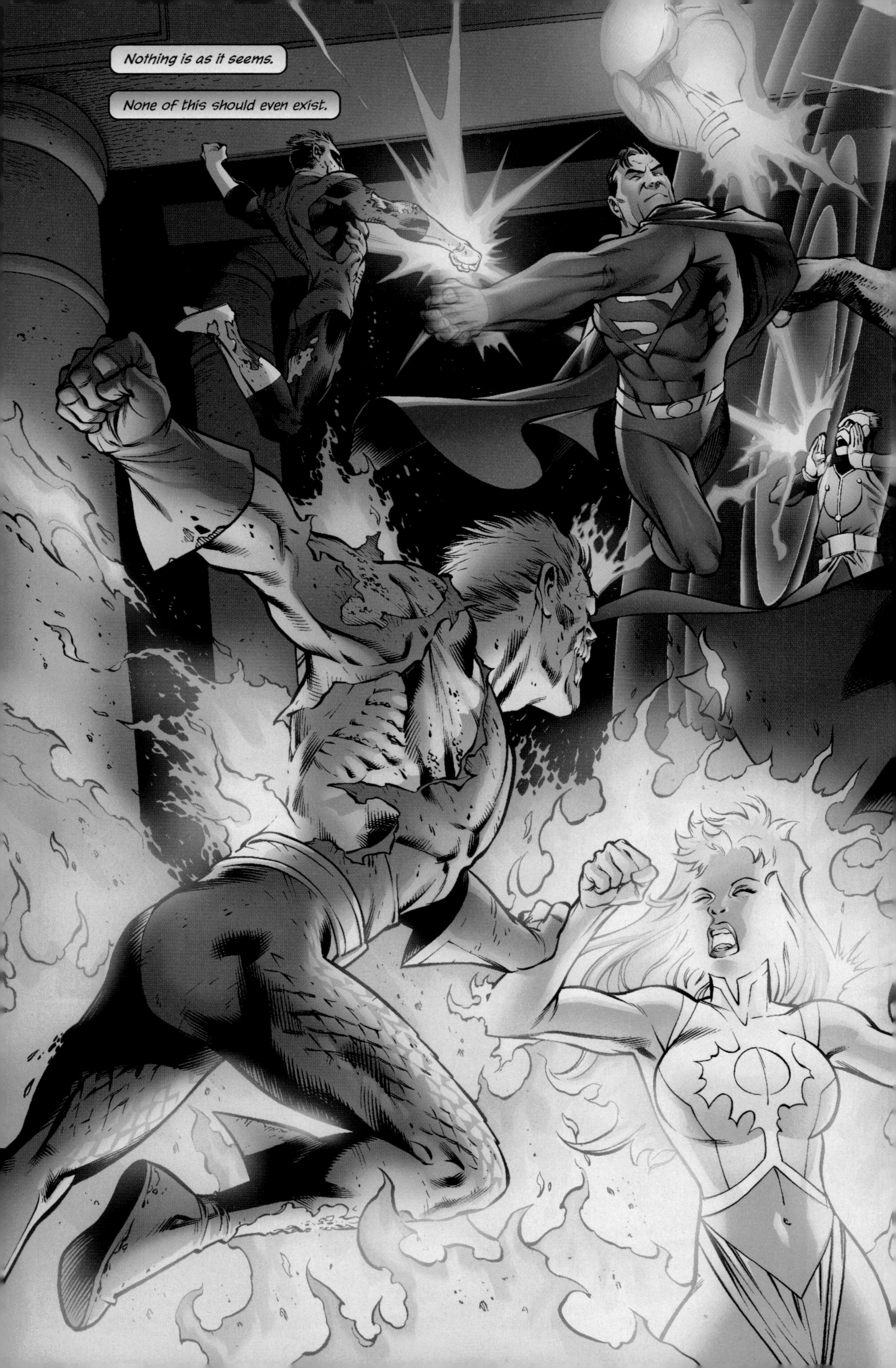
Nothing is as it seems.
None of this should even exist.

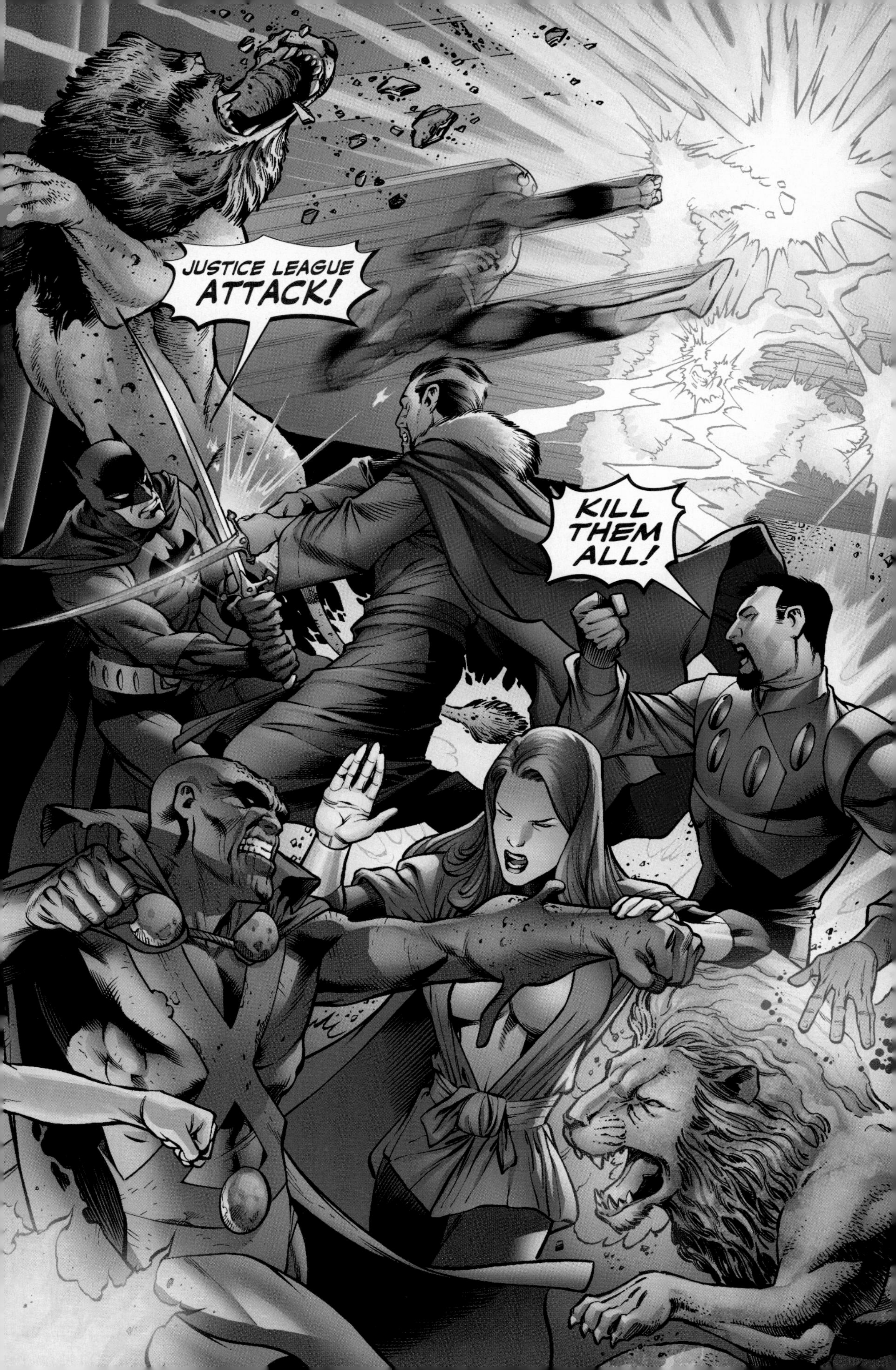
JUSTICE LEAGUE ATTACK!
KILL THEM ALL!

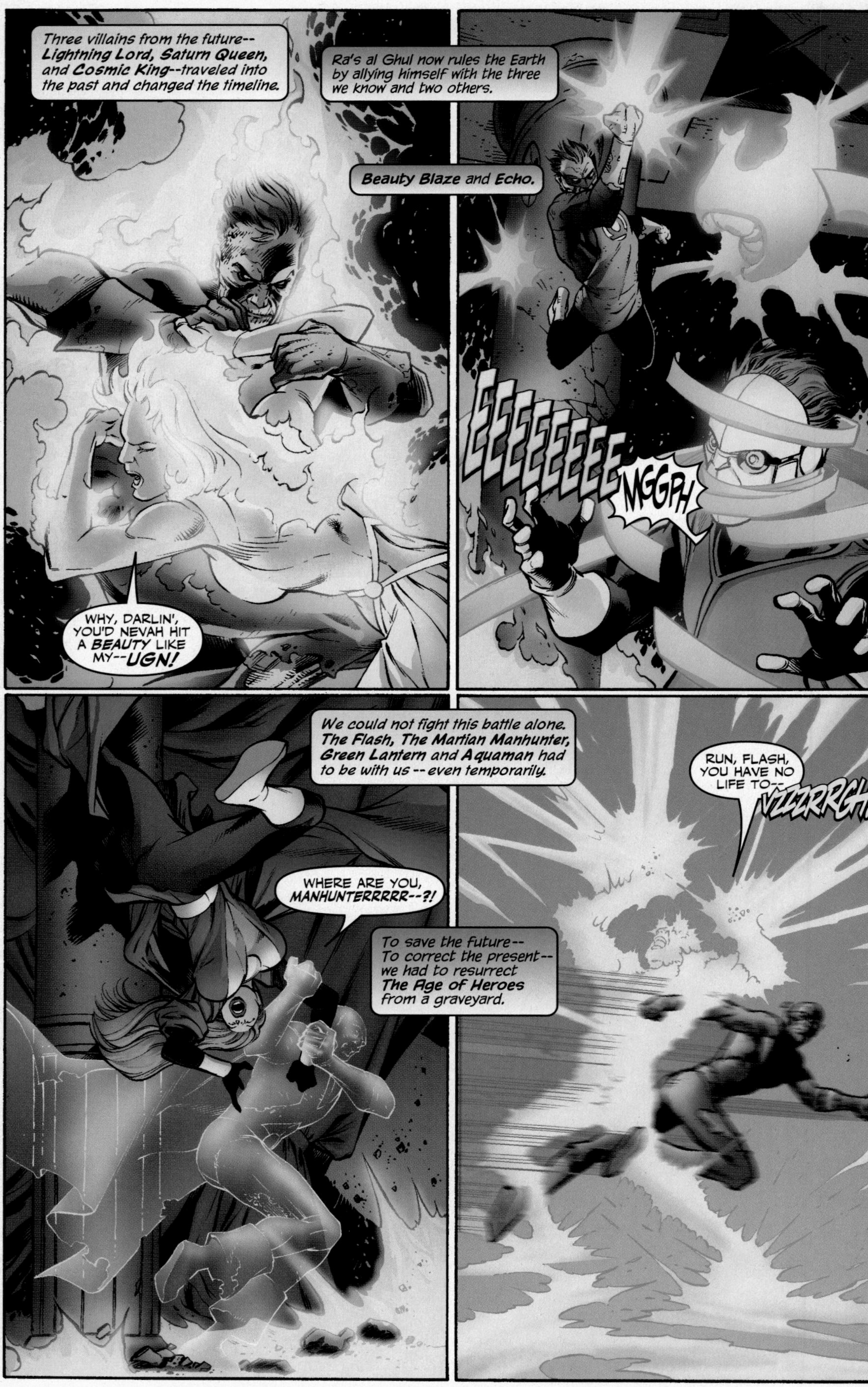
Three villains from the future--Lightning Lord, Saturn Queen, and Cosmic King--traveled into the past and changed the timeline.
WHY, DARLIN', YOU'D NEVAH HIT A BEAUTY LIKE MY--UGN!
Ra's al Ghul now rules the Earth by allying himself with the three we know and two others.
Beauty Blaze and Echo.
EEEEEEEEE
MGGPH
We could not fight this battle alone. The Flash, The Martian Manhunter, Green Lantern and Aquaman had to be with us -- even temporarily.
WHERE ARE YOU, MANHUNTERRRR--?!
To save the future-- To correct the present-- we had to resurrect The Age of Heroes from a graveyard.
RUN, FLASH, YOU HAVE NO LIFE TO--VZZZRRRGH!

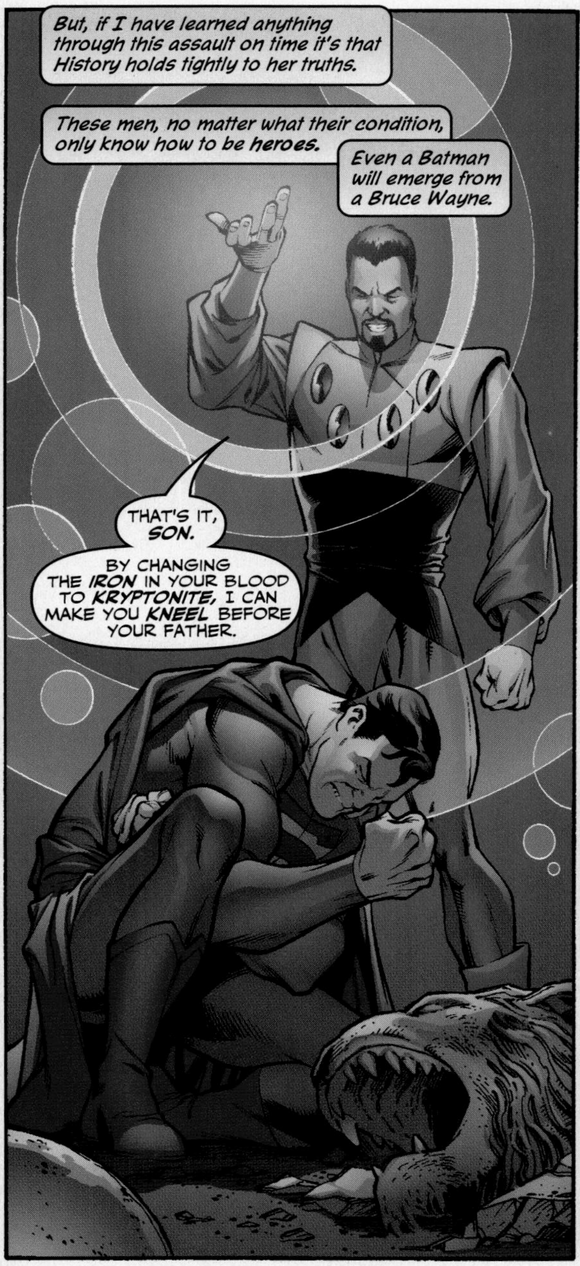
But, if I have learned anything through this assault on time it's that History holds tightly to her truths.
These men, no matter what their condition, only know how to be heroes.
Even a Batman will emerge from a Bruce Wayne.
THAT'S IT, SON.
BY CHANGING THE IRON IN YOUR BLOOD TO KRYPTONITE, I CAN MAKE YOU KNEEL BEFORE YOUR FATHER.

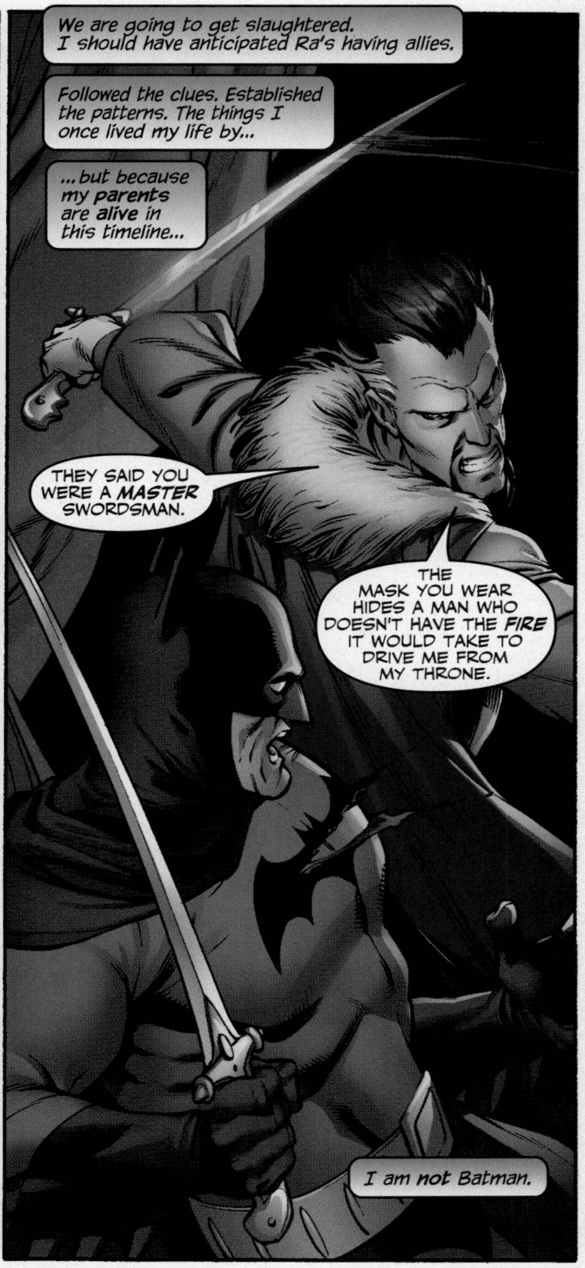
We are going to get slaughtered. I should have anticipated Ra's having allies.
Followed the clues. Established the patterns. The things I once lived my life by...
...but because my parents are alive in this timeline...
THEY SAID YOU WERE A MASTER SWORDSMAN.
THE MASK YOU WEAR HIDES A MAN WHO DOESN'T HAVE THE FIRE IT WOULD TAKE TO DRIVE ME FROM MY THRONE.
I am not Batman.

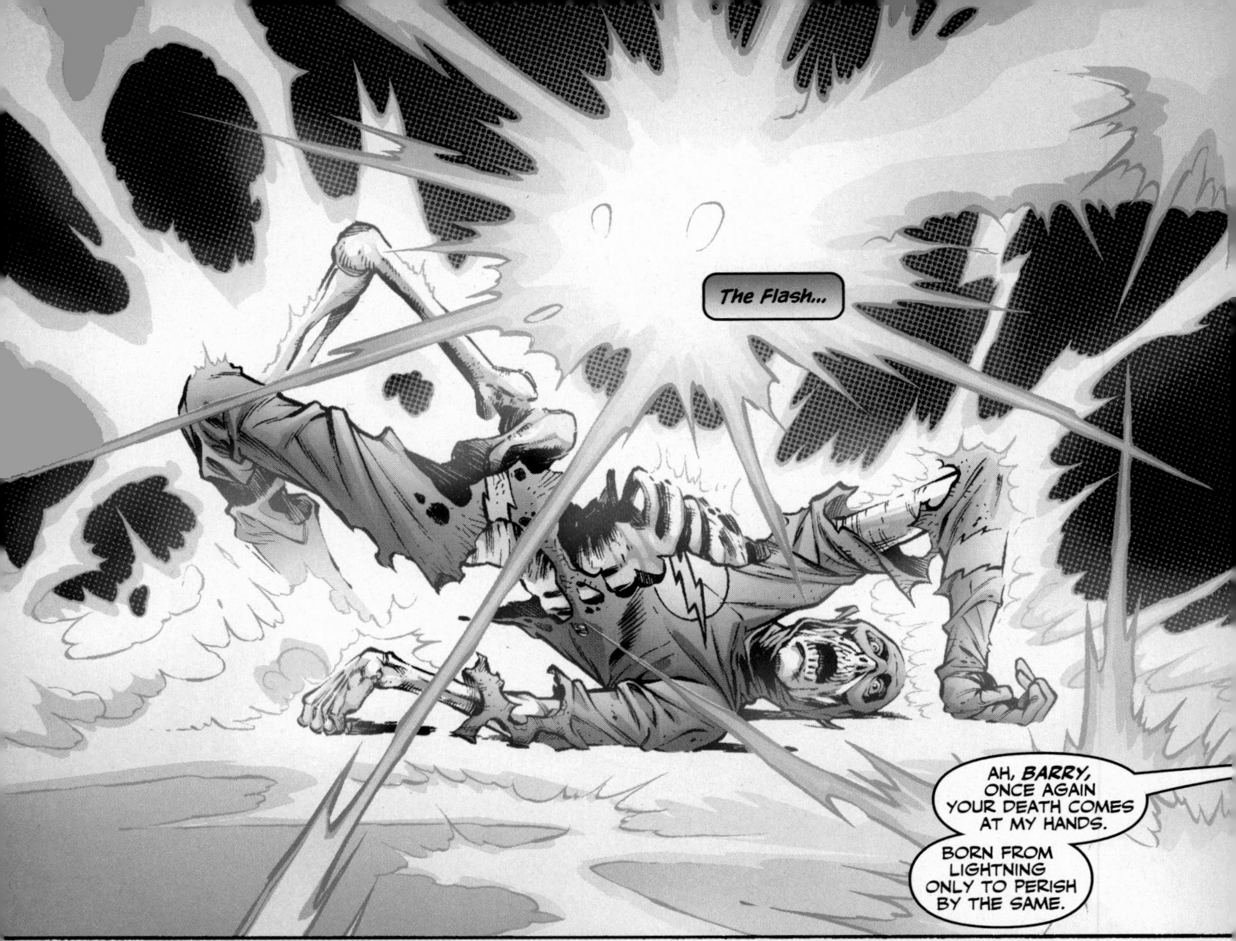
The Flash...
AH, BARRY, ONCE AGAIN YOUR DEATH COMES AT MY HANDS.
BORN FROM LIGHTNING ONLY TO PERISH BY THE SAME.
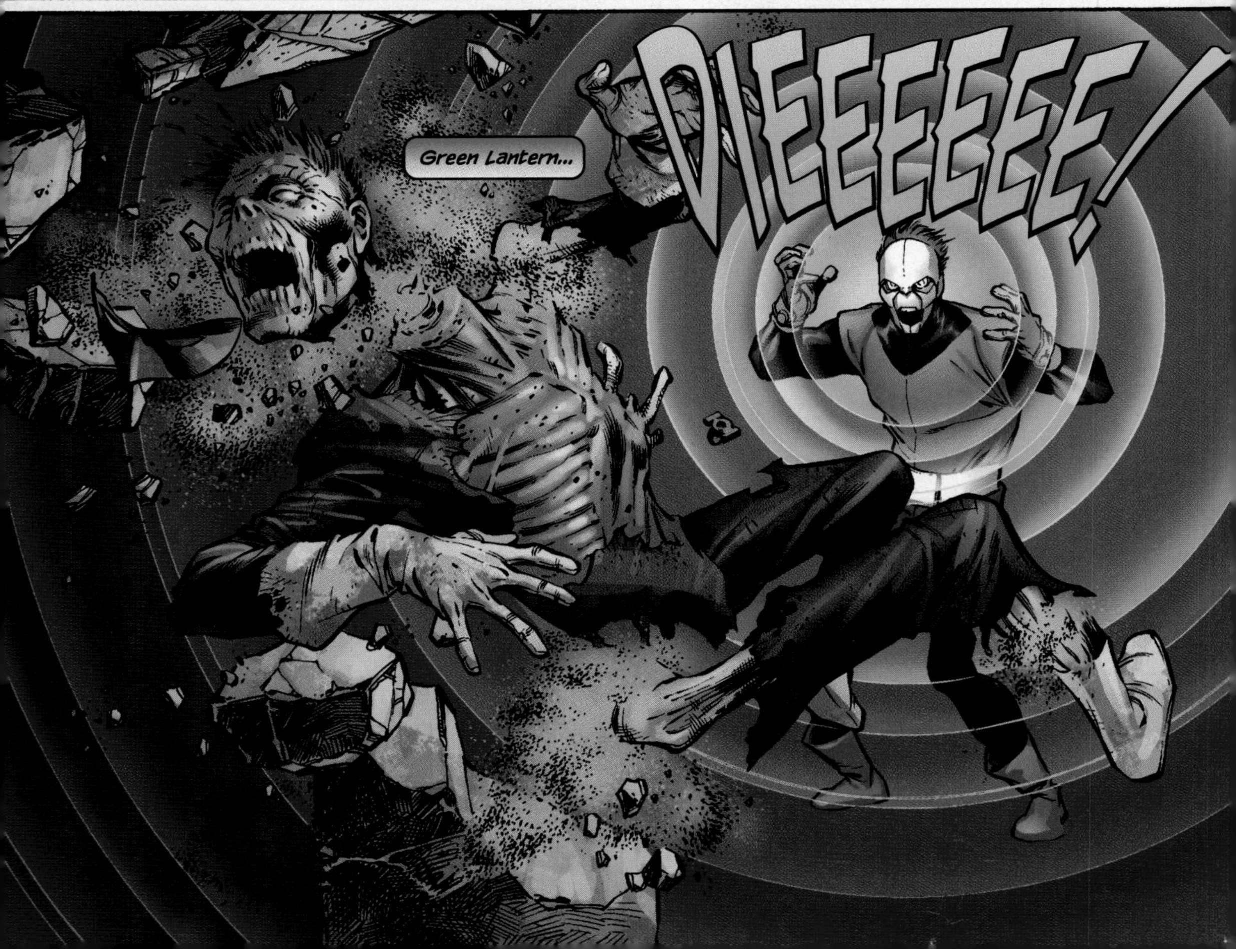
Green Lantern...
DIEEEEEEE!

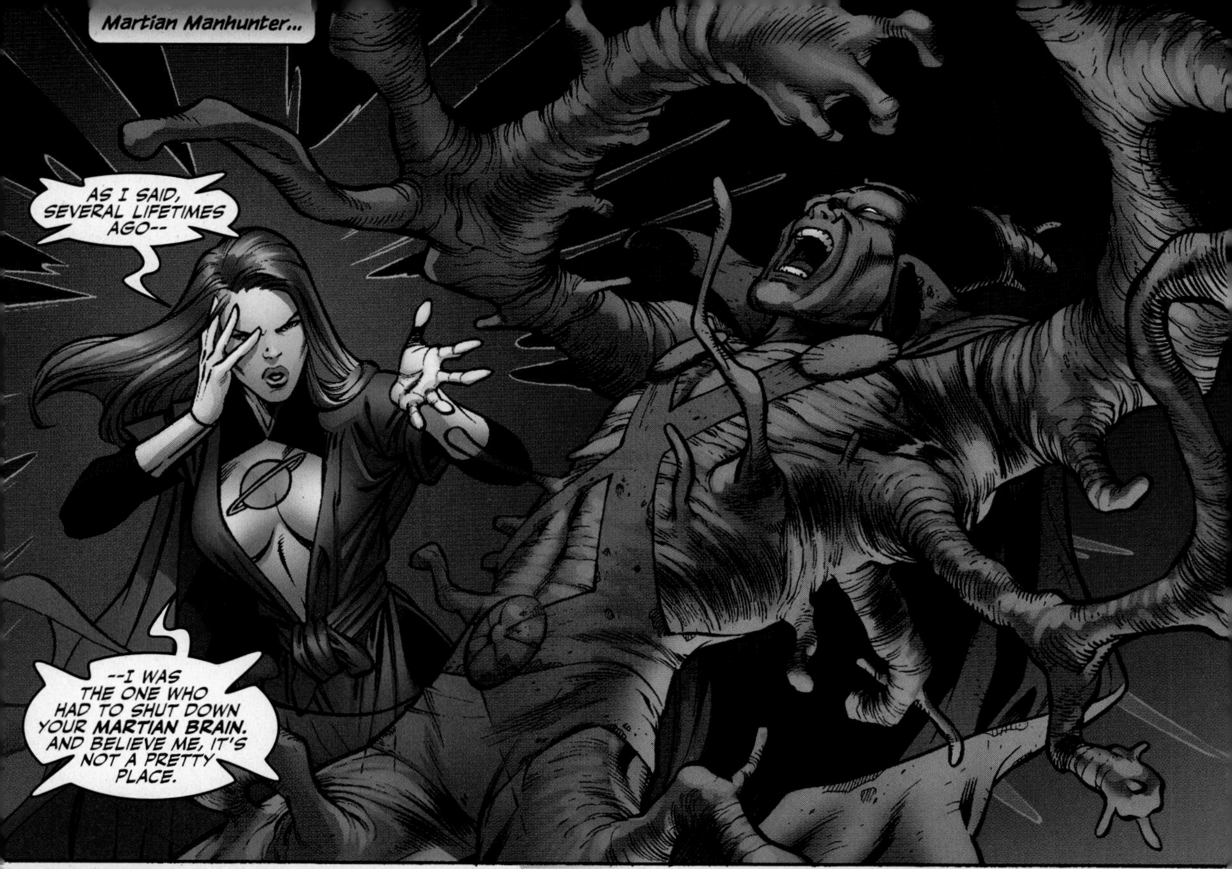
Martian Manhunter...
AS I SAID, SEVERAL LIFETIMES AGO--
--I WAS THE ONE WHO HAD TO SHUT DOWN YOUR MARTIAN BRAIN. AND BELIEVE ME, IT'S NOT A PRETTY PLACE.

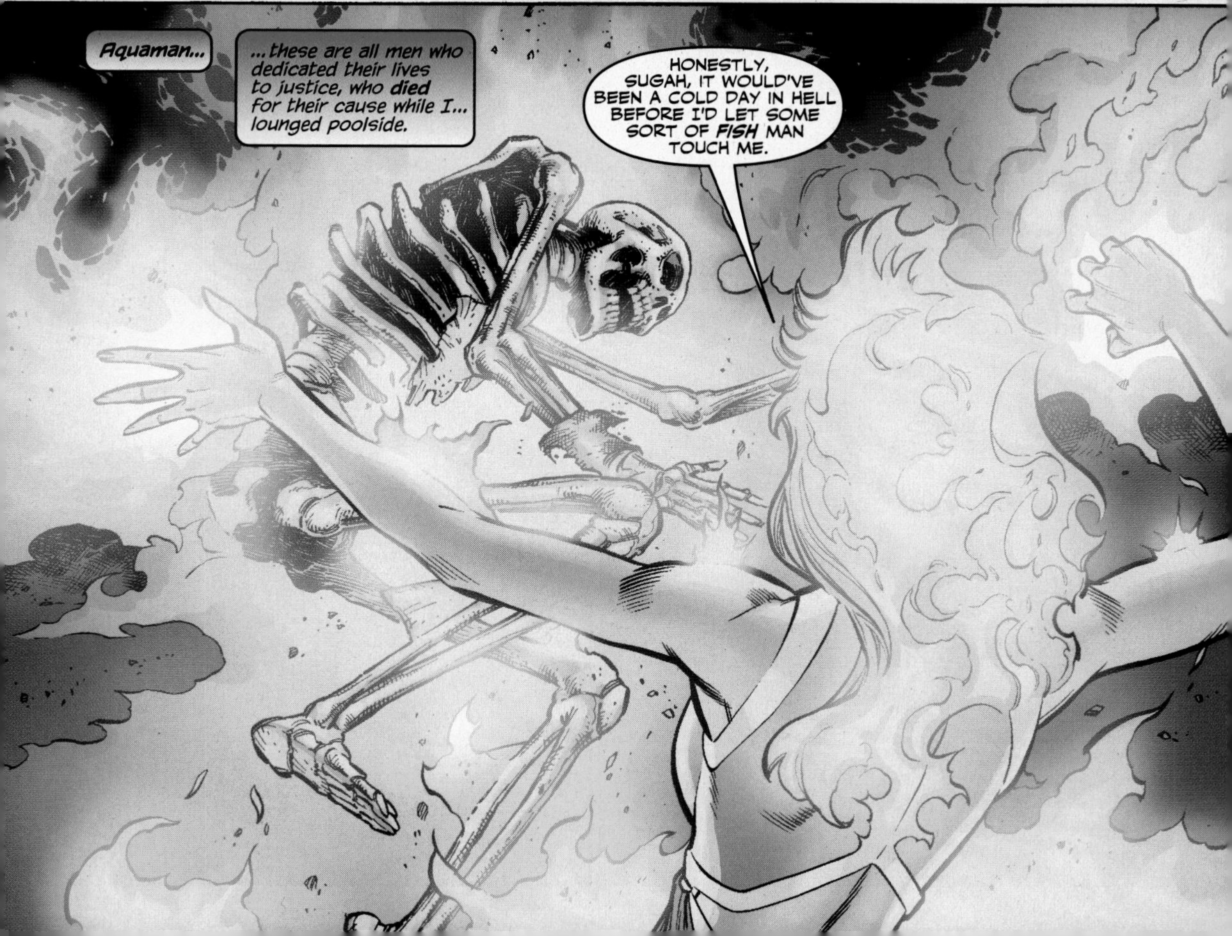
Aquaman...
...these are all men who dedicated their lives to justice, who died for their cause while I... lounged poolside.
HONESTLY, SUGAH, IT WOULD'VE BEEN A COLD DAY IN HELL BEFORE I'D LET SOME SORT OF FISH MAN TOUCH ME.

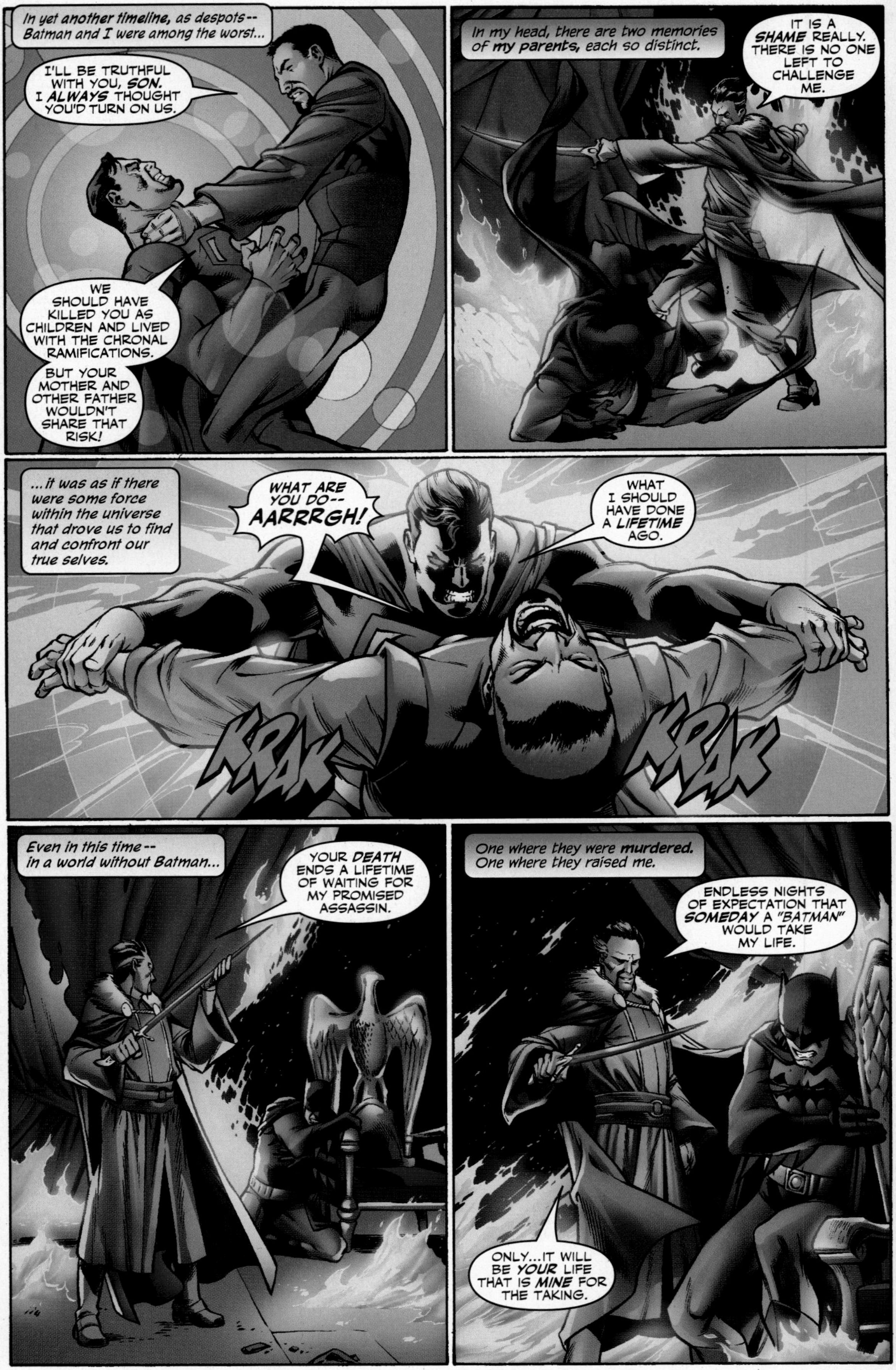
In yet another timeline, as despots--
Batman and I were among the worst...
I'LL BE TRUTHFUL WITH YOU, SON. I ALWAYS THOUGHT YOU'D TURN ON US.
WE SHOULD HAVE KILLED YOU AS CHILDREN AND LIVED WITH THE CHRONAL RAMIFICATIONS.
BUT YOUR MOTHER AND OTHER FATHER WOULDN'T SHARE THAT RISK!
In my head, there are two memories of my parents, each so distinct.
IT IS A SHAME REALLY. THERE IS NO ONE LEFT TO CHALLENGE ME.
...it was as if there were some force within the universe that drove us to find and confront our true selves.
WHAT ARE YOU DO-- AARRRGH!
WHAT I SHOULD HAVE DONE A LIFETIME AGO.
KRAK
KRAK
Even in this time --
in a world without Batman...
YOUR DEATH ENDS A LIFETIME OF WAITING FOR MY PROMISED ASSASSIN.
One where they were murdered.
One where they raised me.
ENDLESS NIGHTS OF EXPECTATION THAT SOMEDAY A "BATMAN" WOULD TAKE MY LIFE.
ONLY...IT WILL BE YOUR LIFE THAT IS MINE FOR THE TAKING.

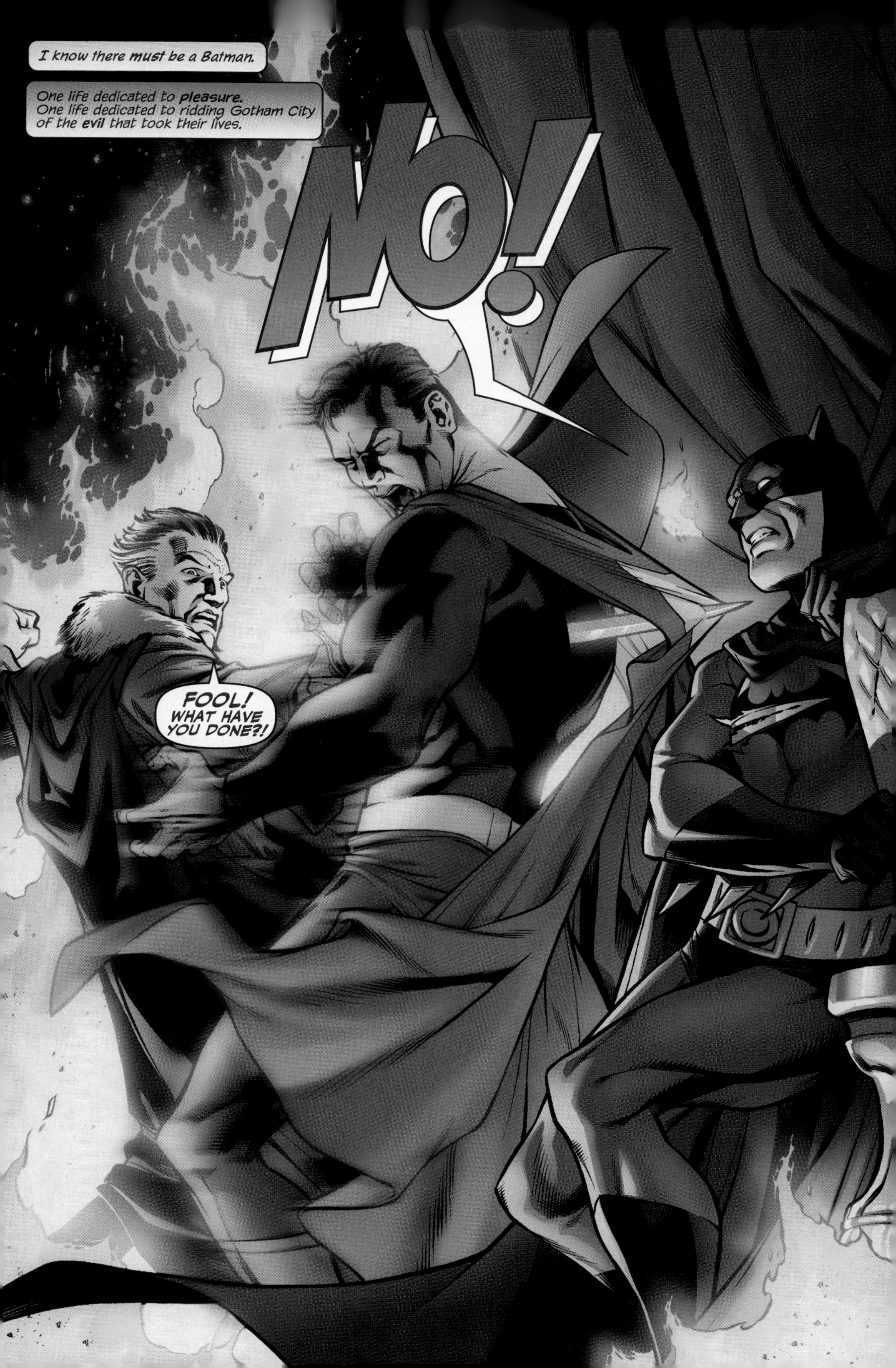
I know there must be a Batman.
One life dedicated to pleasure. One life dedicated to ridding Gotham City of the evil that took their lives.
NO!
FOOL! WHAT HAVE YOU DONE?!

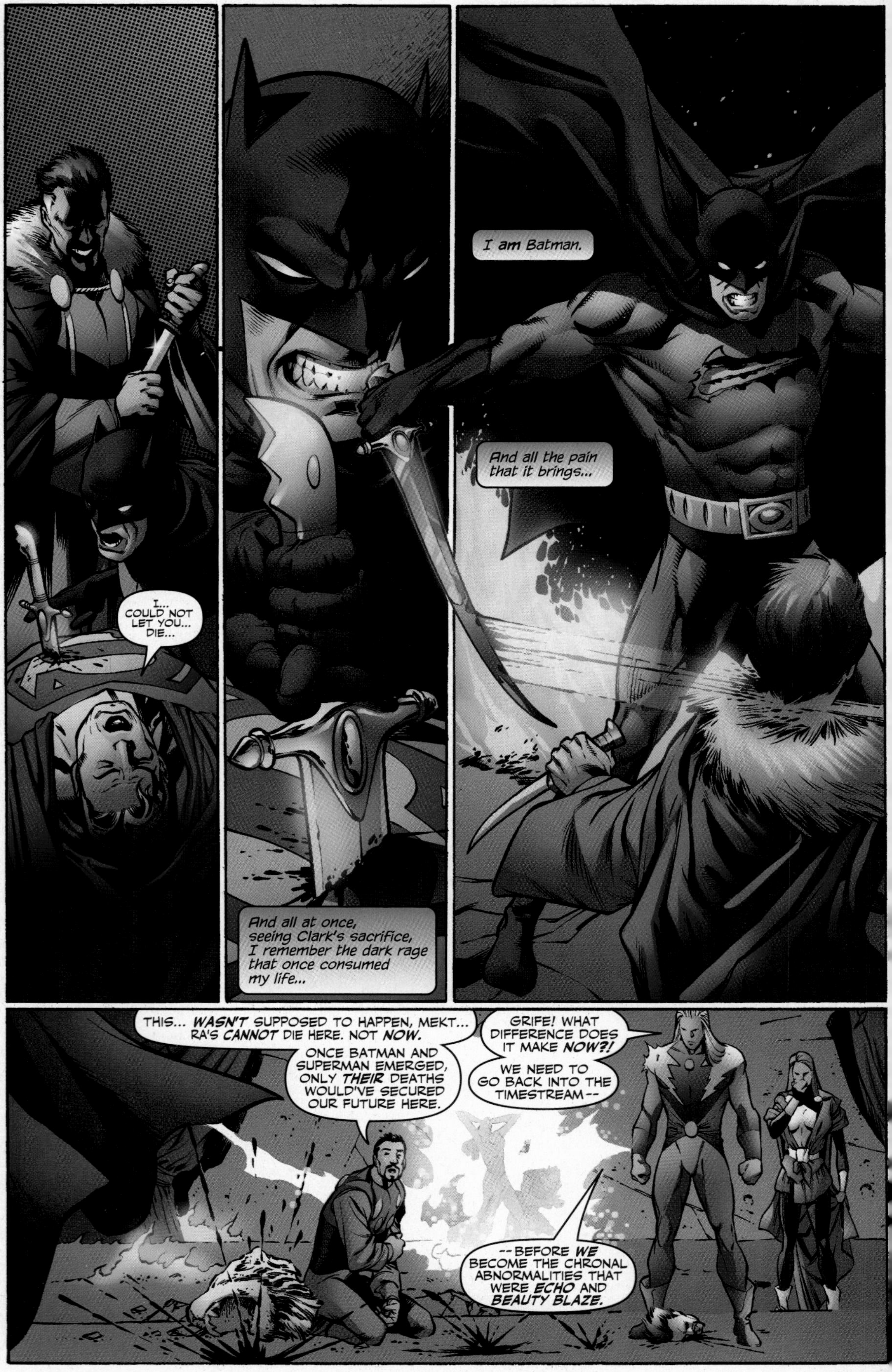

I... COULD NOT LET YOU... DIE...
And all at once, seeing Clark's sacrifice, I remember the dark rage that once consumed my life...
I am Batman.
And all the pain that it brings...
THIS... WASN'T SUPPOSED TO HAPPEN, MEKT... RA'S CANNOT DIE HERE. NOT NOW.
ONCE BATMAN AND SUPERMAN EMERGED, ONLY THEIR DEATHS WOULD'VE SECURED OUR FUTURE HERE.
GRIFE! WHAT DIFFERENCE DOES IT MAKE NOW?!
WE NEED TO GO BACK INTO THE TIMESTREAM--
--BEFORE WE BECOME THE CHRONAL ABNORMALITIES THAT WERE ECHO AND BEAUTY BLAZE.

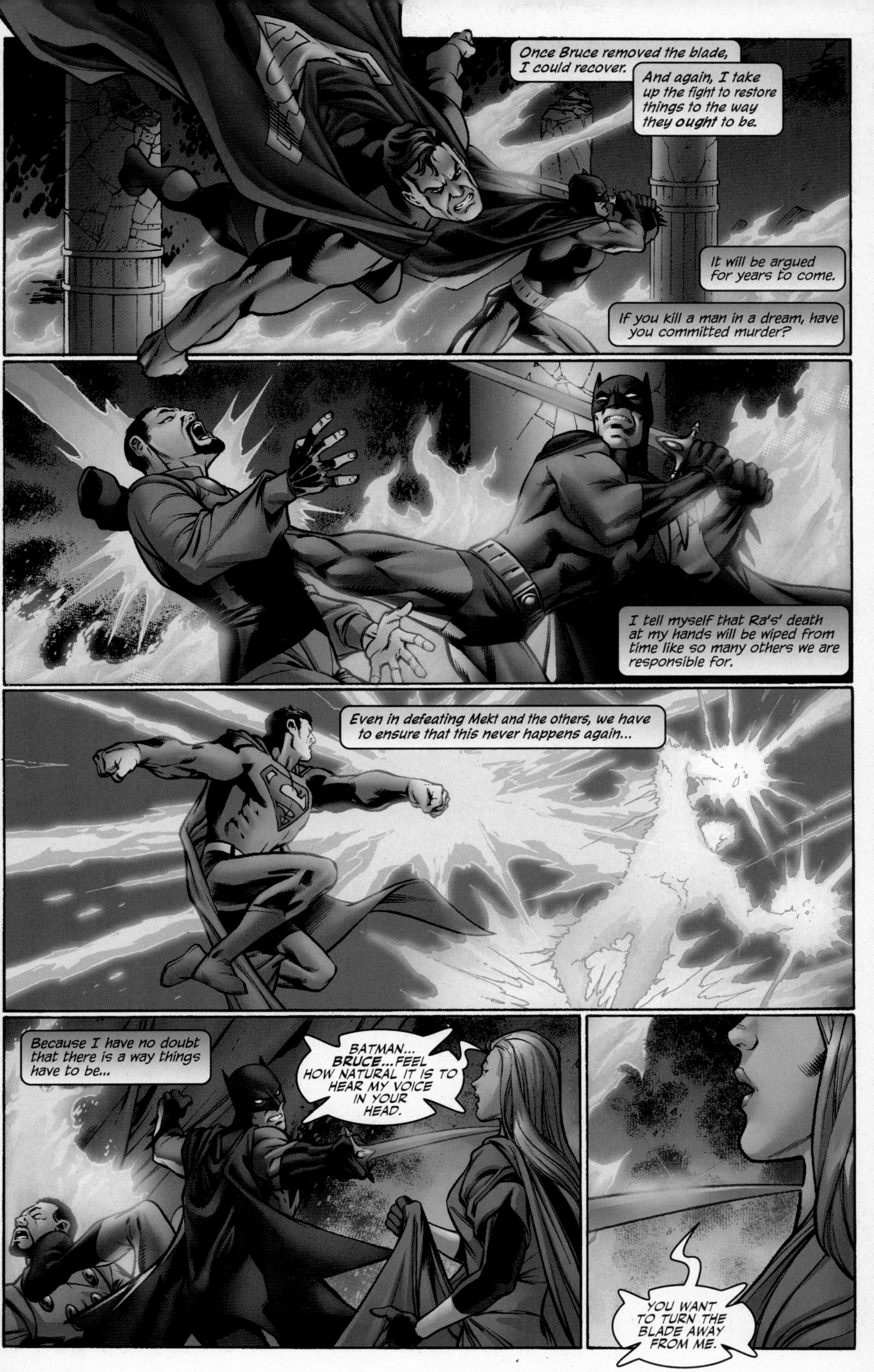
Once Bruce removed the blade, I could recover.
And again, I take up the fight to restore things to the way they ought to be.
It will be argued for years to come.
If you kill a man in a dream, have you committed murder?
I tell myself that Ra's' death at my hands will be wiped from time like so many others we are responsible for.
Even in defeating Mekt and the others, we have to ensure that this never happens again...
Because I have no doubt that there is a way things have to be...
BATMAN... BRUCE...FEEL HOW NATURAL IT IS TO HEAR MY VOICE IN YOUR HEAD.
YOU WANT TO TURN THE BLADE AWAY FROM ME.

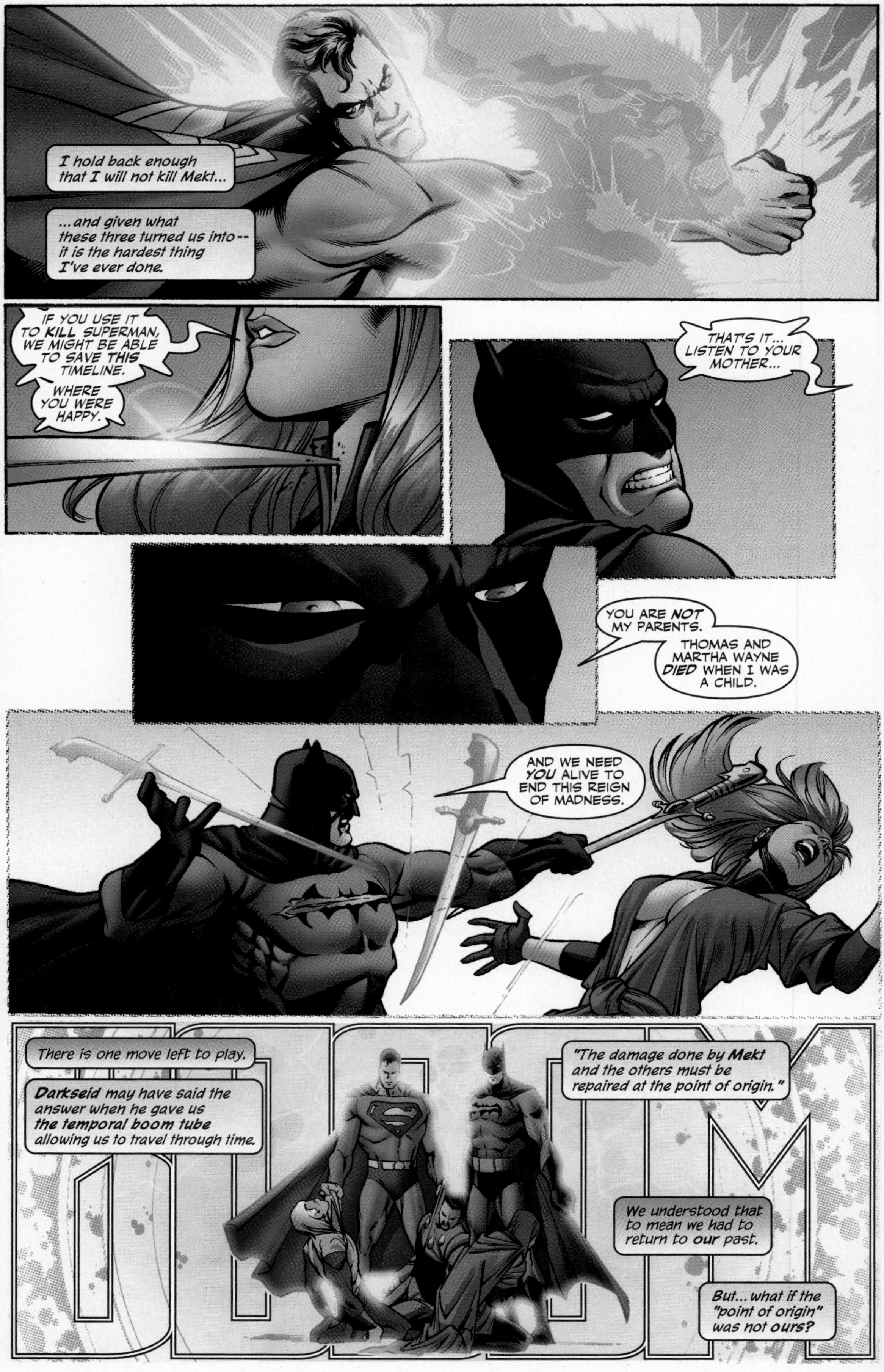
I hold back enough that I will not kill Mekt...
...and given what these three turned us into-- it is the hardest thing I've ever done.
IF YOU USE IT TO KILL SUPERMAN, WE MIGHT BE ABLE TO SAVE THIS TIMELINE.
WHERE YOU WERE HAPPY.
THAT'S IT... LISTEN TO YOUR MOTHER...
YOU ARE NOT MY PARENTS.
THOMAS AND MARTHA WAYNE DIED WHEN I WAS A CHILD.
AND WE NEED YOU ALIVE TO END THIS REIGN OF MADNESS.
There is one move left to play.
Darkseid may have said the answer when he gave us the temporal boom tube allowing us to travel through time.
"The damage done by Mekt and the others must be repaired at the point of origin."
We understood that to mean we had to return to our past.
But... what if the "point of origin" was not ours?

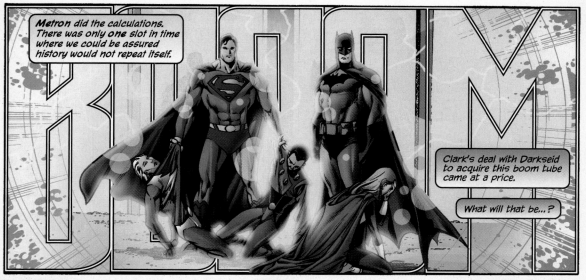

Metron did the calculations. There was only **one** slot in time where we could be assured history would not repeat itself.

Clark's deal with Darkseid to acquire this boom tube came at a price.

What will that be...?

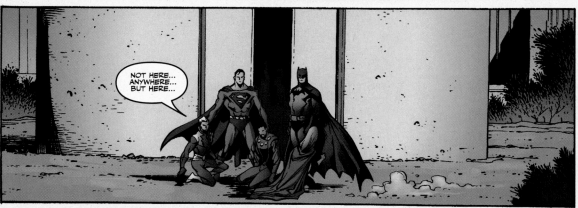

NOT HERE... ANYWHERE... BUT HERE...

WE'VE BEEN **EXPECTING** YOU.

NOT THE TIME WHENCE WE CAME...

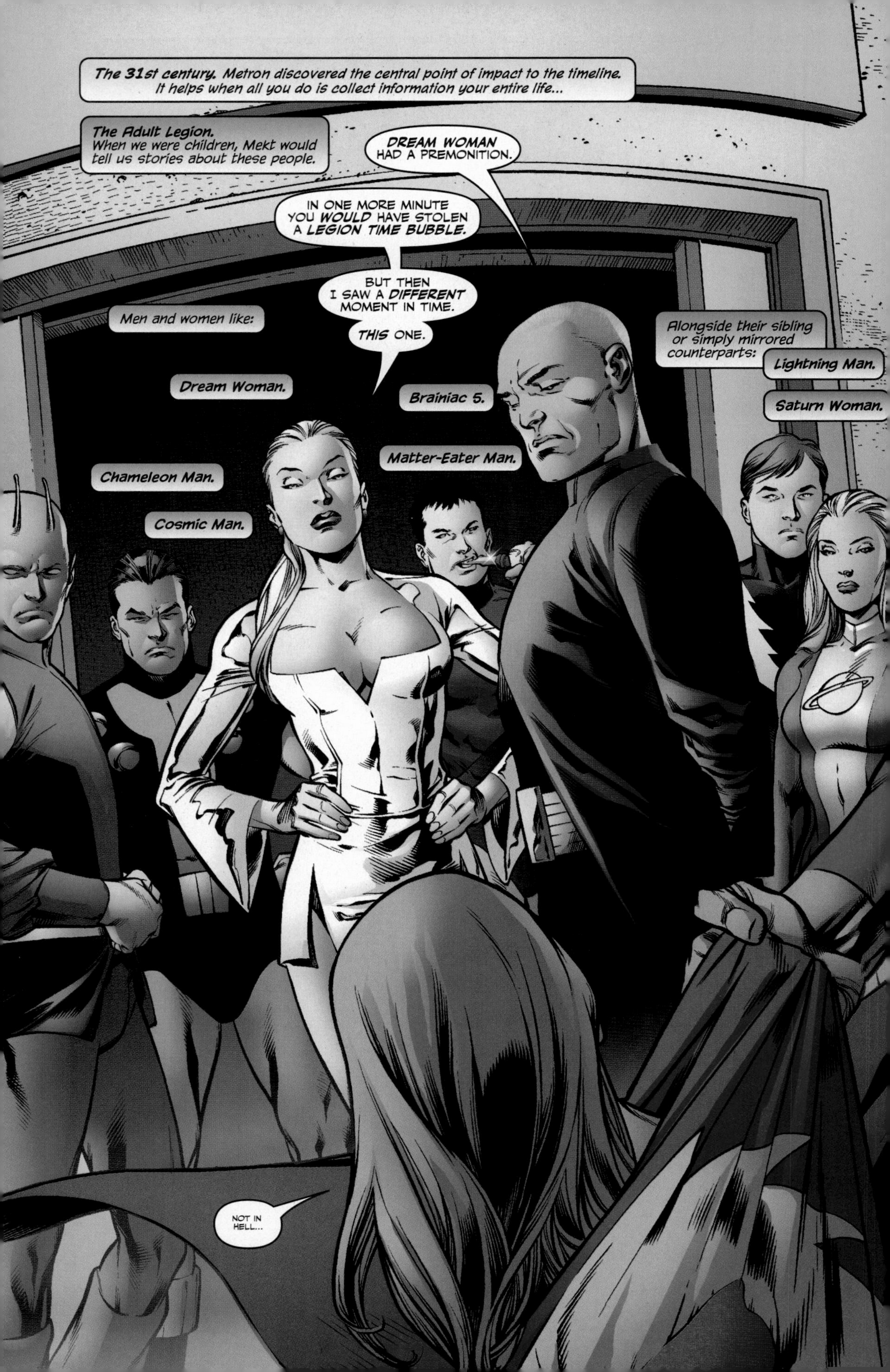

The 31st century. Metron discovered the central point of impact to the timeline. It helps when all you do is collect information your entire life...
The Adult Legion. When we were children, Mekt would tell us stories about these people.
DREAM WOMAN HAD A PREMONITION.
IN ONE MORE MINUTE YOU WOULD HAVE STOLEN A LEGION TIME BUBBLE.
BUT THEN I SAW A DIFFERENT MOMENT IN TIME.
THIS ONE.
Men and women like:
Dream Woman.
Brainiac 5.
Matter-Eater Man.
Chameleon Man.
Cosmic Man.
Alongside their sibling or simply mirrored counterparts:
Lightning Man.
Saturn Woman.
NOT IN HELL...

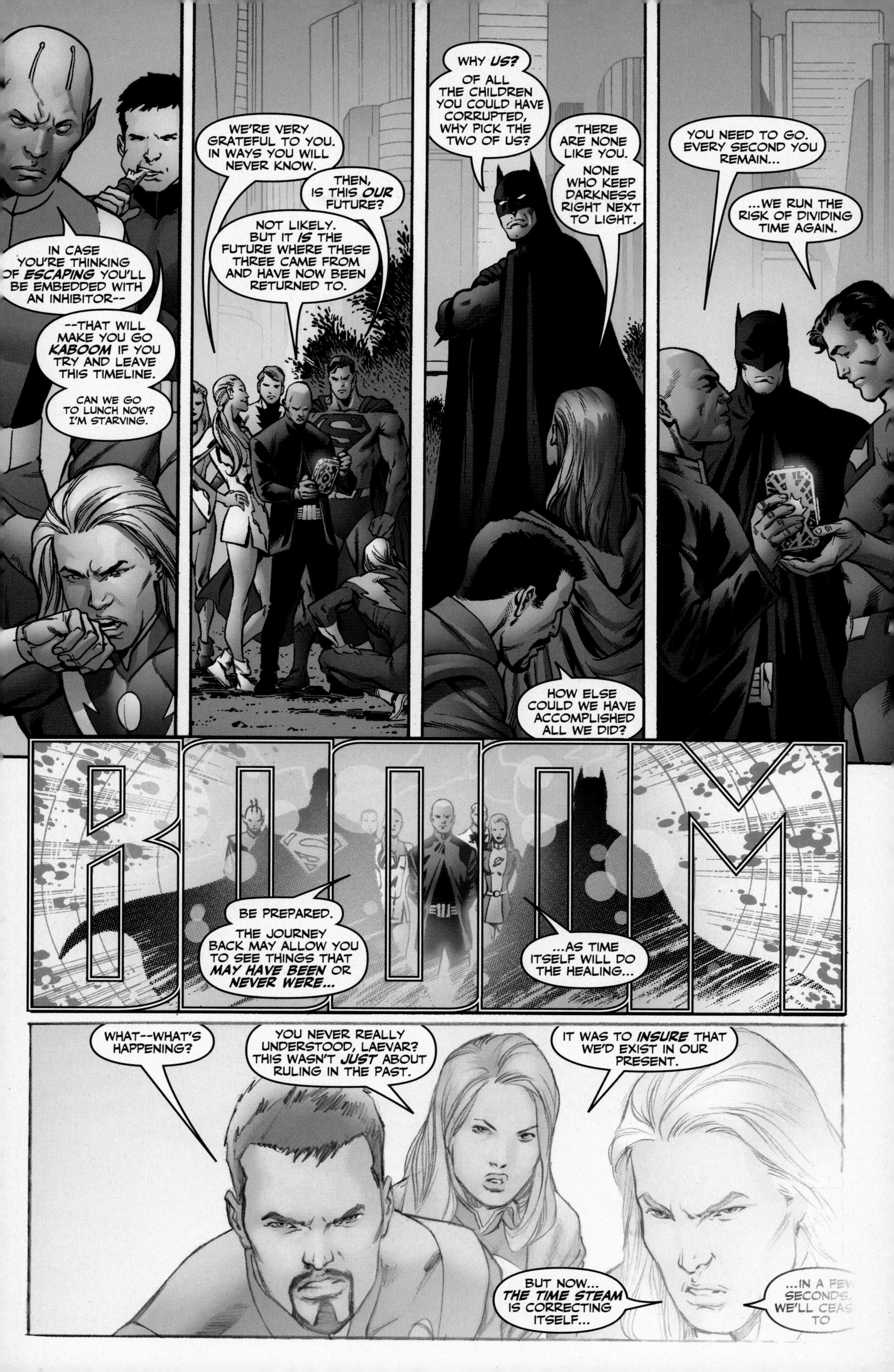
IN CASE YOU'RE THINKING OF ESCAPING YOU'LL BE EMBEDDED WITH AN INHIBITOR--
--THAT WILL MAKE YOU GO KABOOM IF YOU TRY AND LEAVE THIS TIMELINE.
CAN WE GO TO LUNCH NOW? I'M STARVING.
WE'RE VERY GRATEFUL TO YOU. IN WAYS YOU WILL NEVER KNOW.
THEN, IS THIS OUR FUTURE?
NOT LIKELY. BUT IT IS THE FUTURE WHERE THESE THREE CAME FROM AND HAVE NOW BEEN RETURNED TO.
WHY US? OF ALL THE CHILDREN YOU COULD HAVE CORRUPTED, WHY PICK THE TWO OF US?
THERE ARE NONE LIKE YOU. NONE WHO KEEP DARKNESS RIGHT NEXT TO LIGHT.
HOW ELSE COULD WE HAVE ACCOMPLISHED ALL WE DID?
YOU NEED TO GO. EVERY SECOND YOU REMAIN...
...WE RUN THE RISK OF DIVIDING TIME AGAIN.
BOOM
BE PREPARED. THE JOURNEY BACK MAY ALLOW YOU TO SEE THINGS THAT MAY HAVE BEEN OR NEVER WERE...
...AS TIME ITSELF WILL DO THE HEALING...
WHAT--WHAT'S HAPPENING?
YOU NEVER REALLY UNDERSTOOD, LAEVAR? THIS WASN'T JUST ABOUT RULING IN THE PAST.
IT WAS TO INSURE THAT WE'D EXIST IN OUR PRESENT.
BUT NOW... THE TIME STEAM IS CORRECTING ITSELF...
...IN A FEW SECONDS, WE'LL CEASE TO

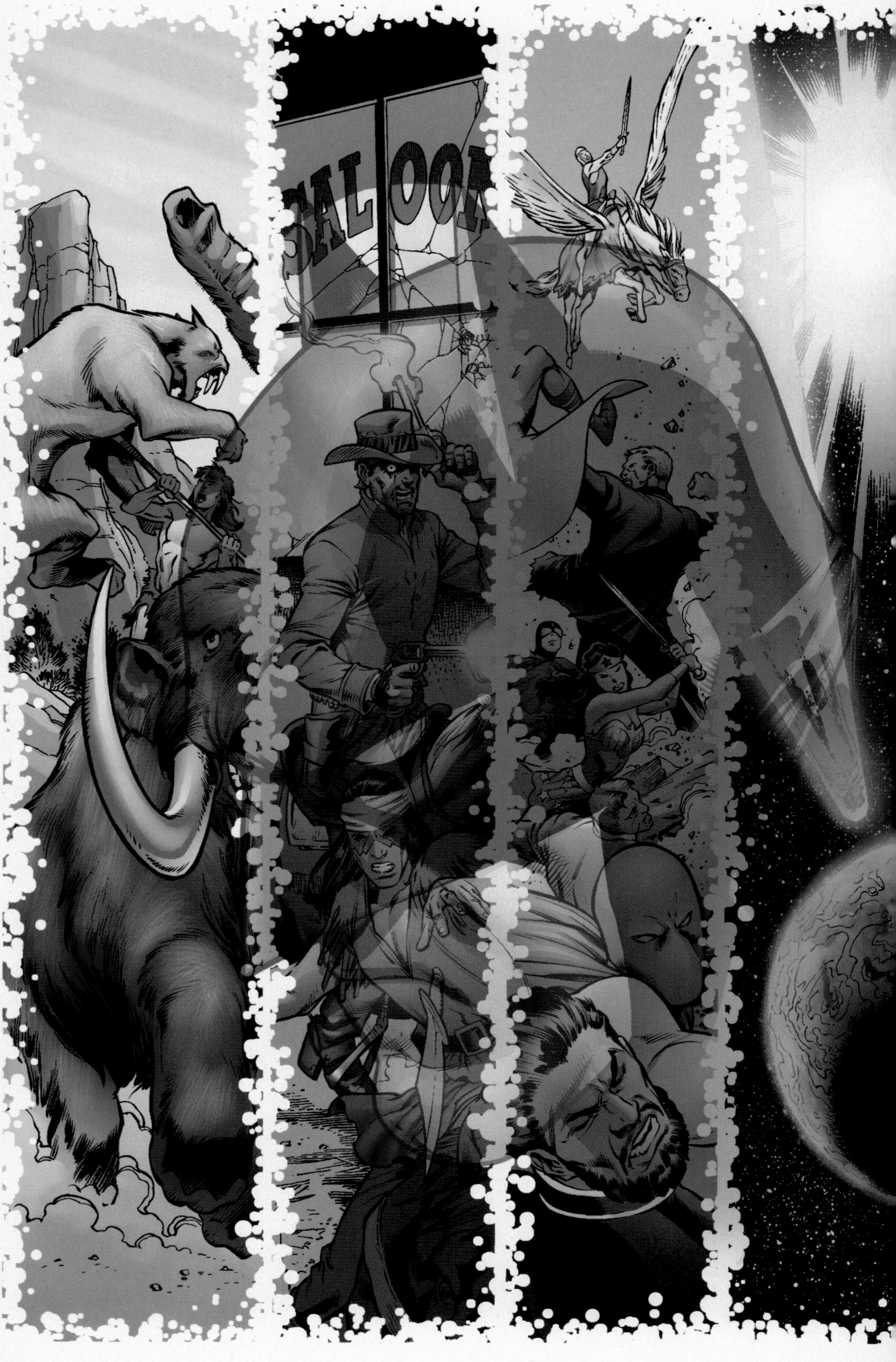
SAL OON

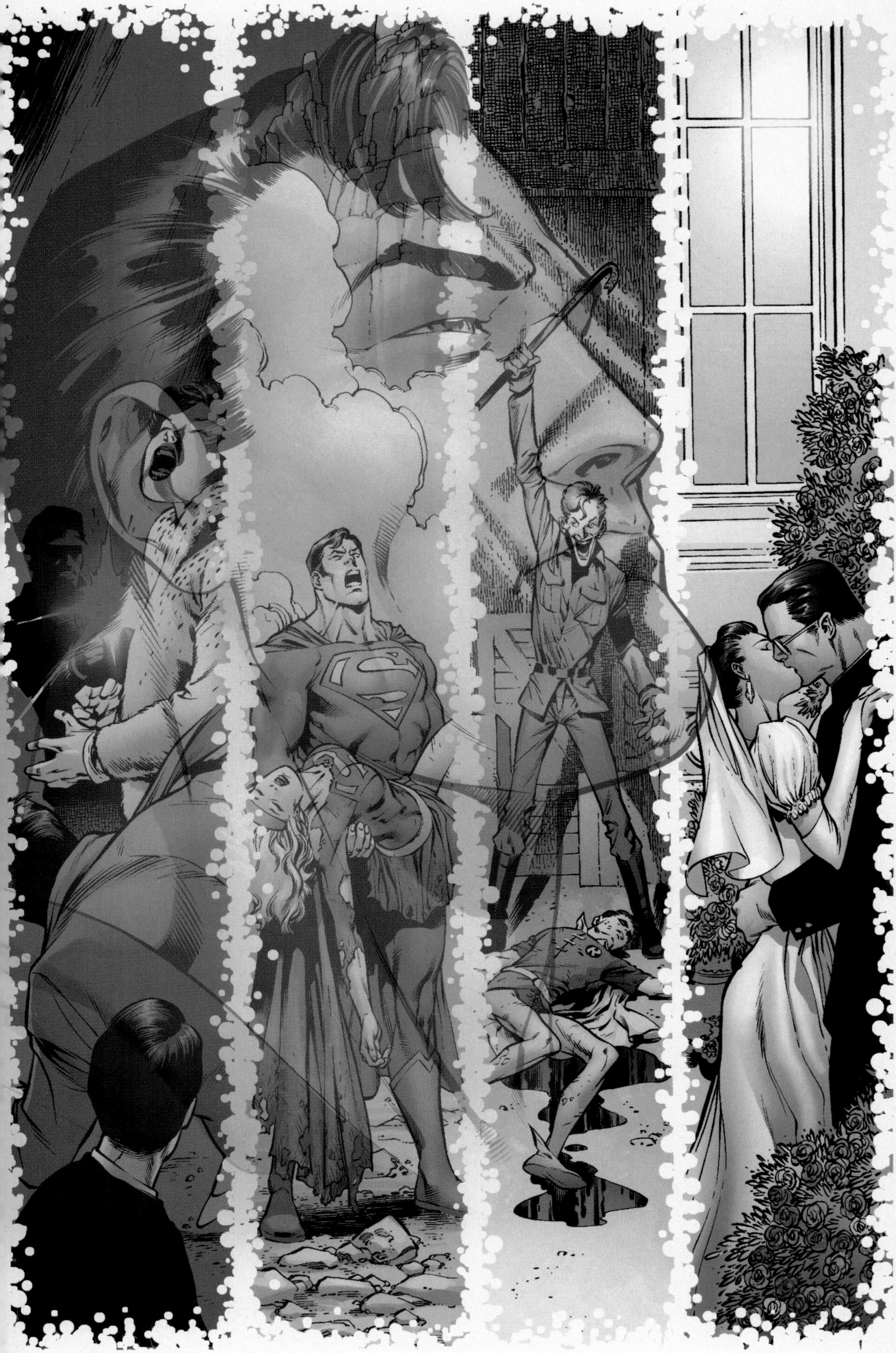

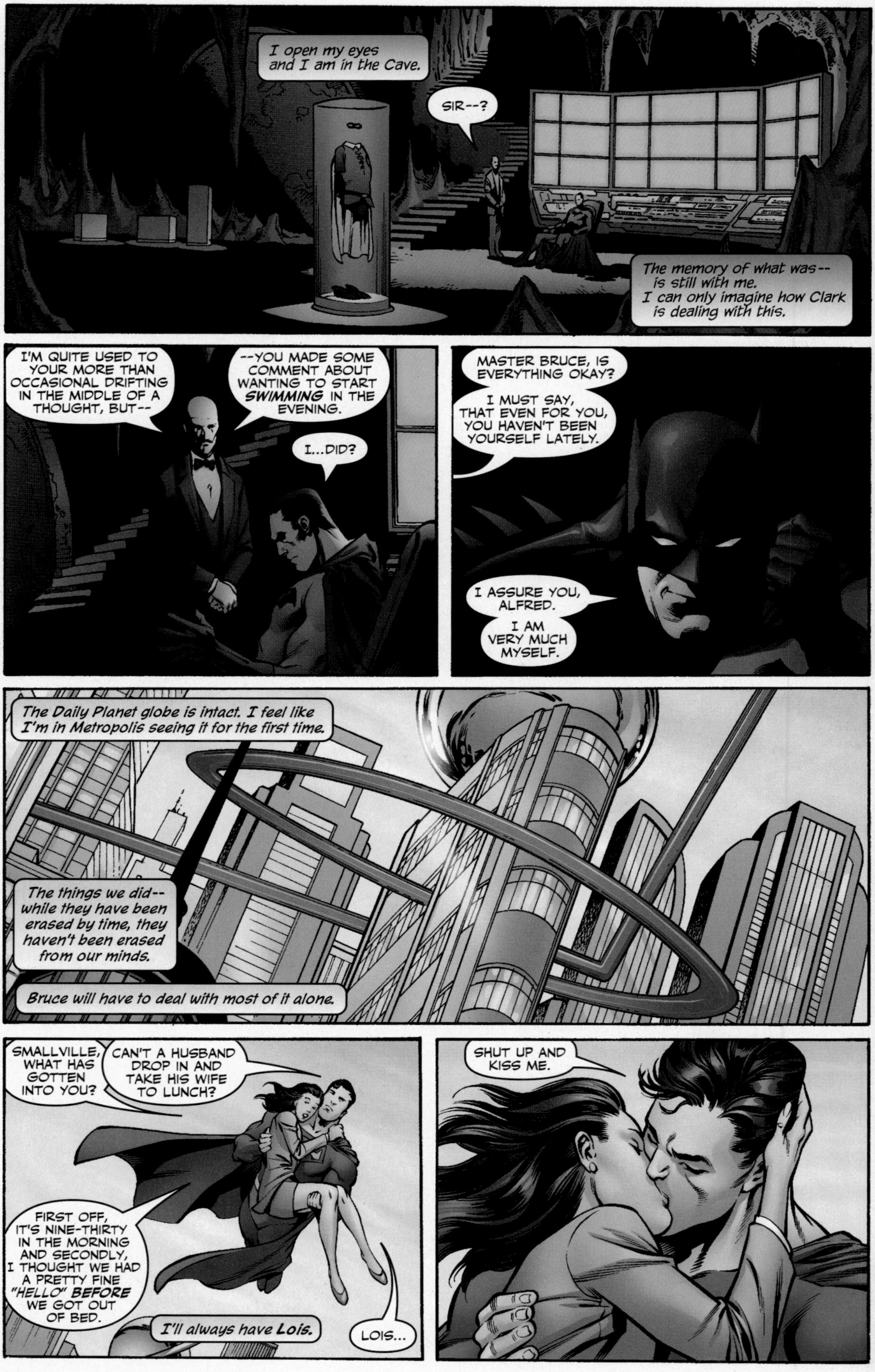
I open my eyes and I am in the Cave.
SIR--?
The memory of what was-- is still with me. I can only imagine how Clark is dealing with this.
I'M QUITE USED TO YOUR MORE THAN OCCASIONAL DRIFTING IN THE MIDDLE OF A THOUGHT, BUT--
--YOU MADE SOME COMMENT ABOUT WANTING TO START SWIMMING IN THE EVENING.
I...DID?
MASTER BRUCE, IS EVERYTHING OKAY?
I MUST SAY, THAT EVEN FOR YOU, YOU HAVEN'T BEEN YOURSELF LATELY.
I ASSURE YOU, ALFRED.
I AM VERY MUCH MYSELF.
The Daily Planet globe is intact. I feel like I'm in Metropolis seeing it for the first time.
The things we did-- while they have been erased by time, they haven't been erased from our minds.
Bruce will have to deal with most of it alone.
SMALLVILLE, WHAT HAS GOTTEN INTO YOU?
CAN'T A HUSBAND DROP IN AND TAKE HIS WIFE TO LUNCH?
FIRST OFF, IT'S NINE-THIRTY IN THE MORNING AND SECONDLY, I THOUGHT WE HAD A PRETTY FINE "HELLO" BEFORE WE GOT OUT OF BED.
I'll always have Lois.
LOIS...
SHUT UP AND KISS ME.

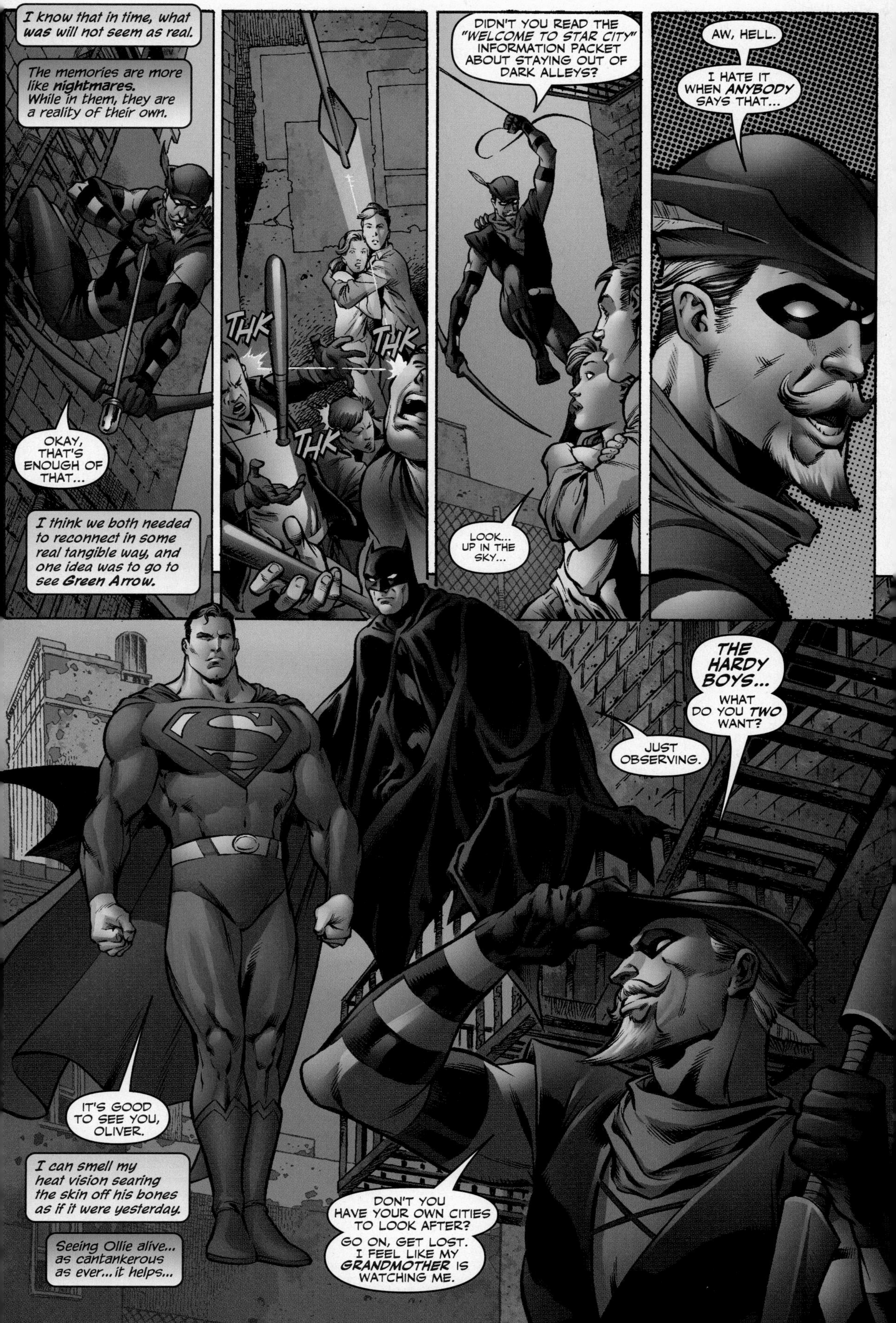

I know that in time, what was will not seem as real.
The memories are more like nightmares. While in them, they are a reality of their own.
OKAY, THAT'S ENOUGH OF THAT...
I think we both needed to reconnect in some real tangible way, and one idea was to go to see Green Arrow.
THK
THK
THK
DIDN'T YOU READ THE "WELCOME TO STAR CITY" INFORMATION PACKET ABOUT STAYING OUT OF DARK ALLEYS?
LOOK... UP IN THE SKY...
AW, HELL.
I HATE IT WHEN ANYBODY SAYS THAT...
THE HARDY BOYS... WHAT DO YOU TWO WANT?
JUST OBSERVING.
IT'S GOOD TO SEE YOU, OLIVER.
I can smell my heat vision searing the skin off his bones as if it were yesterday.
Seeing Ollie alive... as cantankerous as ever... it helps...
DON'T YOU HAVE YOUR OWN CITIES TO LOOK AFTER?
GO ON, GET LOST. I FEEL LIKE MY GRANDMOTHER IS WATCHING ME.

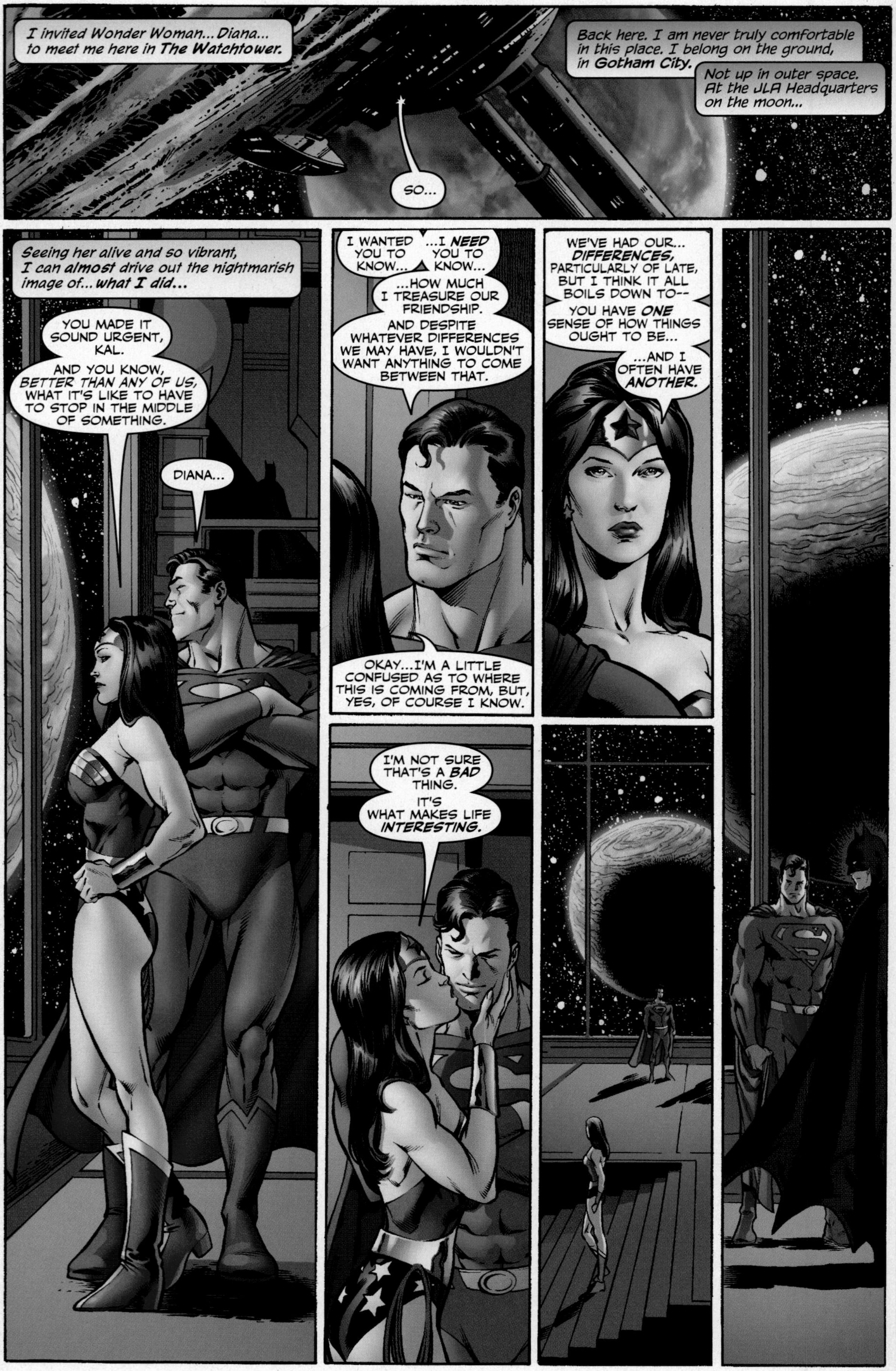
I invited Wonder Woman... Diana... to meet me here in The Watchtower.
Back here. I am never truly comfortable in this place. I belong on the ground, in Gotham City.
Not up in outer space. At the JLA Headquarters on the moon...
SO...
Seeing her alive and so vibrant, I can almost drive out the nightmarish image of... what I did...
YOU MADE IT SOUND URGENT, KAL.
AND YOU KNOW, BETTER THAN ANY OF US, WHAT IT'S LIKE TO HAVE TO STOP IN THE MIDDLE OF SOMETHING.
DIANA...
I WANTED YOU TO KNOW...
...I NEED YOU TO KNOW...
...HOW MUCH I TREASURE OUR FRIENDSHIP.
AND DESPITE WHATEVER DIFFERENCES WE MAY HAVE, I WOULDN'T WANT ANYTHING TO COME BETWEEN THAT.
OKAY...I'M A LITTLE CONFUSED AS TO WHERE THIS IS COMING FROM, BUT, YES, OF COURSE I KNOW.
WE'VE HAD OUR... DIFFERENCES, PARTICULARLY OF LATE, BUT I THINK IT ALL BOILS DOWN TO--
YOU HAVE ONE SENSE OF HOW THINGS OUGHT TO BE...
...AND I OFTEN HAVE ANOTHER.
I'M NOT SURE THAT'S A BAD THING.
IT'S WHAT MAKES LIFE INTERESTING.

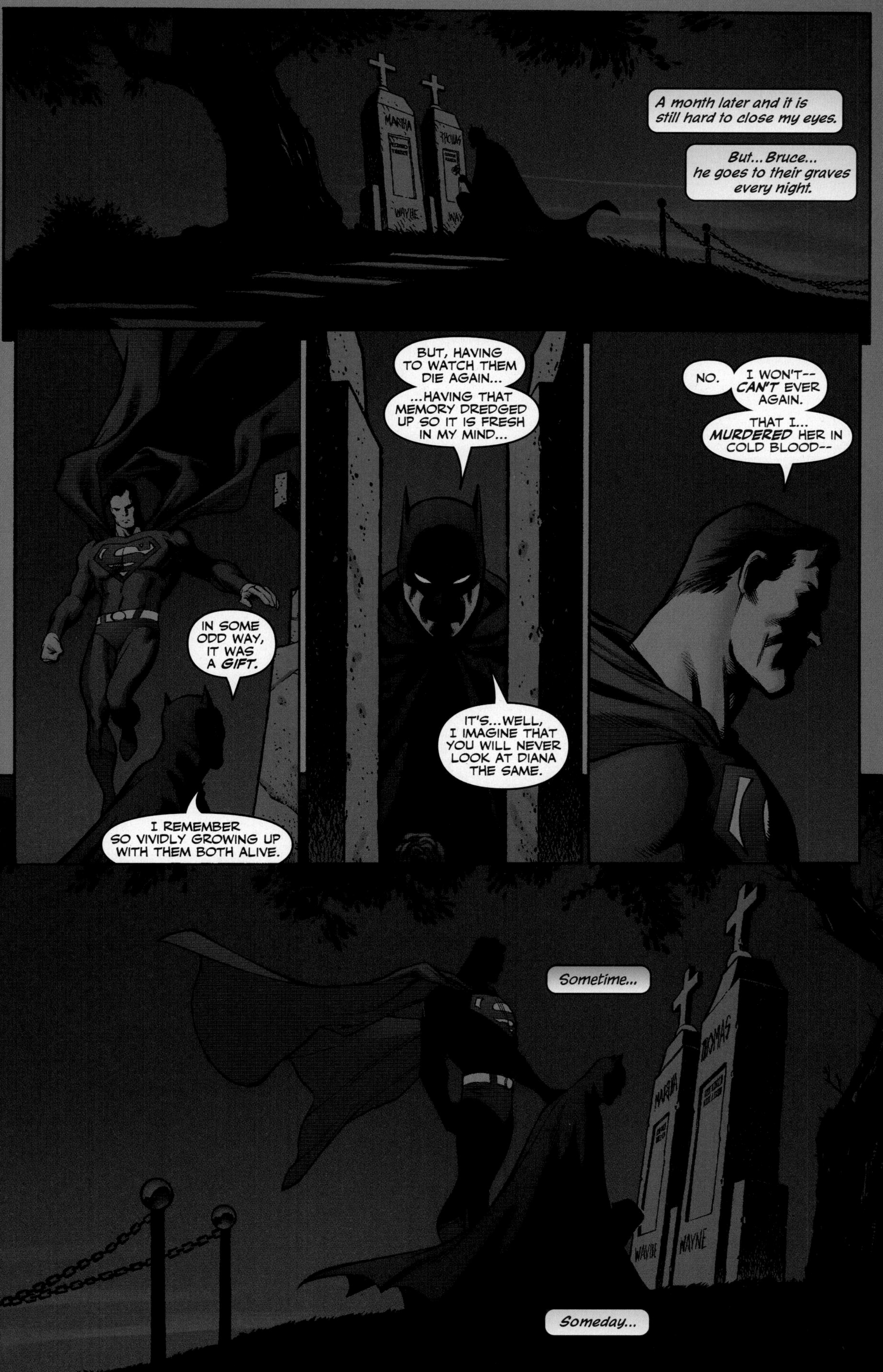
A month later and it is still hard to close my eyes.
But... Bruce... he goes to their graves every night.
I REMEMBER SO VIVIDLY GROWING UP WITH THEM BOTH ALIVE.
IN SOME ODD WAY, IT WAS A GIFT.
BUT, HAVING TO WATCH THEM DIE AGAIN...
...HAVING THAT MEMORY DREDGED UP SO IT IS FRESH IN MY MIND...
IT'S...WELL, I IMAGINE THAT YOU WILL NEVER LOOK AT DIANA THE SAME.
NO.
I WON'T-- CAN'T EVER AGAIN.
THAT I... MURDERED HER IN COLD BLOOD--
Sometime...
Someday...

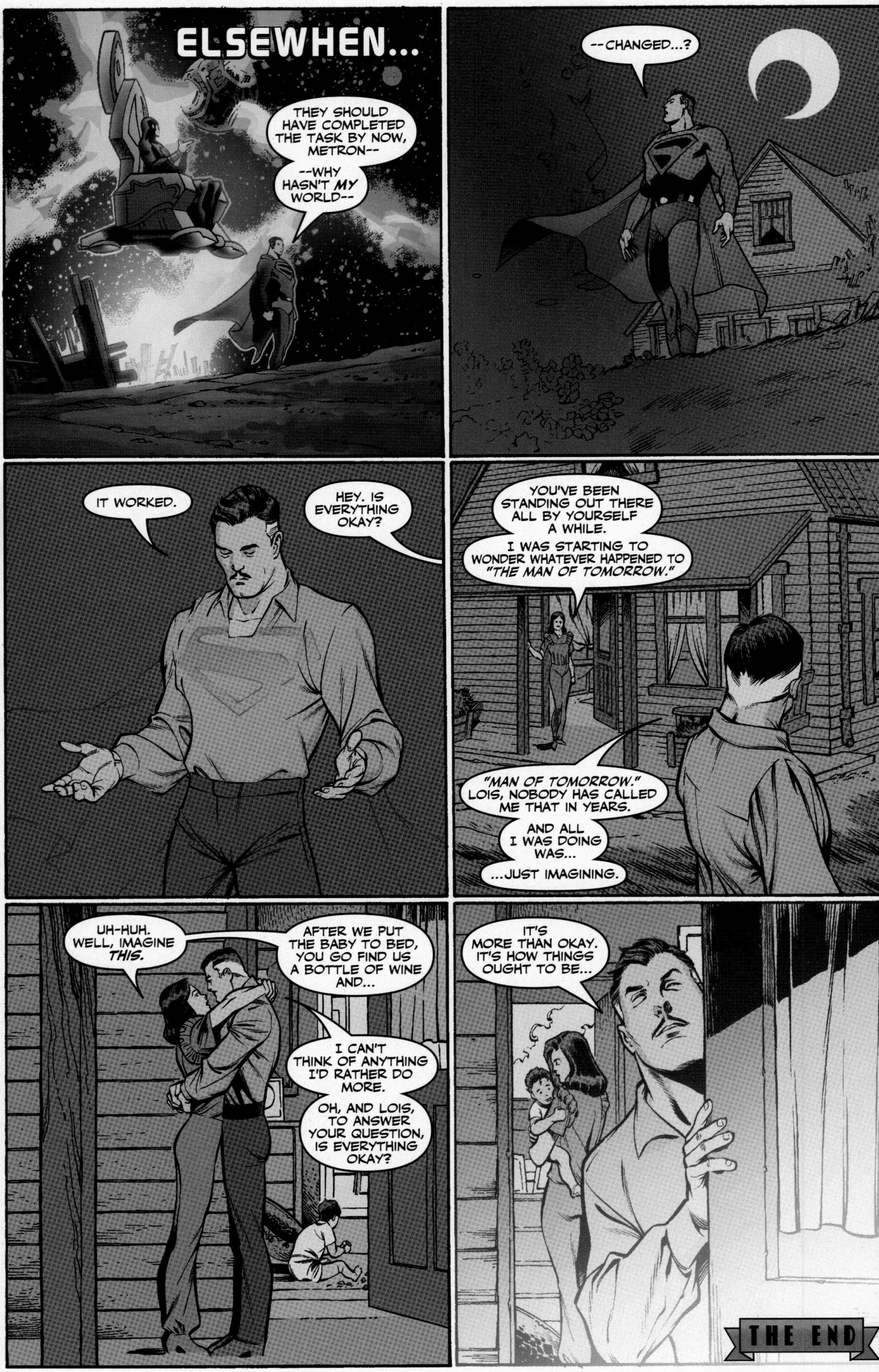
ELSEWHEN...
THEY SHOULD HAVE COMPLETED THE TASK BY NOW, METRON--
--WHY HASN'T *MY* WORLD--
--CHANGED...?
IT WORKED.
HEY. IS EVERYTHING OKAY?
YOU'VE BEEN STANDING OUT THERE ALL BY YOURSELF A WHILE.
I WAS STARTING TO WONDER WHATEVER HAPPENED TO *"THE MAN OF TOMORROW."*
"MAN OF TOMORROW." LOIS, NOBODY HAS CALLED ME THAT IN YEARS.
AND ALL I WAS DOING WAS...
...JUST IMAGINING.
UH-HUH. WELL, IMAGINE *THIS.*
AFTER WE PUT THE BABY TO BED, YOU GO FIND US A BOTTLE OF WINE AND...
I CAN'T THINK OF ANYTHING I'D RATHER DO MORE.
OH, AND LOIS, TO ANSWER YOUR QUESTION, IS EVERYTHING OKAY?
IT'S MORE THAN OKAY. IT'S HOW THINGS OUGHT TO BE...
THE END

BIOGRAPHIES

JEPH LOEB is the author of BATMAN: THE LONG HALLOWEEN, BATMAN: DARK VICTORY, SUPERMAN FOR ALL SEASONS, CATWOMAN: WHEN IN ROME, CHALLENGERS OF THE UNKNOWN MUST DIE!, *Spider-Man: Blue*, *Daredevil: Yellow* and *Hulk: Gray* — all of which were collaborations with artist Tim Sale. He has also written SUPERMAN, THE WITCHING HOUR, *Cable, X-Man, X-Force*, and various other books. A writer/producer living in Los Angeles, his credits include *Teen Wolf, Commando* and *Smallville*.

CARLOS PACHECO is a veteran of the comics industry hailing from Cadiz, Spain, and has pencilled numerous projects for Marvel Comics such as *Excalibur, X-Men, Avengers Forever,* and *Fantastic Four* (which he also wrote for a spell). Most recently his work has been seen at DC, where he and writer Kurt Busiek co-created ARROWSMITH for the Homage imprint. He has paired with writer Geoff Johns on the JLA/JSA: VIRTUE & VICE graphic novel, and is currently working with Johns again on the new GREEN LANTERN monthly.

JESÚS MERINO has been inking the pencils of Carlos Pacheco for several years now, having worked with Carlos on *Avengers Forever, Fantastic Four,* ARROWSMITH, JLA/JSA: VIRTUE & VICE, and numerous other titles.

IVAN REIS has worked for Marvel, Dark Horse, Chaos!, and most recently DC Comics — where he recently completed a successful run on ACTION COMICS. Recently, he pencilled the pivotal miniseries RANN-THANAGAR WAR and will become the regular penciller on TEEN TITANS.

LAURA MARTIN is an Eisner Award-winning colorist whose work has received raves and much notice on titles such as THE AUTHORITY, PLANETARY, JLA, *Ruse, Astonishing X-Men,* and *The Ultimates.*

RICHARD STARKINGS is best known as the creator of the Comicraft studio, purveyors of unique design and fine lettering — and a copious catalogue of comic-book fonts — since 1992. He is less well known as the creator and publisher of Hip Flask and his semi-autobiographical cartoon strip, *Hedge Backwards.*

SUPERMAN COLLECTIONS

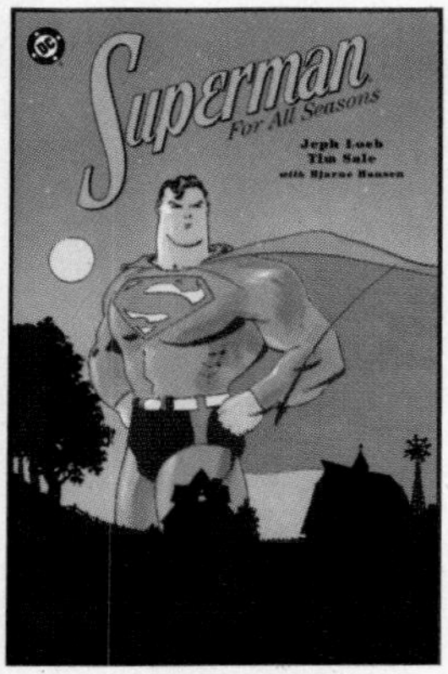
Superman
For All Seasons
Jeph Loeb
Tim Sale
with Bjarne Hansen

SUPERMAN FOR ALL SEASONS

Jeph Loeb/Tim Sale

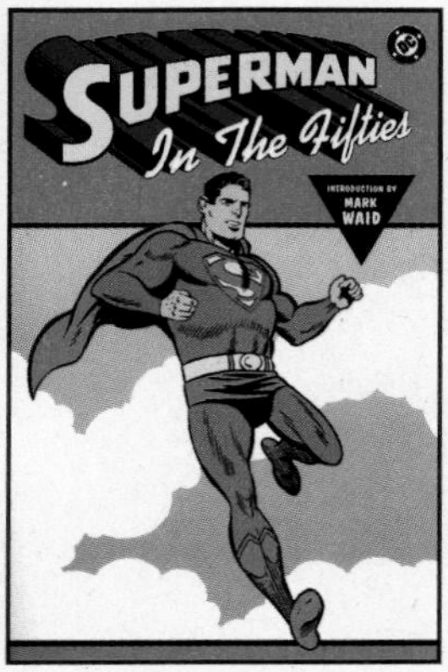
SUPERMAN
In The Fifties
INTRODUCTION BY MARK WAID

SUPERMAN IN THE FIFTIES

various

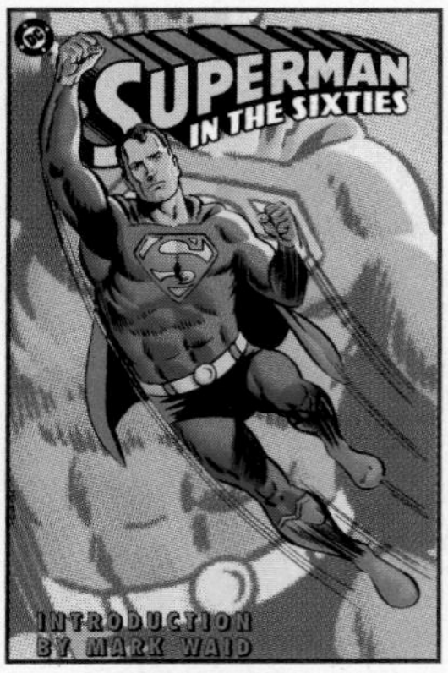
SUPERMAN
IN THE SIXTIES
INTRODUCTION BY MARK WAID

SUPERMAN IN THE SIXTIES

various

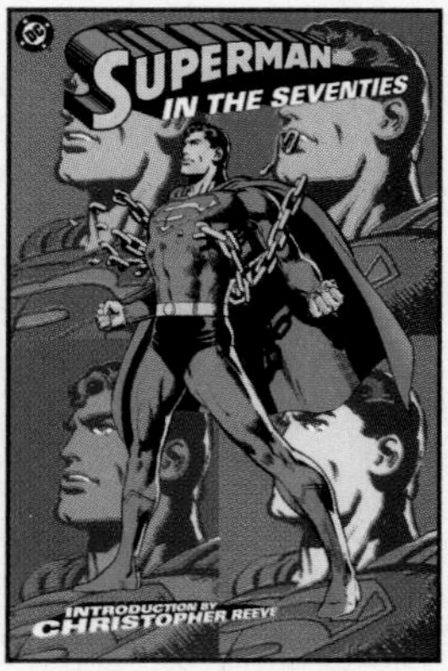
SUPERMAN
IN THE SEVENTIES
INTRODUCTION BY CHRISTOPHER REEVE

SUPERMAN IN THE SEVENTIES

various

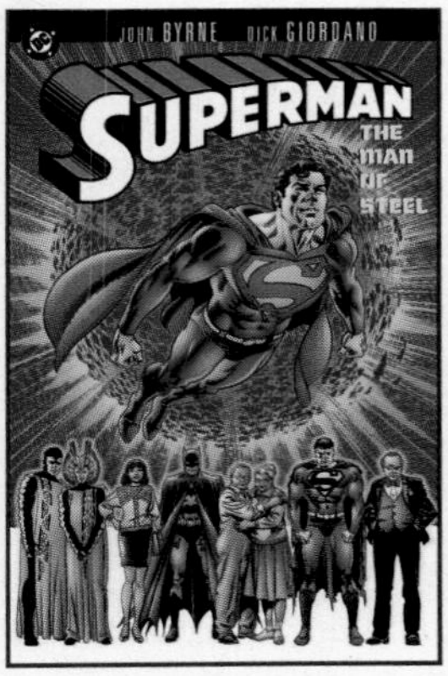
JOHN BYRNE DICK GIORDANO
SUPERMAN
THE MAN OF STEEL

SUPERMAN: THE MAN OF STEEL VOLUMES 1 - 4

John Byrne/Marv Wolfman/
Jerry Ordway

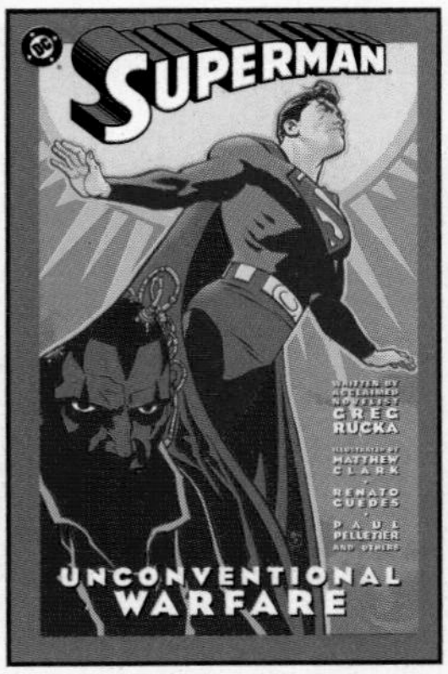
SUPERMAN
UNCONVENTIONAL WARFARE

SUPERMAN: UNCONVENTIONAL WARFARE

Greg Rucka/various

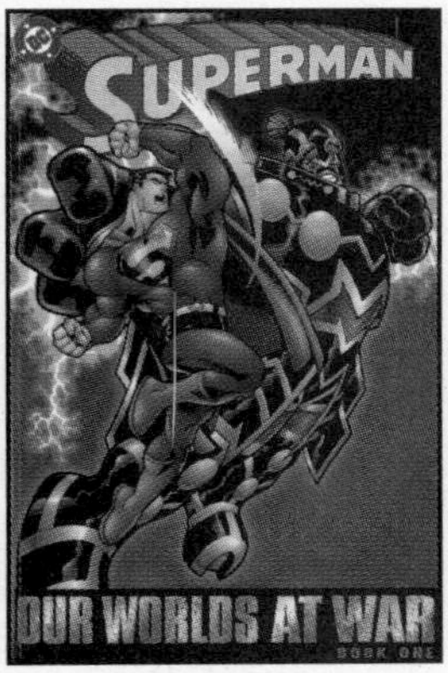
SUPERMAN
OUR WORLDS AT WAR
BOOK ONE

SUPERMAN: OUR WORLDS AT WAR VOLUMES 1 & 2

various

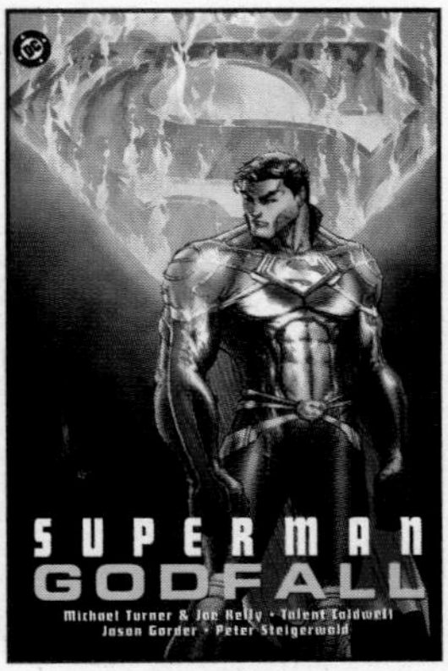
SUPERMAN
GODFALL
Michael Turner & Joe Kelly • Talent Caldwell
Jason Gorder • Peter Steigerwald

SUPERMAN: GODFALL

Michael Turner/Joe Kelly/Talent Caldwell/
Jason Gorder/Peter Steigerwald

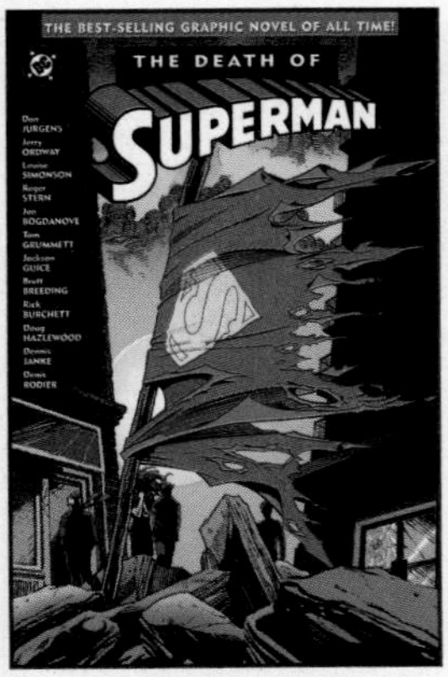
THE BEST-SELLING GRAPHIC NOVEL OF ALL TIME!
THE DEATH OF
SUPERMAN

THE DEATH OF SUPERMAN

various

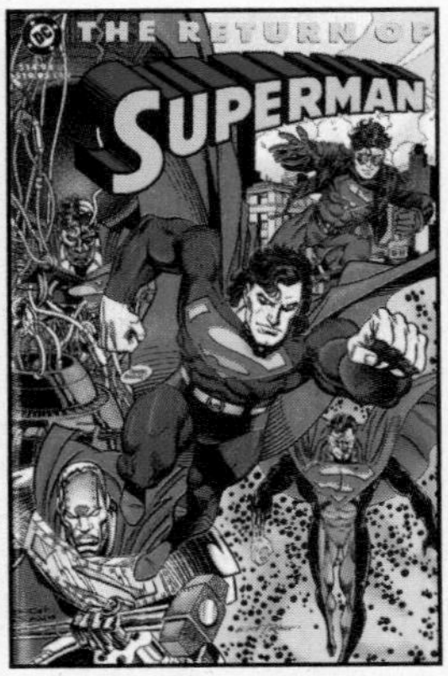
THE RETURN OF
SUPERMAN

THE RETURN OF SUPERMAN

various

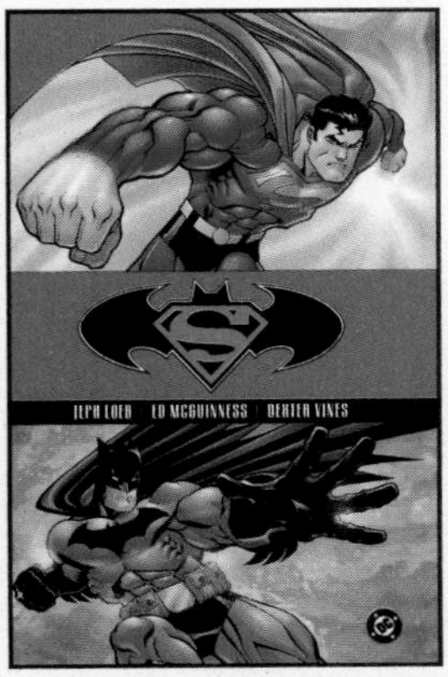
JEPH LOEB | ED MCGUINNESS | DEXTER VINES

SUPERMAN/BATMAN: PUBLIC ENEMIES

Jeph Loeb/Ed McGuinness

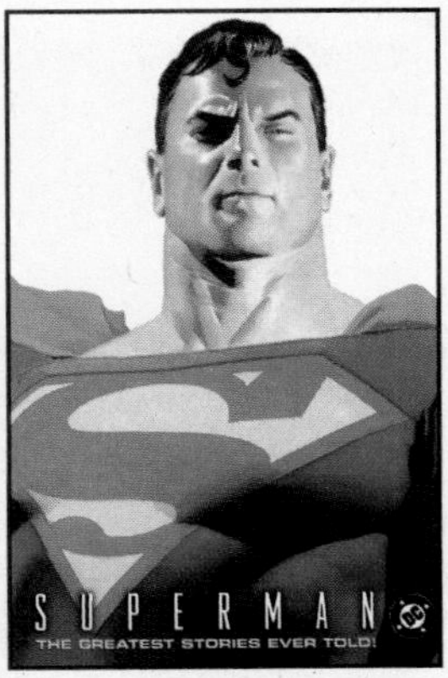
SUPERMAN
THE GREATEST STORIES EVER TOLD!

SUPERMAN: THE GREATEST STORIES EVER TOLD!

various